Roadside Photography Guide to Glacier National Park

photography and text by Dr. Jack Walker

RIGHT: This beautiful panorama of the peaks surrounding Lake McDonald was taken from a lakeside dock. The mountains, from the left, are Stanton Mountain, Mount Vaught, The Garden Wall, Mount Cannon, Mount Brown, Snyder Ridge, Edwards Mountain, and Gunsight Mountain, with the Little Matterhorn Mountain in the background.

FRONT COVER: Dr. Jack Walker stands on the shore of Lake McDonald, accompanied by three of his loves: his Corvette, his camera, and the mountains of Glacier National Park.

TITLE PAGE: Dr. Jack Walker calls this shot on the Going-to-the-Sun Road "Almost There." It appears that you literally are almost to the sun itself. This image, which seems to be a forest fire but is a sunrise, was taken in mid-July about 4:30 A.M., while he was in a class with the late Galen Rowell. He submits this photo as a remembrance in Rowell's honor.

Acknowledgments

I wish to thank Joel Brann, Paul Menssen, and staff of Photo Video Plus camera store in Kalispell for their willing and very professional processing, plus their problem-solving help in preparing this book. I also wish to thank Sherry Parmater for taking us to the next step and introducing us to Farcountry Press. The staff at Farcountry Press has provided patient and tireless help in preparing this book. Many thanks to Kathy Springmeyer for directing the production of this book, to Caroline Patterson for her help crafting the captions and organizing the material, to Jessica Solberg for copyediting and proofreading, and to Shirley Machonis for her excellent work designing these pages. More thanks need to go to Teri Bjornrud for providing invaluable technical assistance. Finally, I have to thank my wife, Arlene, for coordinating this project and making it happen—and for being my Nancy Russell.

ISBN-13: 978-1-59152-021-4
ISBN-10: 1-59152-021-5

Created, produced, and designed in the United States.
Printed in Canada.

09 08 07 06 05 1 2 3 4 5

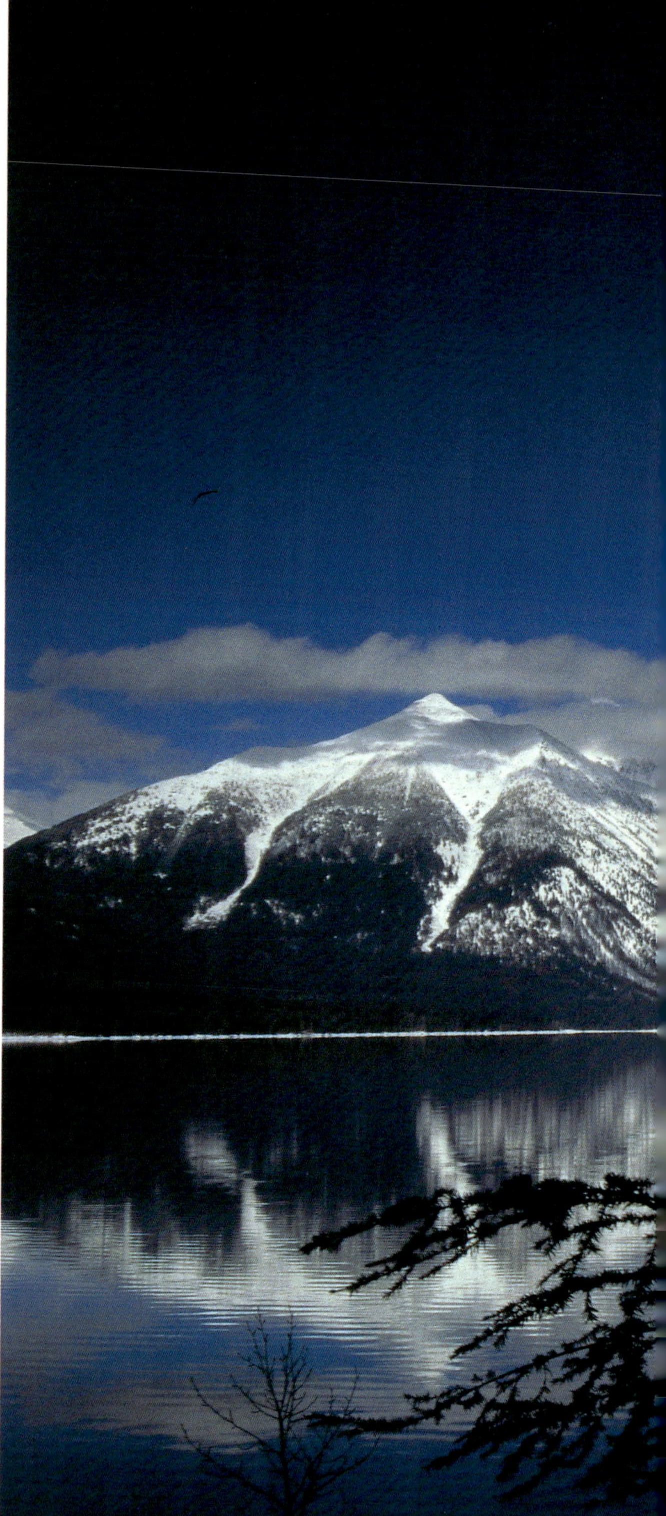

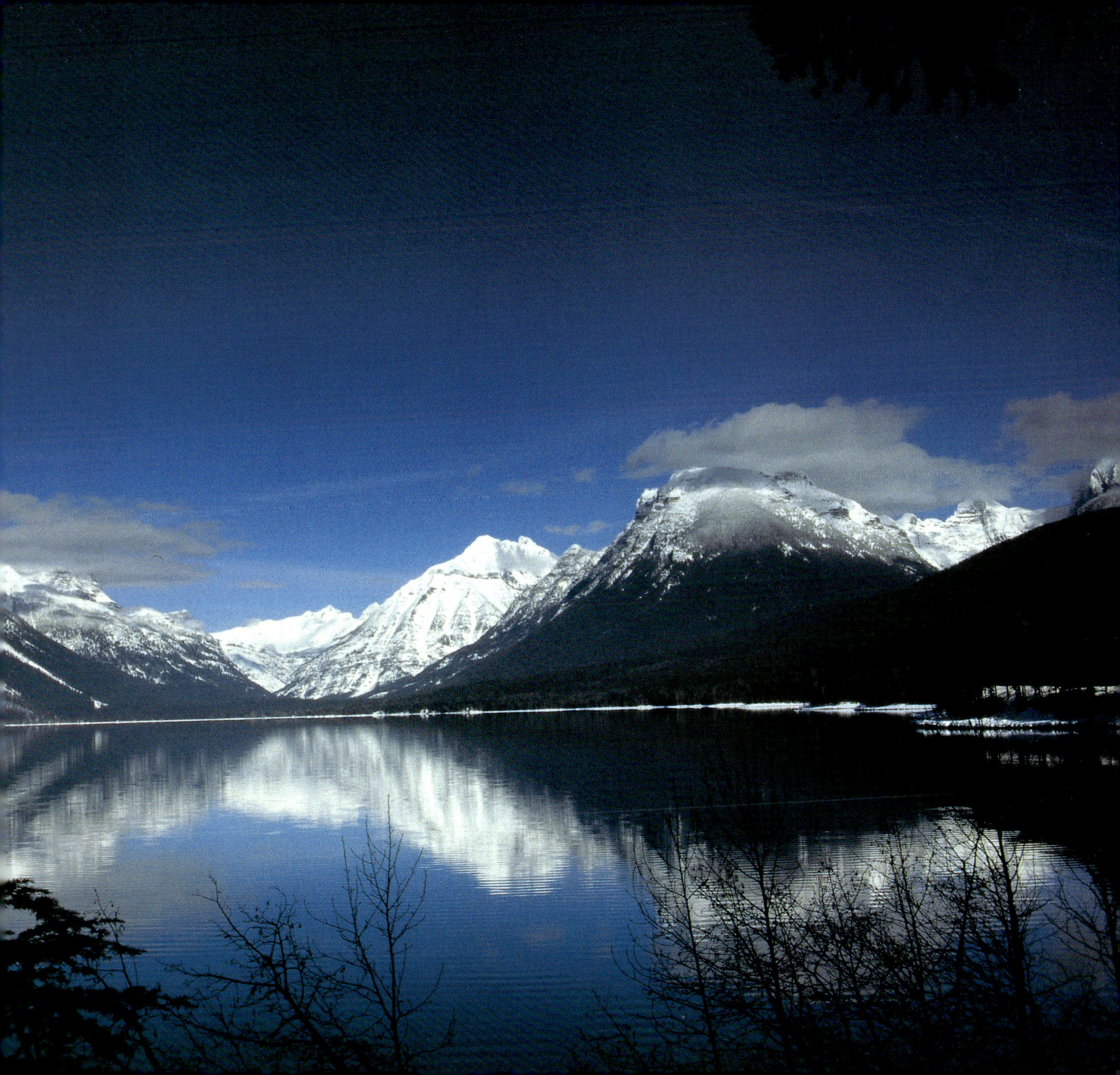

Preface

by Dr. Jack Walker

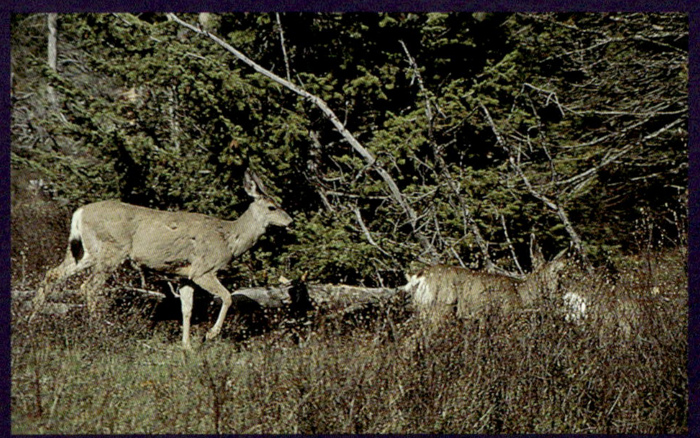

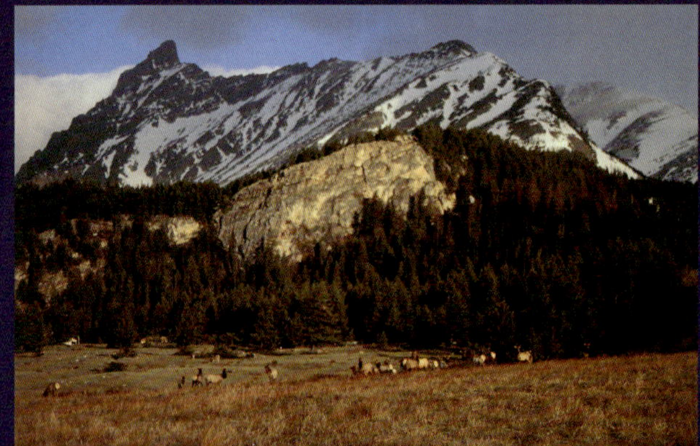

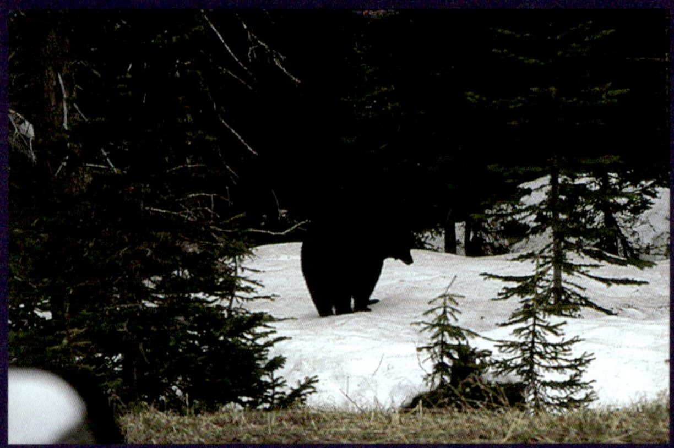

Much of what you will see in Glacier National Park—the sculpted mountains, cirques, glacial moraines, and hanging valleys—is a direct result of the glaciers that covered the area at least 200,000 years ago. The National Park Service has provided numerous exhibits along the way explaining those activities and their resulting landscape features.

This book, however, is a guide to the photographs that you will want to take as you drive through this magnificent scenery. These aren't images that you have to find by hiking or climbing long distances—these are outstanding photographs that you can take from the side of the road!

Along Glacier's narrow Going-to-the-Sun-Road, there is one spectacular scene after another. Even though the park service has made it easier to stop and take pictures by providing pull-outs at almost every possible photo opportunity, it is nevertheless difficult, and sometimes impossible, to backtrack to photograph a spot that you might have missed.

Over the past thirty years, I have photographed the park from many of these stops. I have culled the images in this book from those hundreds of my pictures. A map is included that pinpoints the mile marker of each photograph so you can anticipate each stop.

Over the next few years, it may become mandatory for people to travel in Glacier National Park on the park's red busses. This will make this guide even more essential, because it will help you to plan for what lies ahead on the road. But rest assured, whether you are traveling by bike, car or bus, splendid picture opportunities will remain.

I have also included a number of wildlife photographs in the book. In Glacier National Park, there are at least 70 species of mammals and nearly 260 species of birds, so you are sure to see some of these unique creatures as you drive through the park. This book features roadside photographs of deer, mountain goats, bears, and even moose. I also share some pictures of the wide diversity of flora in Glacier

National Park. There are over 1,400 different plants in the park: 41 of these species are rare in Montana, and 28 species do not exist anywhere else in the state.

To take photographs such as these, no fancy equipment is required. These images were captured with an ordinary 35mm camera, a standard lens, and Ektachrome-VS 100 ASA film. A polarizer filter can be useful in any alpine environment, but is not a necessity. In addition, a tripod will help provide the sharpest photos, but again it is not required.

I hope this book makes it easier to enjoy and appreciate one of the most spectacular areas in our country. Thank goodness for those who had the foresight to preserve this area in 1910. And thank you to the National Park Service for being the keepers of this exquisite region.

Many of these photographs can also be seen at Doc Walker's Photo Gallery in downtown Kalispell, where prints of these photos and others around the world are available.

Future Photo Destinations
The Norwegian Fjords
The Eastern European Alps
The Himalayas
The Italian Dolomites
The French and Spanish Pyrenees

Future Books in Progress
Grand Teton National Park Roadside Photography Guide
Flathead Lake Roadside Photography Guide
Flathead Valley Geology for Kids

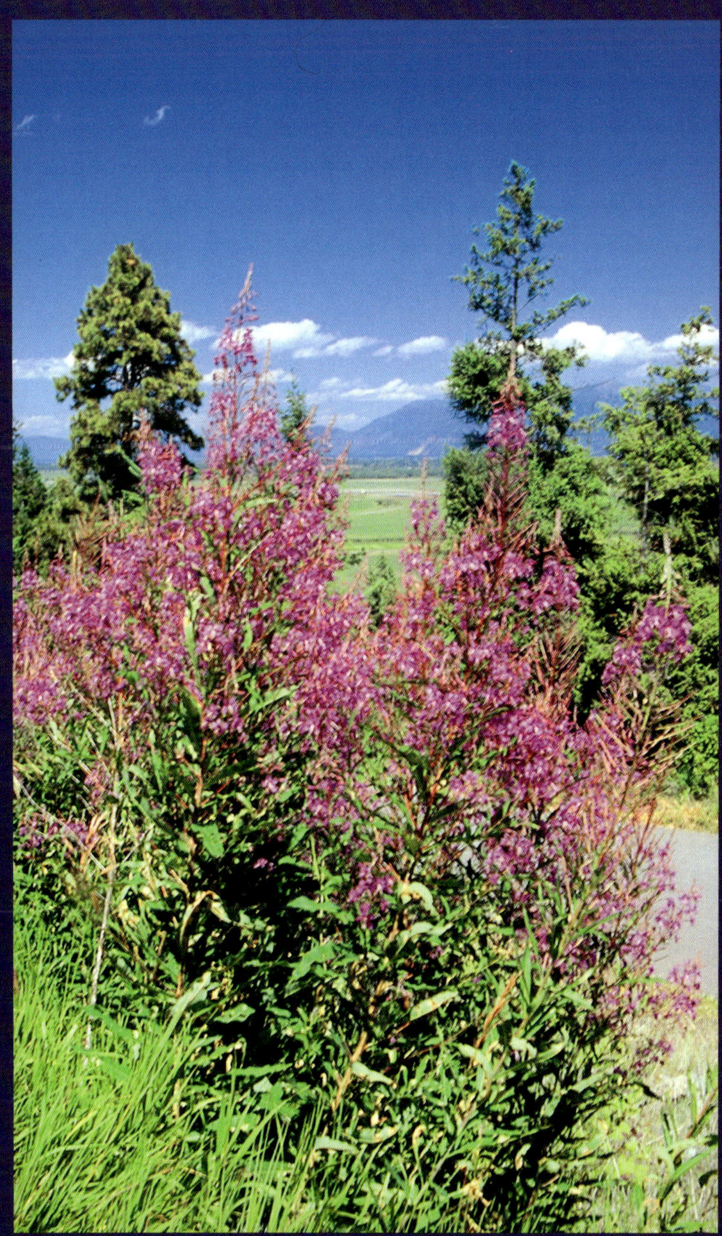

RIGHT: Fireweed in Glacier National Park.

Foreword

by Arlene Zepeda de Walker

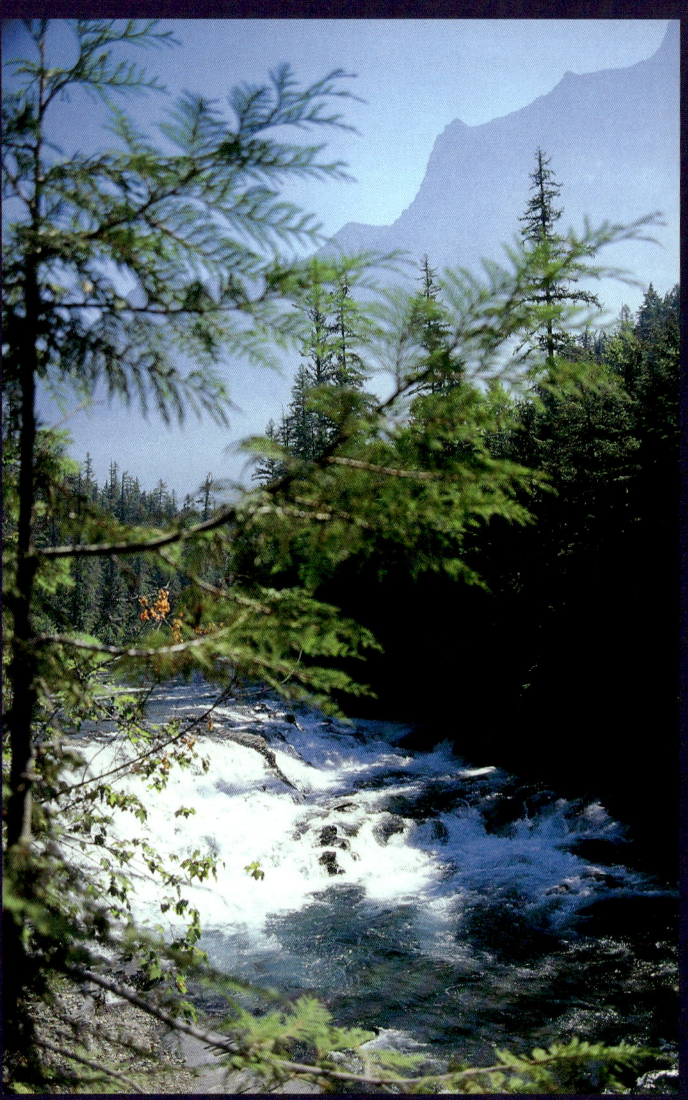

On a ski holiday to Jackson Hole, Wyoming, in January 1974, I met Dr. Jack Walker. We had gathered with friends in the Heidelberg Inn on the evening of a horrendous blizzard. As luck would have it, we fell in love. I quickly discovered on that eventful evening that he was, and still is, an amazing storyteller. The stories that fascinated me most that night were his tales about climbing the Grand Teton, the fourth winter ascent of that 13,970-foot mountain in 1968, the first to include ascents Middle Teton (12,804 feet) and the South Teton (12,514 feet). I had never before heard a story as bone-chilling and thrilling as this one.

And he had stunning photographs to accompany his riveting tales—photographs that depicted in vivid detail his adventures. I could see everything from the wind howling across the face of the Grand Teton to the sculpted tip of its peak.

I realized, soon after that first meeting in Wyoming, that Jack had three loves in his life: mountains, women, and music—in that order! I also found his love and appreciation for the outdoors admirable and unique in my experience.

From the onset of our relationship that fateful evening more than thirty years ago, our adventures have revolved around Jack's photographs. He has photographed our trips around the globe, from our explorations of Montana's Glacier

LEFT: Second cascade at McDonald Creek

National Park to the European Alps, and from the Alaskan Kenai Peninsula to the Andes in South America.

Since 1978, the first time we traveled up the Going-to-the-Sun Highway together, Glacier National Park in Montana has been Jack's passion. After he retired as a doctor in Kalispell in 2003, the park has replaced the hospital emergency room as his "office." At this breath-taking place, he fulfills his passion for capturing fleeting moments of stunning light on landscapes. Whether he's photographing a sunrise-splashed sky over Logan Pass, the knife-edged Garden Wall, or the ice-clear terraces along Logan Creek, Jack captures and celebrates the beauty of nature.

I have had the privilege to observe Jack's many talents throughout our years together. He brings to his photography the qualities that distinguish him as a person: patience, calm, loving, perceptiveness, intelligence, tenacity, humor, and wit. He gives each photograph the time it deserves—waiting for the right light, returning again to create the best possible image, and keeping a good attitude about the perfectionism it takes to be an accomplished landscape photographer.

When it was time to publish these photographs as a book, I volunteered to tie up the loose ends. As this book took shape over the past ten years, I knew that finishing the project would be a labor of love for Jack and me. He took the photographs and created the captions; and I helped him organize the material and work with the editor and designer. But seeing Jack's writing and photography, page by page, brought tears of joy into my heart. It wasn't an easy job collaborating to get the details straight, but Jack and his works of art motivated me, and we made it happen.

Jack has made it easier for me to drive, point, and shoot with a camera. He has inspired me—as I hope he will you—to take to the road in Glacier National Park, to drive slowly through this national treasure, and to stop and photograph unforgettable sights such as Lake McDonald, the Weeping Wall, and Chief Mountain. I am thrilled and honored to have shared in this wonderful experience.

Vaya con Dios.

Photographing Glacier

The public's primary and most extensive exposure to Glacier National Park is along the 52-mile Going-to-the-Sun Road, which runs between West Glacier and East Glacier. The park's west and east sides are divided by Logan Pass, which crosses the Continental Divide at 6,646 feet—and is a spectacle not to be missed! The trip from west to east is also a climb up through forests of aspen, lodgepole pine, and western larch to the open, drier alpine climate.

This guide covers the Going-to-the-Sun Road, mile by mile, with each site pinpointed on the accompanying map. At many of these locations, the National Park Service has provided pullouts for cars as well as interpretive signs with information on the area's geology, natural history, flora, and fauna. In this book, photographs of the flora and fauna that abound in these specific spots are interspersed with landscape images in order to provide you with a more detailed portrait of the area.

In addition, I have included several photographs of Many Glacier and Chief Mountain, two glorious areas that are north of the main part of Glacier National Park. Both sites are located just off of U.S. 89 north of Saint Mary and south of Waterton Lakes National Park in Canada.

I have grouped these photographs into sections, with each section beginning at the odometer setting of zero. These two sections cover the park's west side from Lake McDonald to Logan Pass, and the park's east side from Lunch Creek (just east of Logan Pass) to the town of Saint Mary. This will make it easier for you to retrace your steps and accommodate the starts and stops that inevitably happen on a trip through Glacier National Park.

The park is generally open year round on the west side up to Avalanche Creek, and to Rising Sun Lodge on the east side, depending on the weather. Glacier's climate can change in minutes—especially in the higher elevations—so be prepared with proper winter clothing and gear, even in summer.

On the Road

To reach Glacier National Park, head north on U.S. Highway 2 until you reach the small town of West Glacier. Drive through the town's small commercial area, then head north over the bridge spanning the Middle Fork of the Flathead River until you reach the west entrance of Glacier National Park.

If you would like to get maps and other park information to make your park experience more rewarding, stop at the Orientation Center on the right. Otherwise, after you pay your entrance fee, head into the park.

Drive straight until you reach the "T" in the road, then turn left. Drive 0.25 miles, then turn right at the Apgar Village sign. The fun begins at Apgar Village, a small commercial establishment featuring a motel and cabins, a general store, restaurants, gift shops, and boat rentals—and a great ice cream shop with huckleberry ice cream. Follow the signs to the boat ramp just east of Apgar Village Lodge—a drive of 0.7 miles.

The lower end of 10-mile-long Lake McDonald, the largest lake in Glacier National Park, is one of the most scenic and inspiring sights in the northwest (see pages 2 and 3).

As you continue down the road, you will pass the Apgar Campground at the foot of Lake McDonald. You will quickly reach the "T" junction in the road where you turn left at a park sign that says Lake McDonald and Logan Pass. **Note: Here you will set your odometer to zero, which corresponds to the 0 mile marker on the map.**

Lake McDonald to Logan Pass

This is the beginning of the Going-to-the-Sun Road, the roadway that was finished in 1932 to bisect the heart of Glacier National Park. You will see many nice views as you drive along the southeast shore of Lake McDonald, but the best by far is at 3.4 mile marker on your map. Generally, anytime after 9:00 A.M., the light should be good for your photographs.

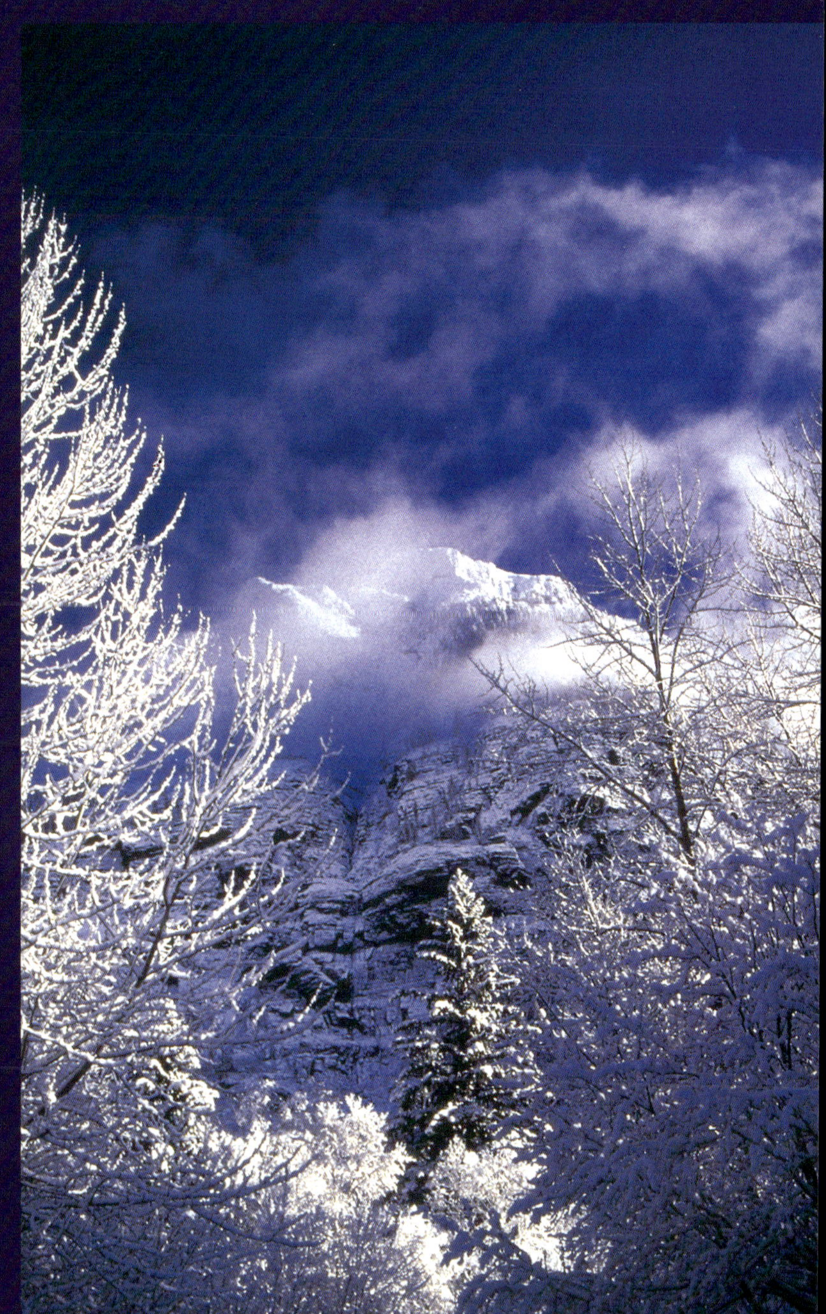

RIGHT: A snowy peak in Glacier in stark relief against a bright blue sky.

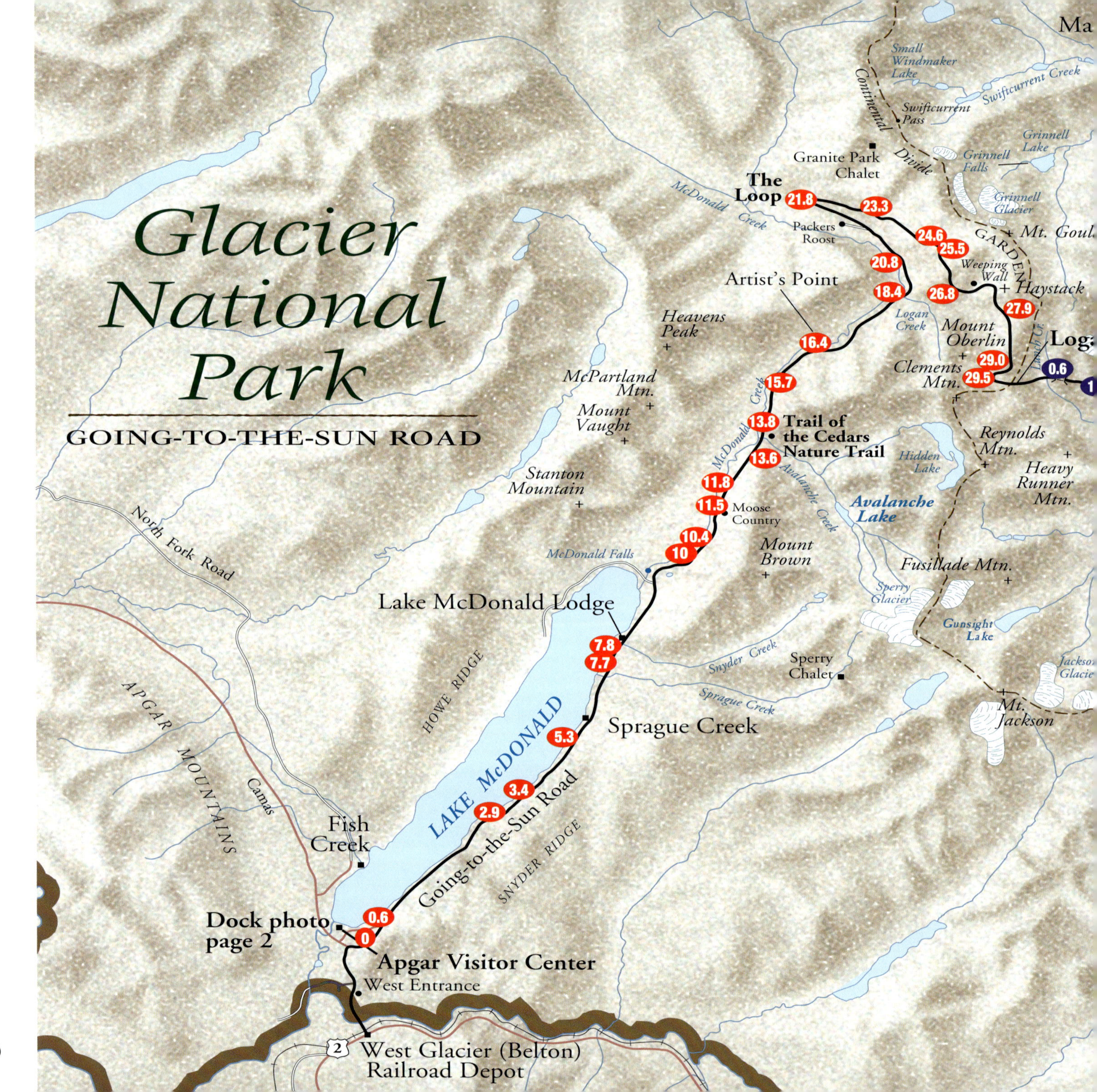

Glacier National Park
GOING-TO-THE-SUN ROAD
The Loop
Granite Park Chalet
Packers Roost
Artist's Point
Heavens Peak
McPartland Mtn.
Mount Vaught
Stanton Mountain
Trail of the Cedars Nature Trail
Moose Country
McDonald Falls
Mount Brown
Lake McDonald Lodge
Sperry Chalet
Sprague Creek
LAKE McDONALD
Going-to-the-Sun Road
HOWE RIDGE
SNYDER RIDGE
APGAR MOUNTAINS
North Fork Road
Fish Creek
Dock photo page 2
Apgar Visitor Center
West Entrance
West Glacier (Belton) Railroad Depot
Continental Divide
Swiftcurrent Pass
Grinnell Glacier
Weeping Wall
Haystack
Logan Creek
Mount Oberlin
Clements Mtn.
Reynolds Mtn.
Heavy Runner Mtn.
Hidden Lake
Avalanche Lake
Fusillade Mtn.
Sperry Glacier
Gunsight Lake
Mt. Jackson
Snyder Creek
Sprague Creek

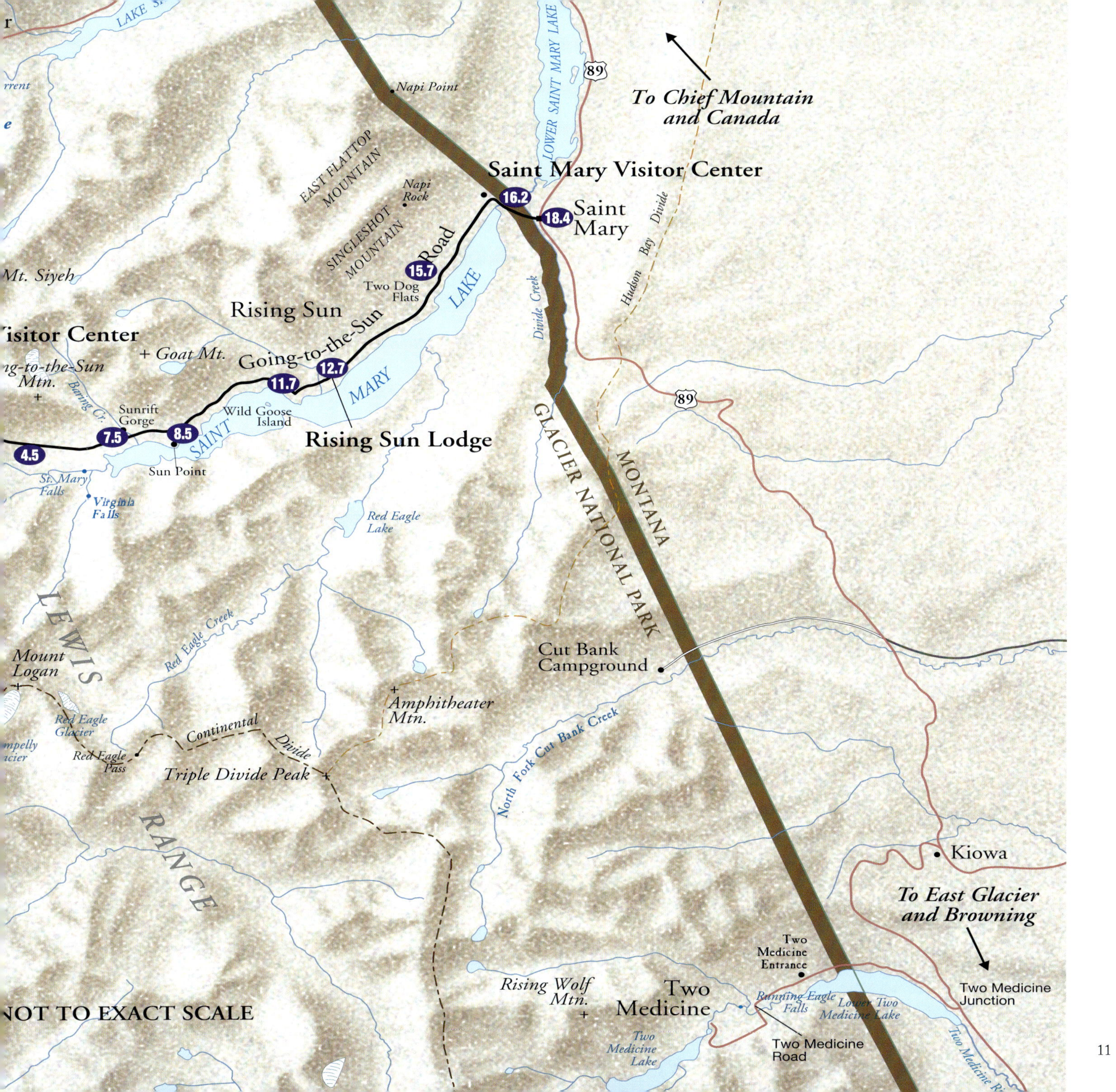
To Chief Mountain and Canada
Napi Point
LOWER SAINT MARY LAKE
89
Saint Mary Visitor Center
EAST FLATTOP MOUNTAIN
Napi Rock
16.2
18.4
Saint Mary
SINGLESHOT MOUNTAIN
Road
15.7
Mt. Siyeh
Two Dog Flats
LAKE
Rising Sun
Divide Creek
Hudson Bay Divide
Visitor Center
Going-to-the-Sun
+ Goat Mt.
12.7
11.7
MARY
Sunrift Gorge
Wild Goose Island
7.5
8.5
SAINT
4.5
Rising Sun Lodge
Sun Point
St. Mary Falls
Virginia Falls
Red Eagle Lake
GLACIER NATIONAL PARK
MONTANA
LEWIS
Red Eagle Creek
Mount Logan
Cut Bank Campground
Amphitheater Mtn.
Red Eagle Glacier
Continental Divide
Red Eagle Pass
Triple Divide Peak
North Fork Cut Bank Creek
RANGE
Kiowa
To East Glacier and Browning
Two Medicine Entrance
Rising Wolf Mtn.
Two Medicine
Running Eagle Falls
Lower Two Medicine Lake
Two Medicine Junction
NOT TO EXACT SCALE
Two Medicine Lake
Two Medicine Road

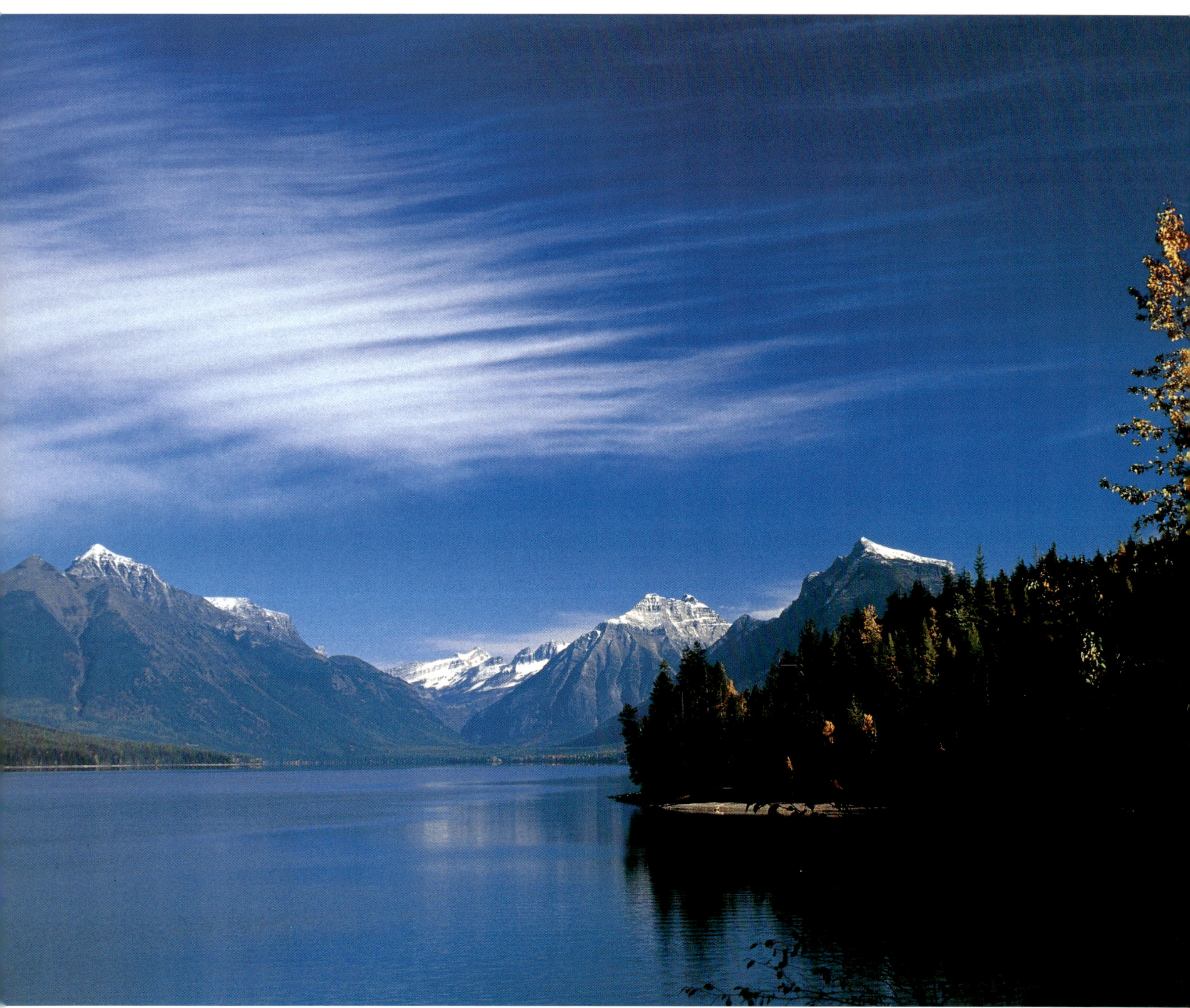

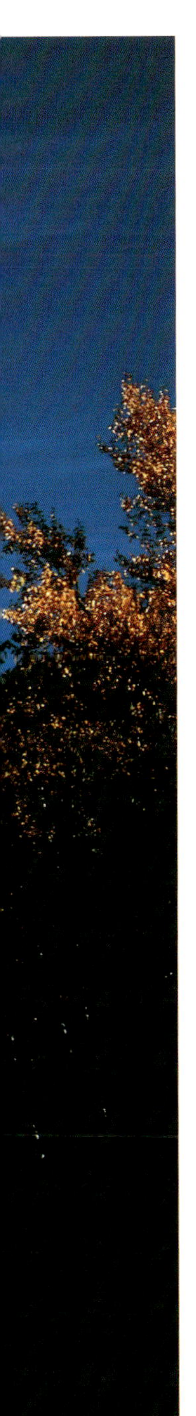

LEFT: ***Mile 0.6.*** With Lake McDonald as a background, this captivating spot is a great site for a family shot.

BELOW: ***Mile 2.9.*** A small beach lends perspective to this summertime image of Lake McDonald and the surrounding mountains.

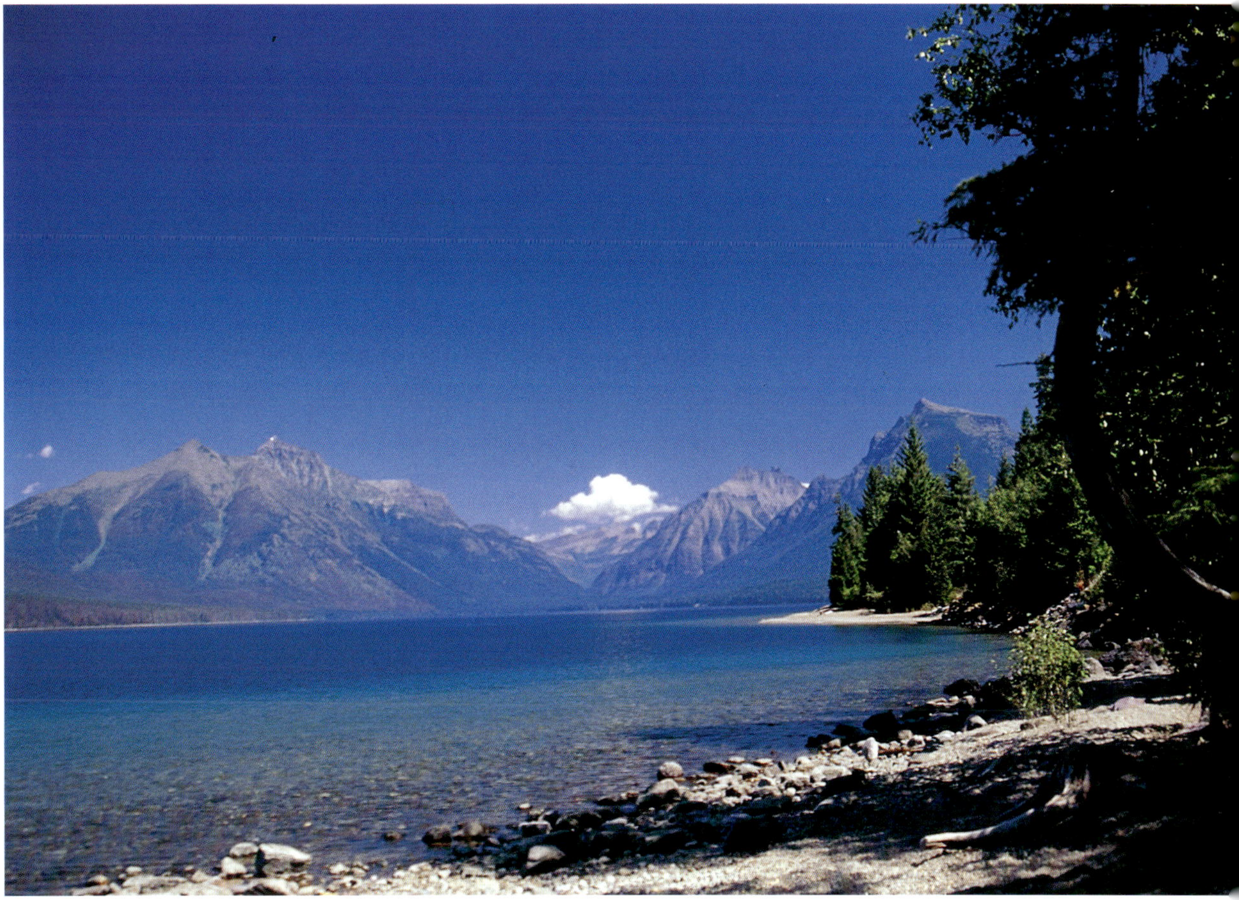

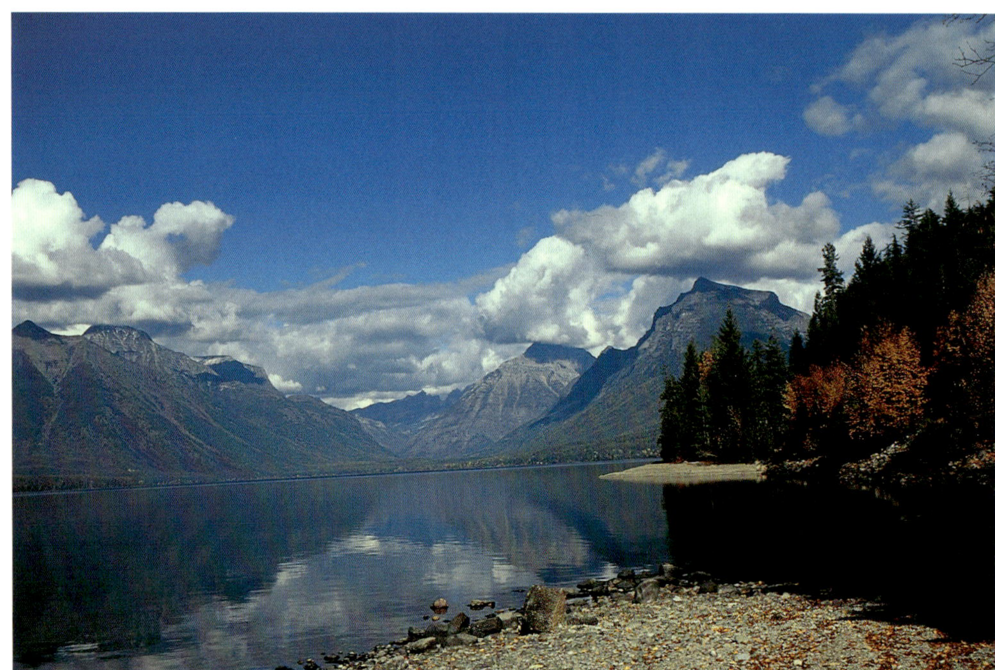

RIGHT: ***Mile 3.4.*** Autumn paints the trees surrounding Lake McDonald in reds and golds.

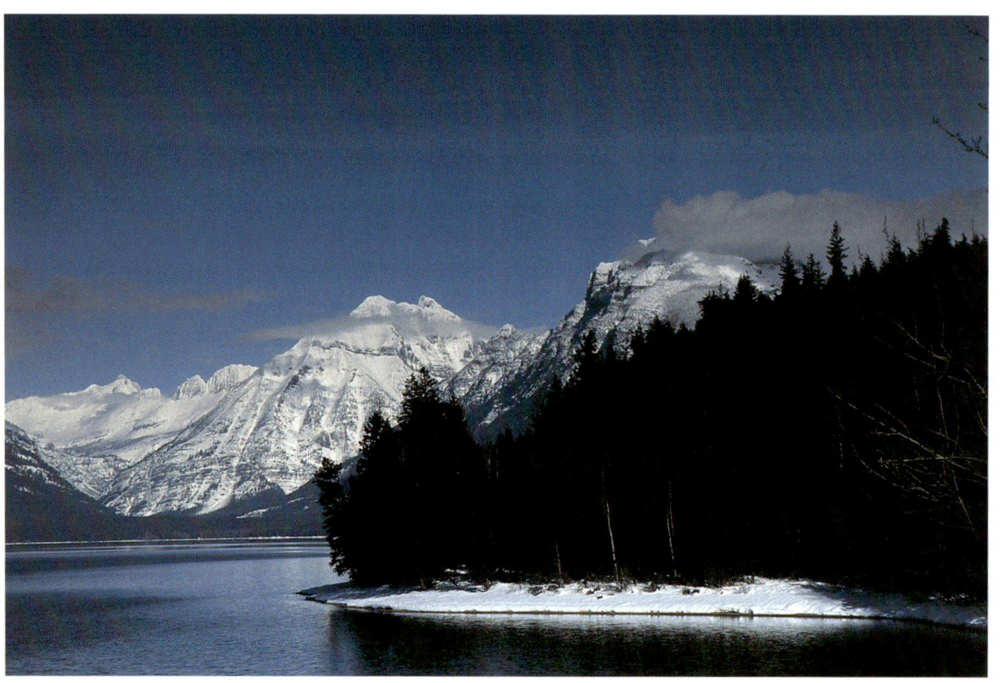

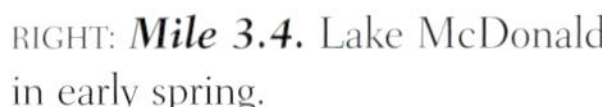

RIGHT: ***Mile 3.4.*** Lake McDonald in early spring.

FACING PAGE: ***Mile 3.4.*** Lake McDonald, pictured here in summer, is framed by western larch and Douglas fir trees, two of the park's nineteen species of trees. From the pullout, you will need to walk down toward the water about twenty feet to frame your photograph of Lake McDonald with the large trees.

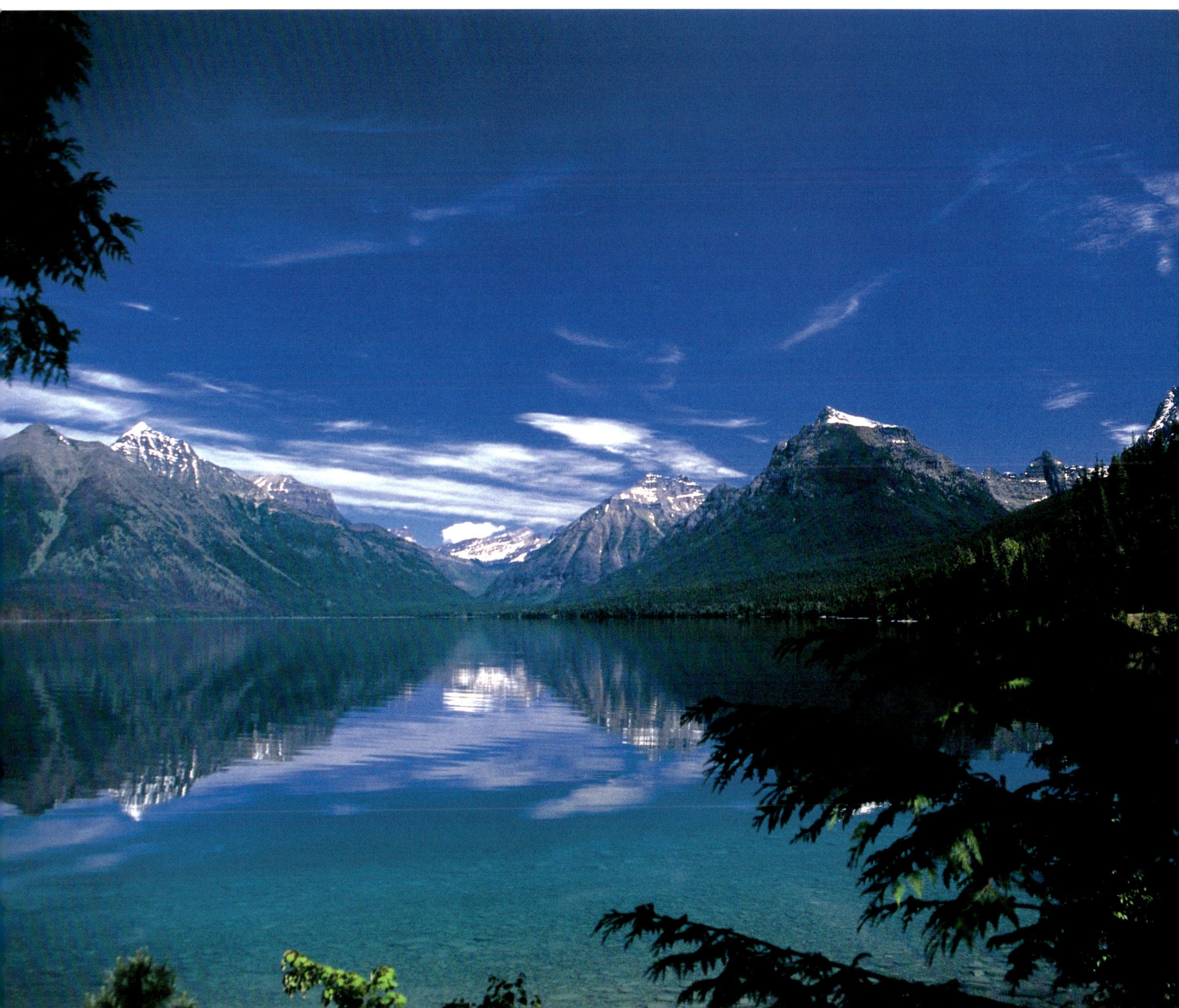

RIGHT: A rainbow over Lake McDonald can occur at any mile marker, should you be so fortunate.

BELOW: ***Mile*** **5.3.** Lake McDonald, from another angle, in early spring with a picture-perfect reflection of the mountains in the lake.

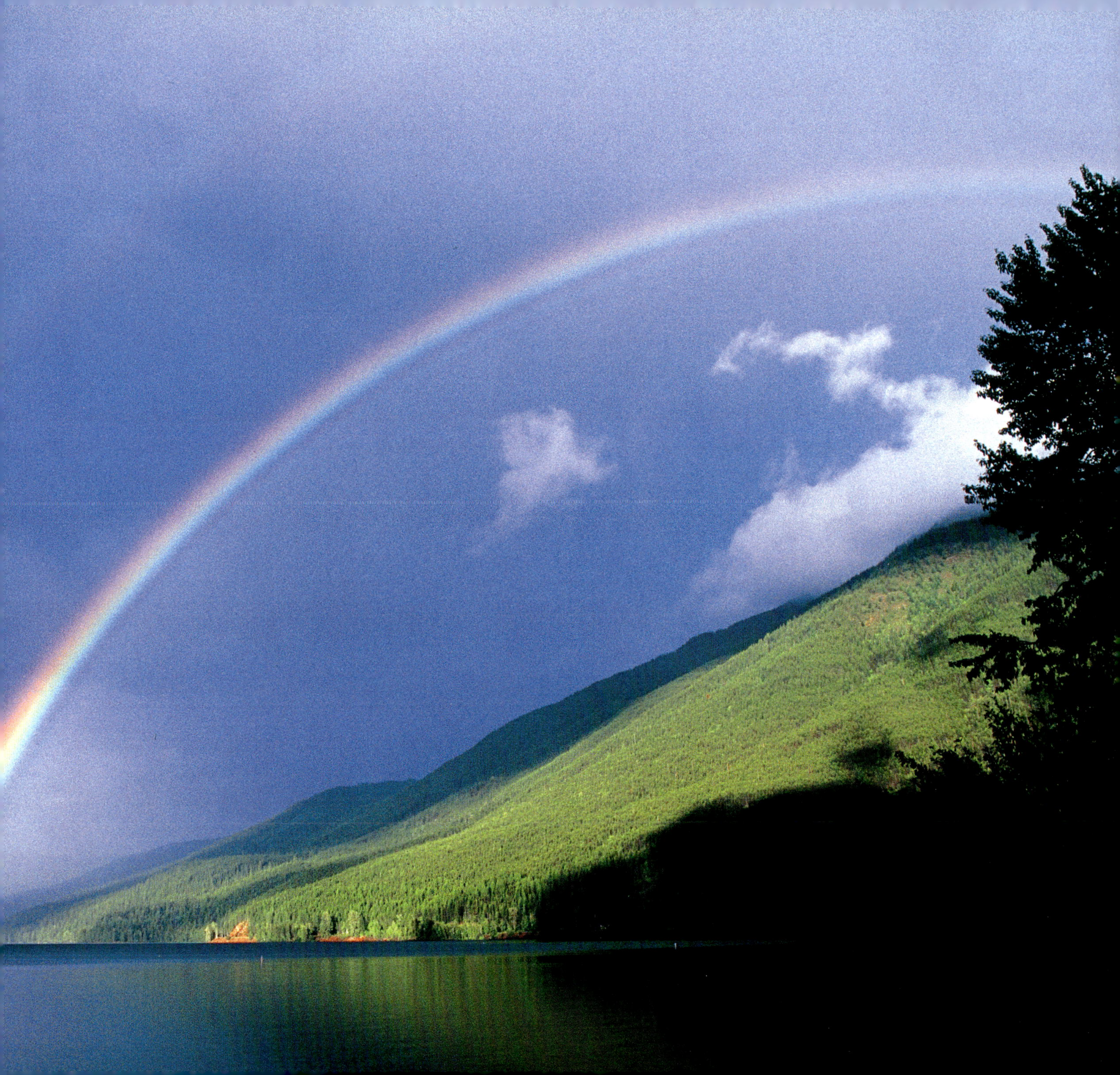

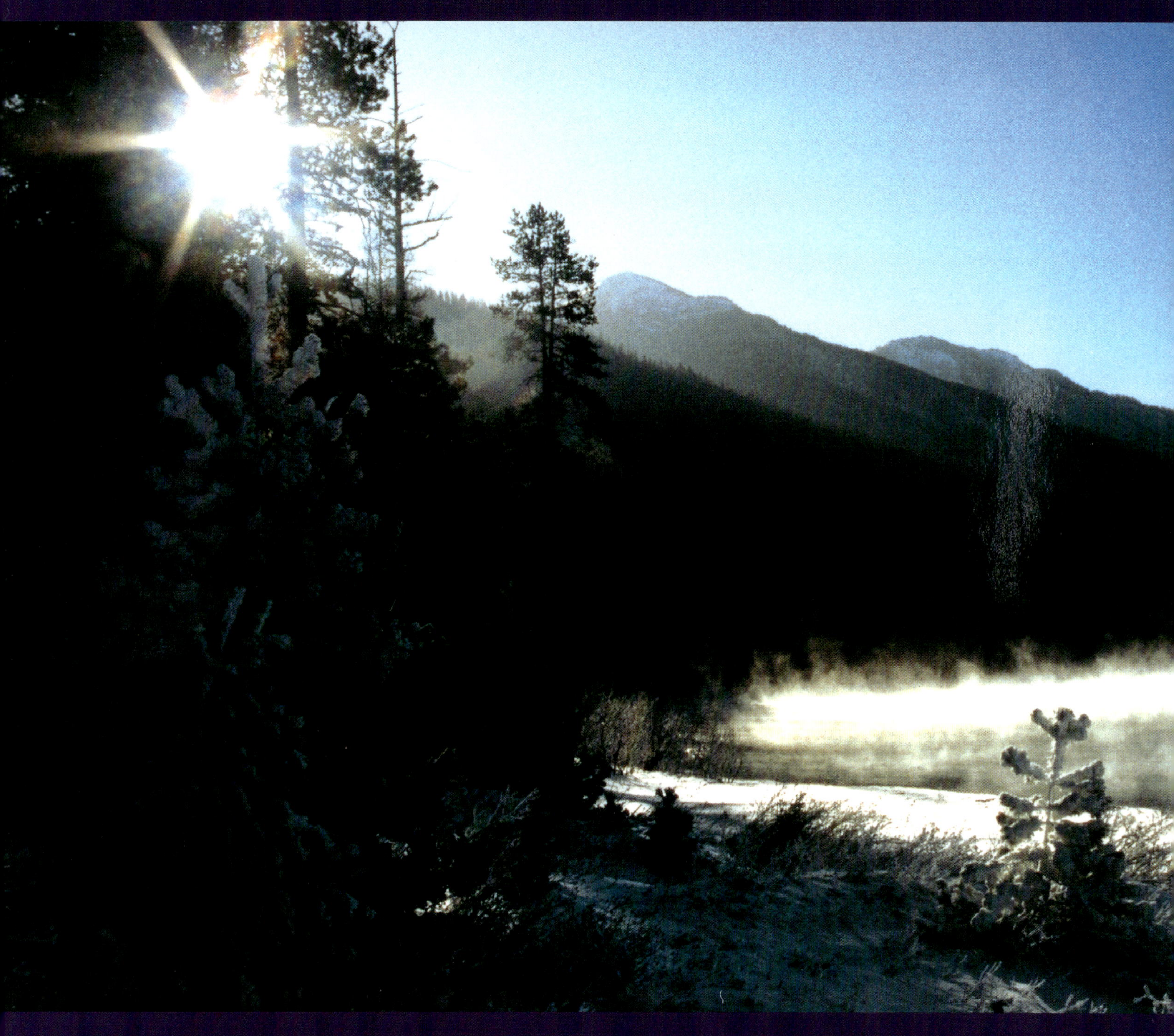

These next three photographs illustrate how light can transform an ordinary scene. The view from this location is not that exceptional, unless you enhance the shot by taking advantage of shafts of sunlight breaking through the clouds or sunsets, as these photos do.

LEFT: ***Mile 7.7.*** I call this shot the "Christmas Star Scene." This pullout, at the north end of the lake, features an exhibit that explains how the lake was formed during the last ice age, when glaciers filled the area. The largest glaciers scoured out Saint Mary and McDonald Valleys, which now hold lakes that feature expansive views of Glacier's glacially carved, craggy peaks.

BELOW: Taken in summer, this is looking at the northern end of Lake McDonald.

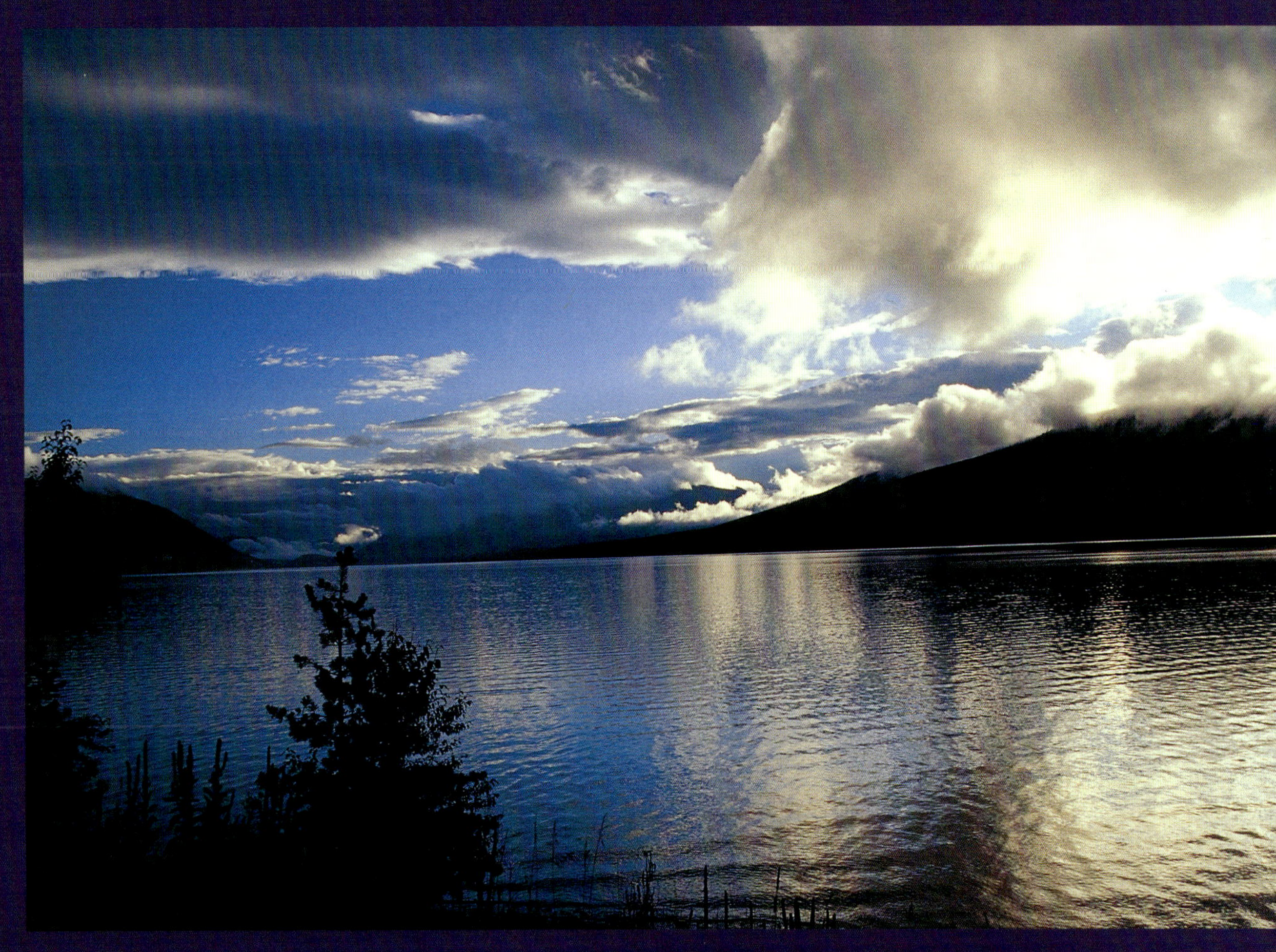

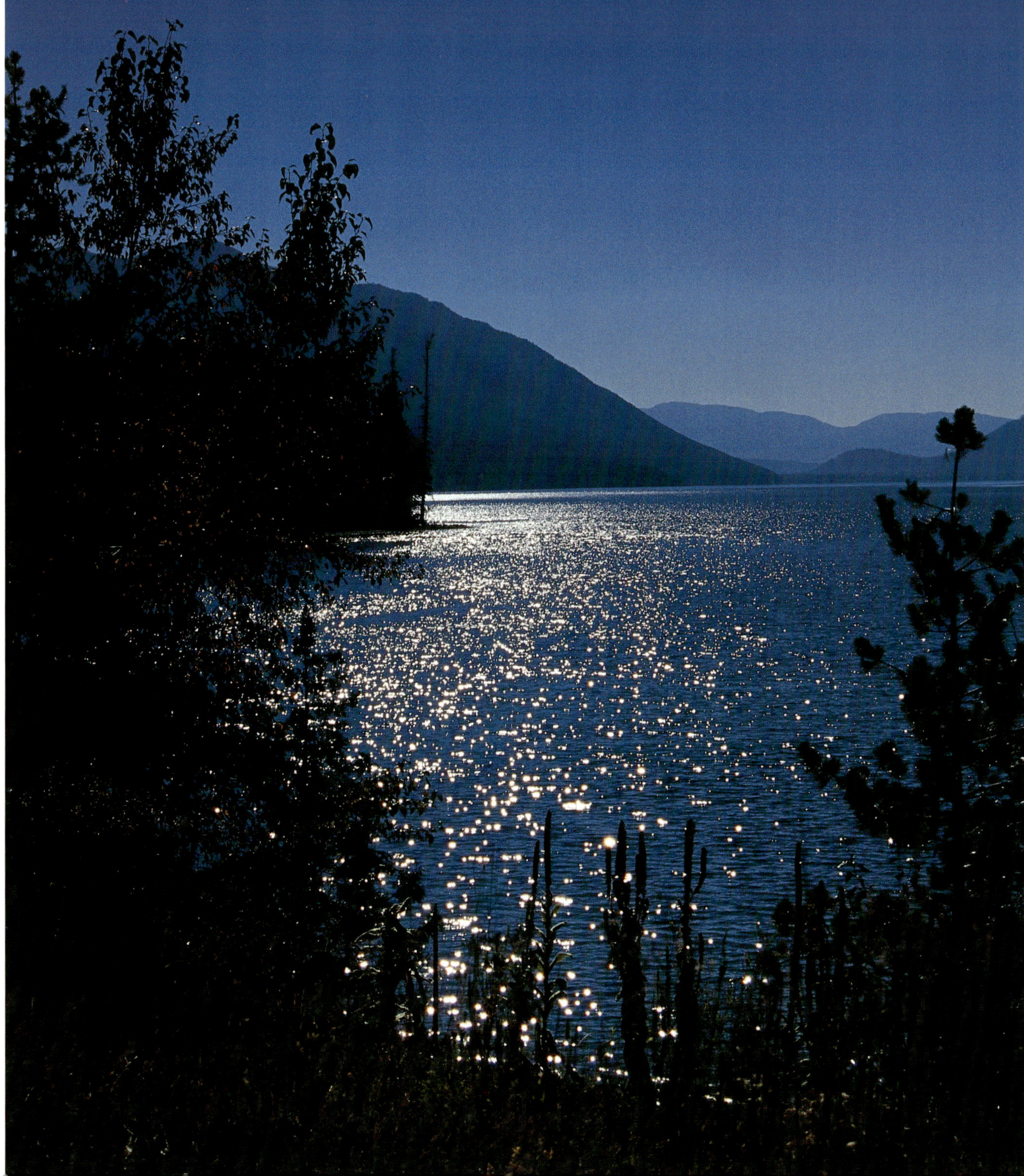

FACING PAGE: ***Mile* 7.7.** Another photo of extraordinary light on Lake McDonald. Lake McDonald Lodge is just around the corner.

RIGHT: ***Mile* 7.8.** Lake McDonald Lodge, nestled in a grove of old cedars, is a wonder of its own just like the other park lodges, which are all historic and stately. The elegant yet rustic Swiss-style structure was built as a hunting lodge in 1913 by John Lewis and was known as Lewis's Glacier Hotel. Today the lodge features a lobby with a massive stone fireplace, a restaurant overlooking the lake, and boat tours. Accommodations are available in the lodge and the quaint cabins.

Note: If you decide to pull into the Lake McDonald Lodge, be sure to add 0.2 miles to each of the following stops. **The sequential mile markers, as they are listed, do not account for a stop at the lodge.**

BELOW: Aquatic plants on Lake McDonald.

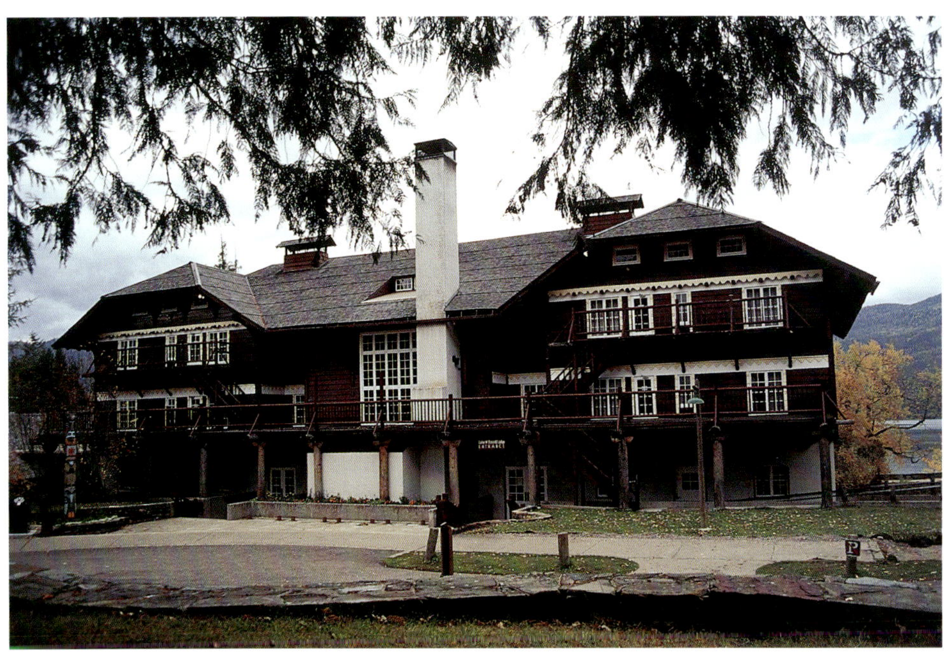

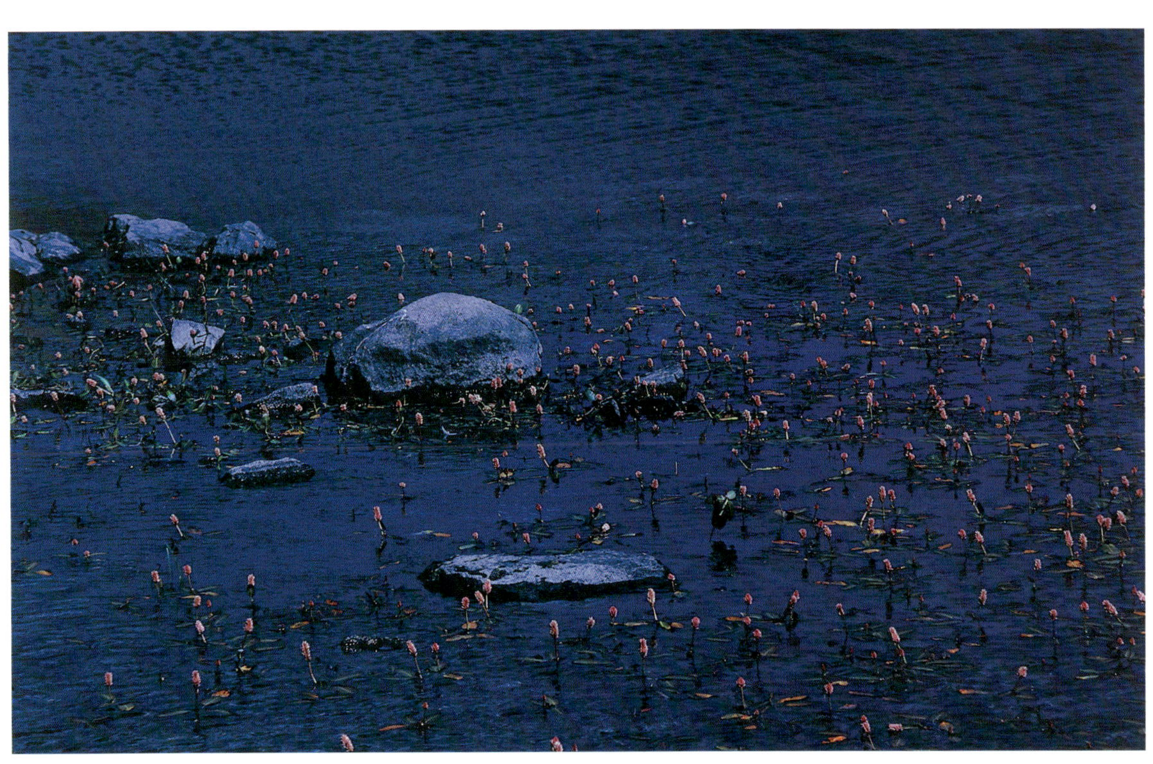

Miles 10.0 to 11.5. ou will drive alongside McDonald Creek, which feeds nto Lake McDonald. he three significant ascades in this lower art of McDonald Creek are the next ites you will pproach. They are vell worth the stops. Each location is beautiful and so different rom the others that t is difficult to select he prettiest. If you lrive on by, you will niss the unique charcteristics of these ister cascades.

IGHT: *Mile 10.0.* ined by banks of noss-covered limestone, the water of he first cascade is hundering and powerful as it travels over he metamorphic ock. You can also nclude Stanton Mountain in the ackground here.

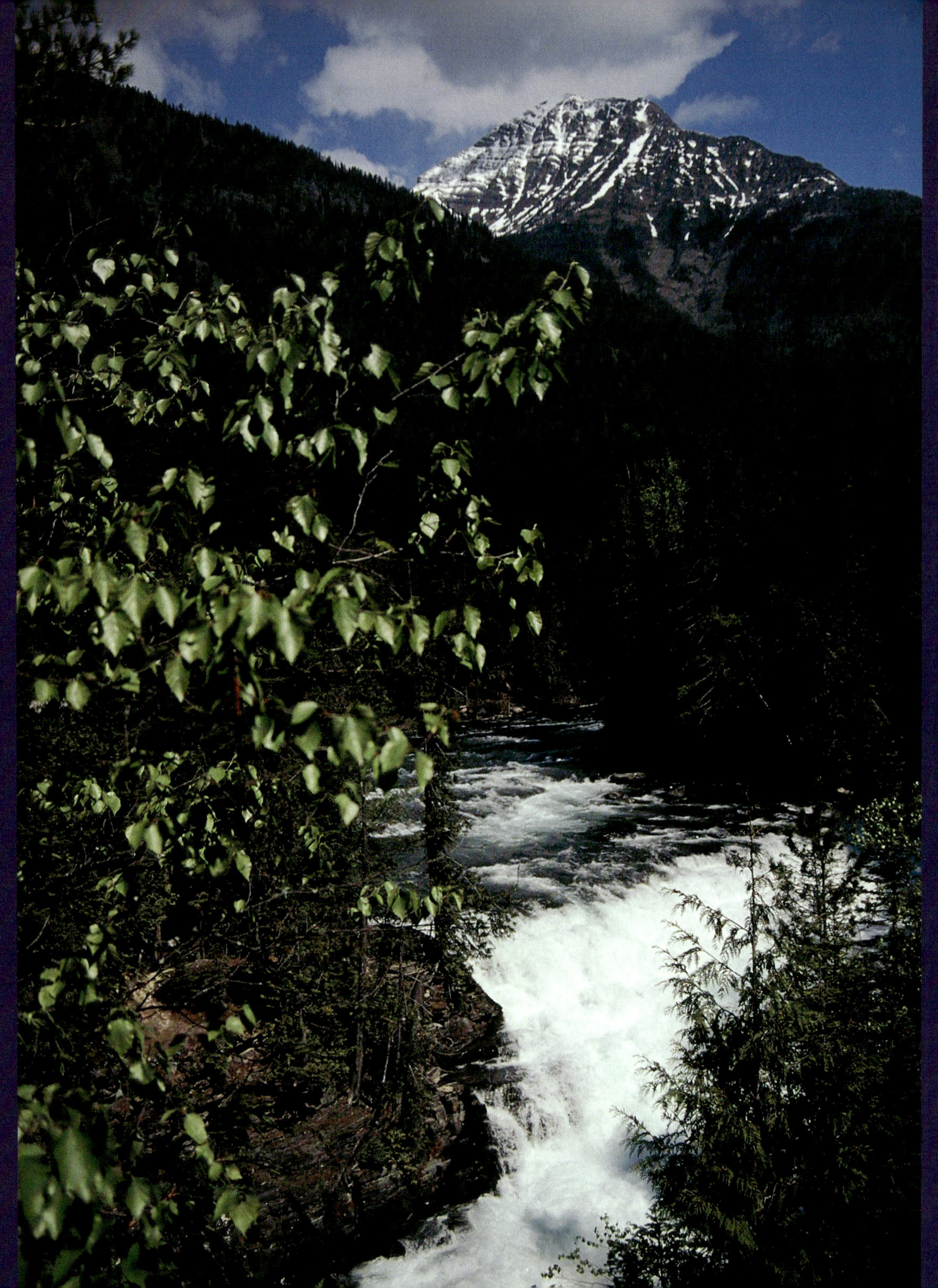

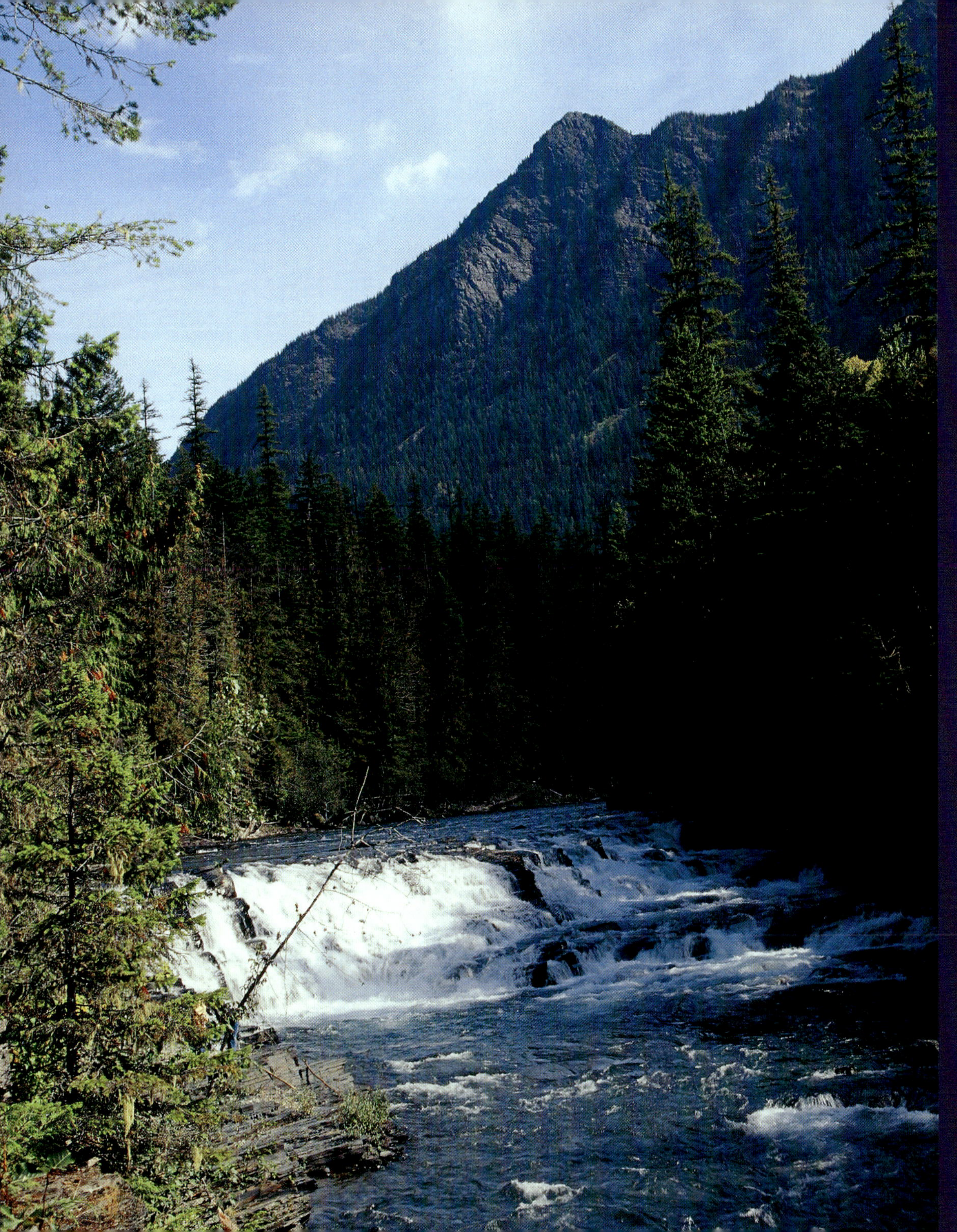

LEFT: ***Mile 10.4.*** Use the mountain in the background to frame this photo from the far end of the footbridge across McDonald Creek, just below McDonald Falls. This is an especially impressive site in the spring when the runoff fills the creek, turning it into a rushing torrent. You can smell the fresh scent of water and pine as you walk down toward the bridge.

RIGHT: ***Mile 11.5.*** In between mile makers 10.4 and 11.8, you will see a lovely group of mountain terraces known as the Ledges above McDonald Creek.

FAR RIGHT: ***Mile 11.8.*** From an overhanging deck provided by the National Park Service, you can see the third cascade of McDonald Falls. In the spring the water is churning and pulsing, but by fall it often slows to a trickle. You can frequently see harlequin ducks at this stop. Be sure to go onto the deck for good photo opportunities up and down this splendid area of McDonald Creek and the surrounding mountains.

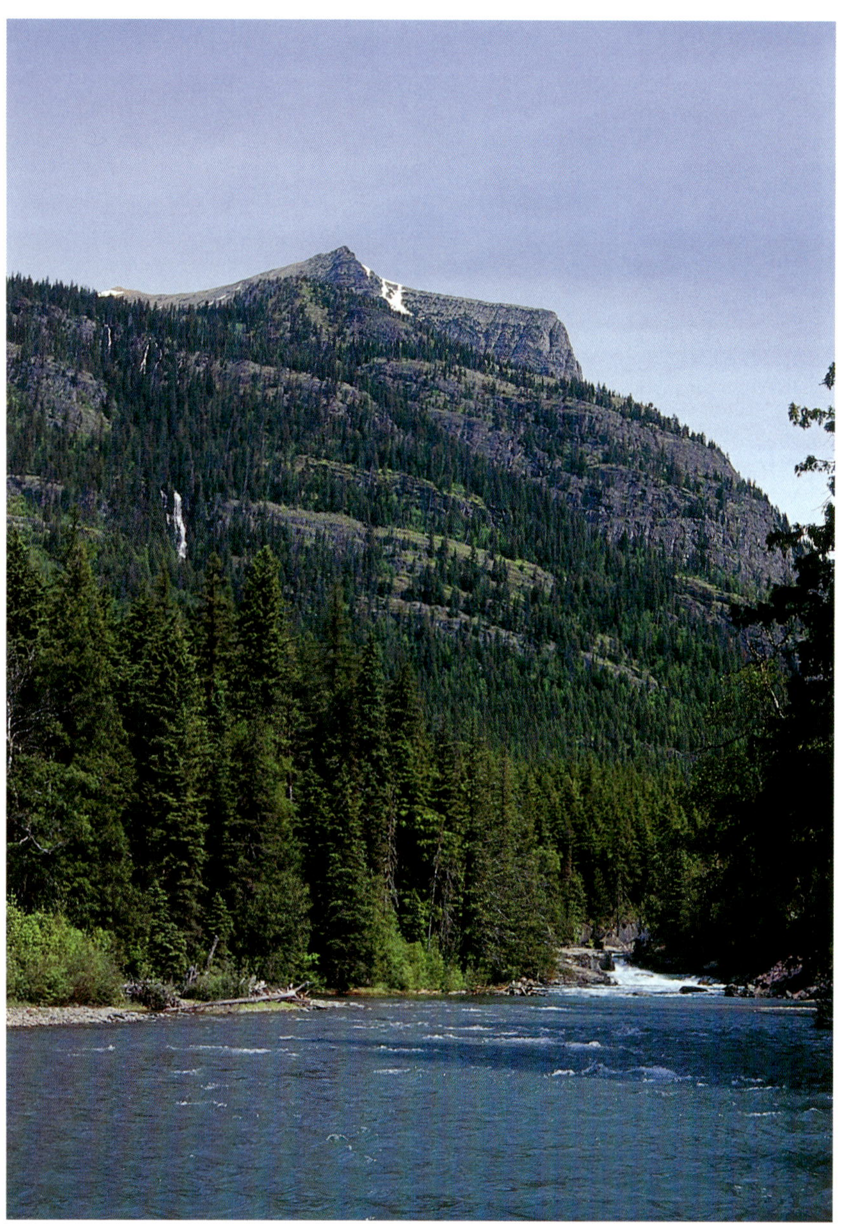

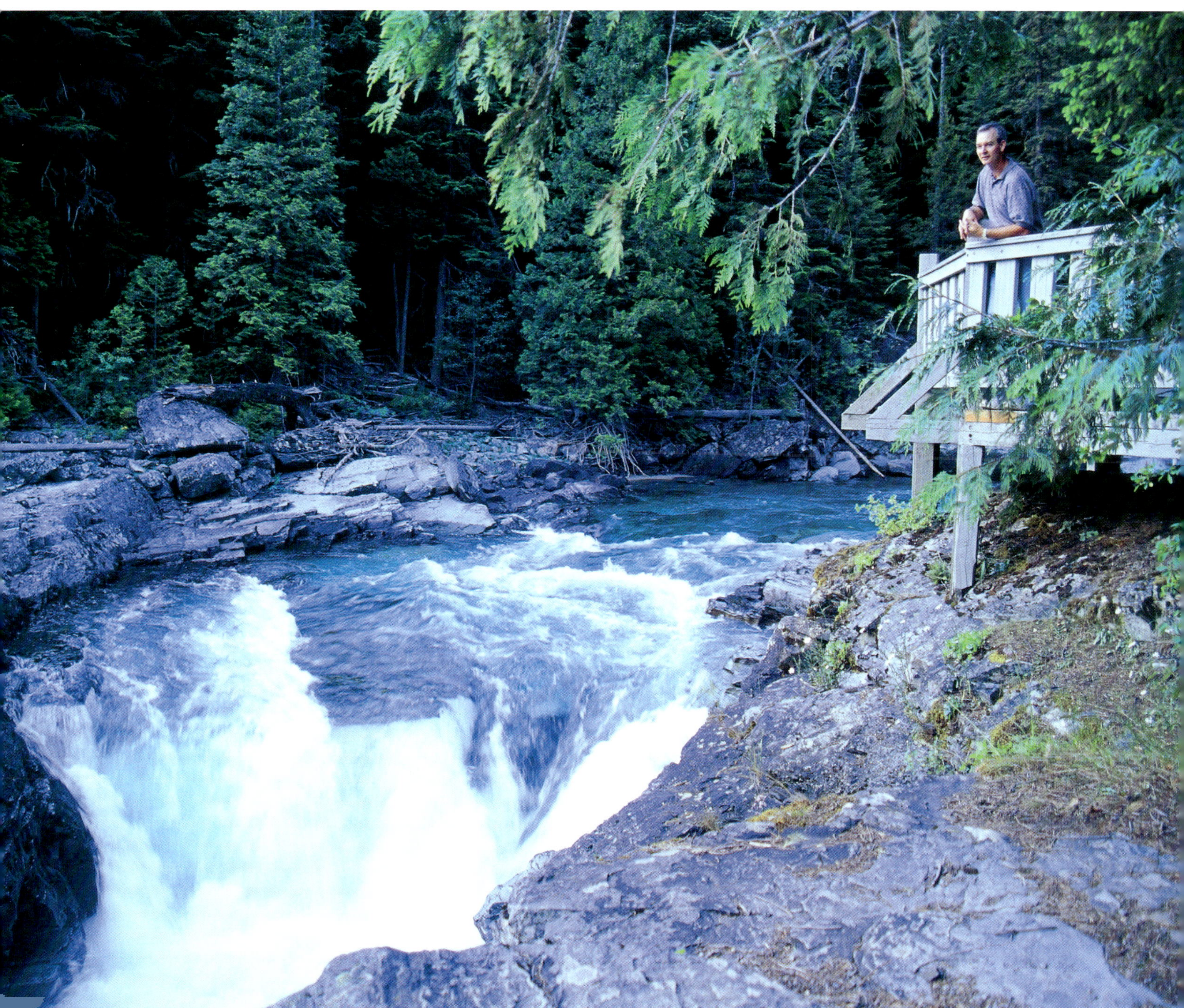

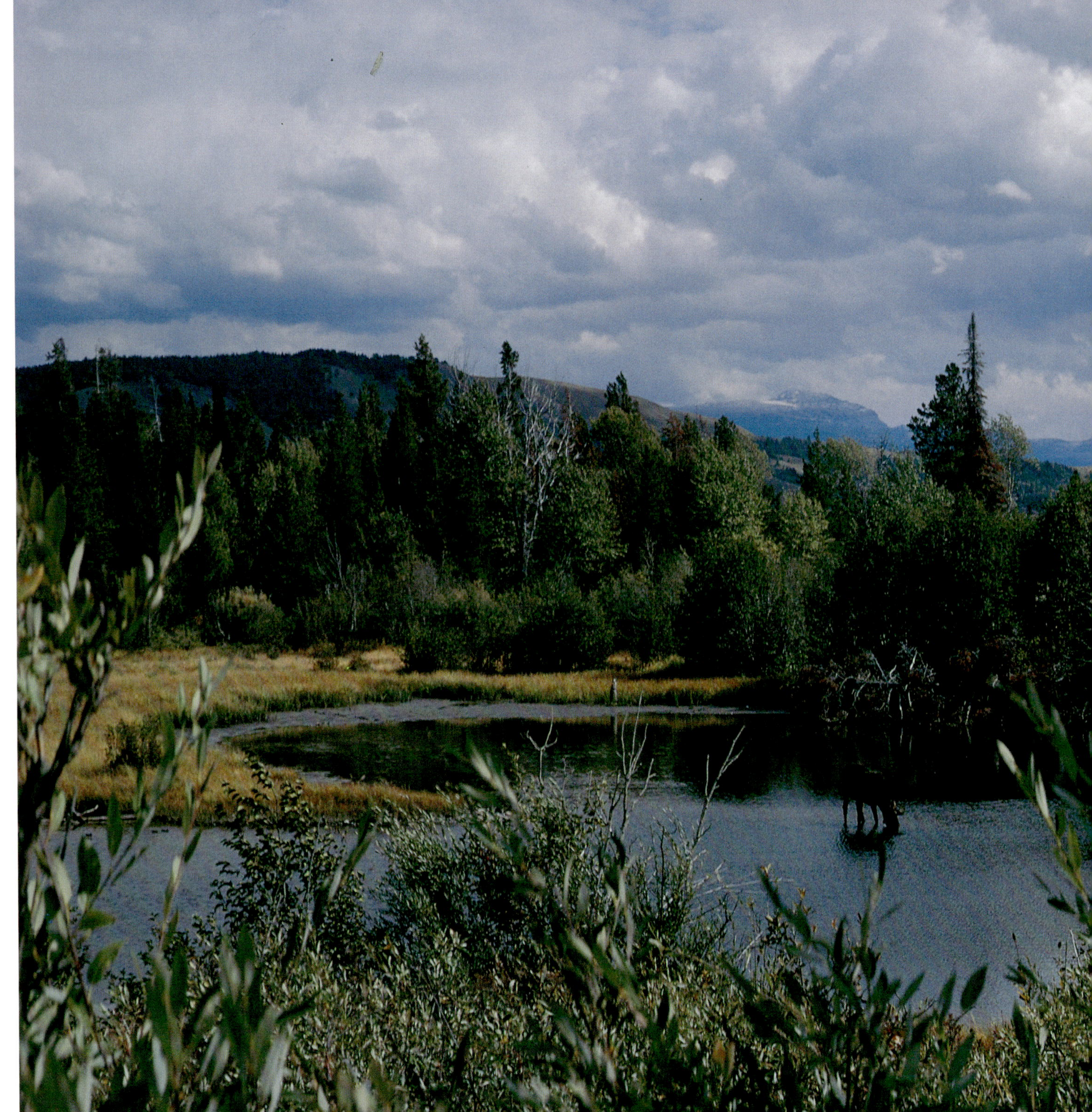

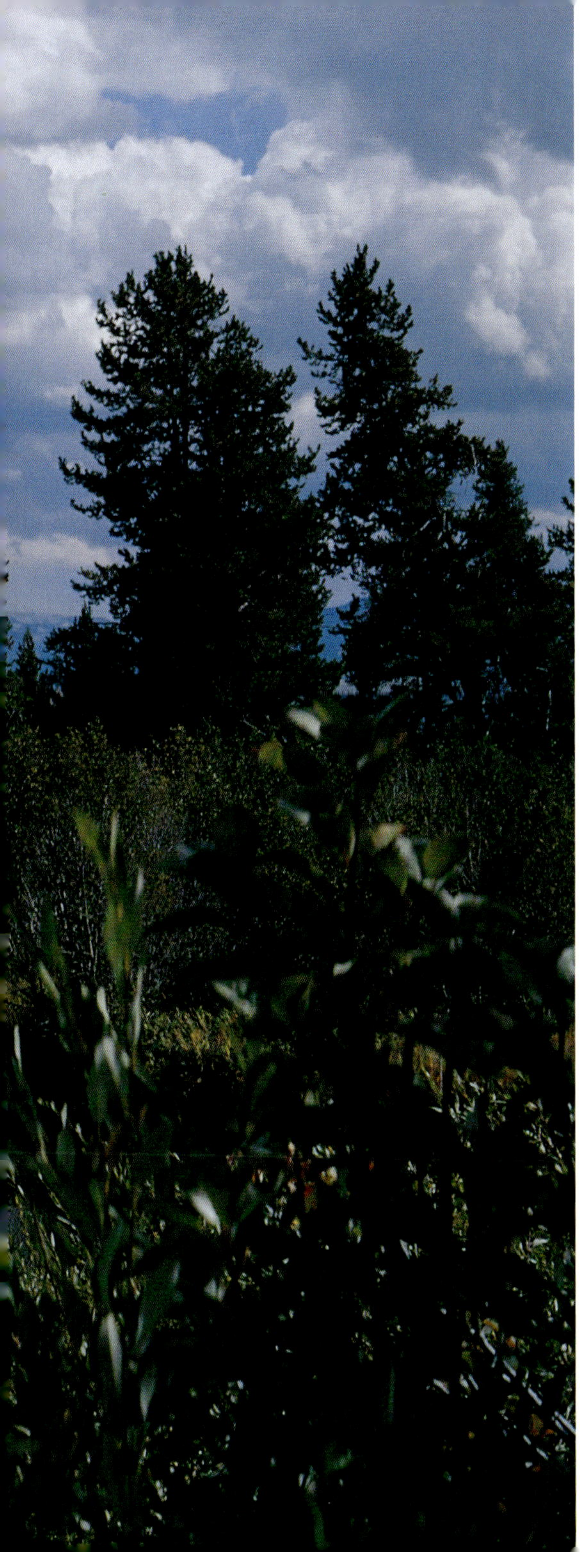

LEFT: ***Mile 13.6.*** As you drive, watch for the pond on the right-hand side of the road. If you are lucky, you may see a moose.

Mile 13.8. If you are interested in a short walk, I suggest stopping at the 0.7-mile Trail of the Cedars, a dark, almost spooky path lined with boulders, tall western red cedars, and small waterfalls along the meandering Avalanche Creek into the Avalanche Gorge. There is an excellent boardwalk along half of the hike; the rest is a well-maintained dirt path. This easy walk, suitable for all ages, has resting benches along the way and is wheelchair accessible.

BELOW: ***Mile 13.8.*** A view of Avalanche Creek along the first part of the Trail of the Cedars hike.

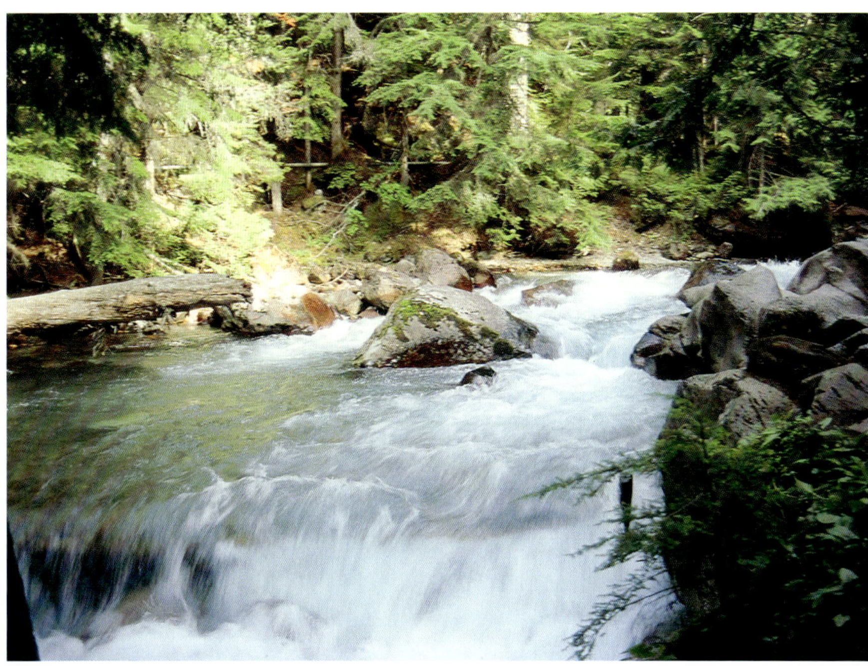

RIGHT: ***Mile 13.8.*** Avalanche Gorge as it can be seen from the loop on the Trail of the Cedars. This is quite spectacular and well worth the short walk.

FAR RIGHT: ***Mile 13.8.*** If you are interested in an afternoon picnic, I recommend taking the moderate, 4.6-mile round-trip hike to Avalanche Lake, a glacial cirque. One of the most popular hikes in the park, the Avalanche Lake hike begins at the apex of the Loop, near the Gorge, and climbs through a forest of western red cedar and western hemlock and borders the western shore of Avalanche Lake. **Don't confuse this hike with the Avalanche Trail hike.**

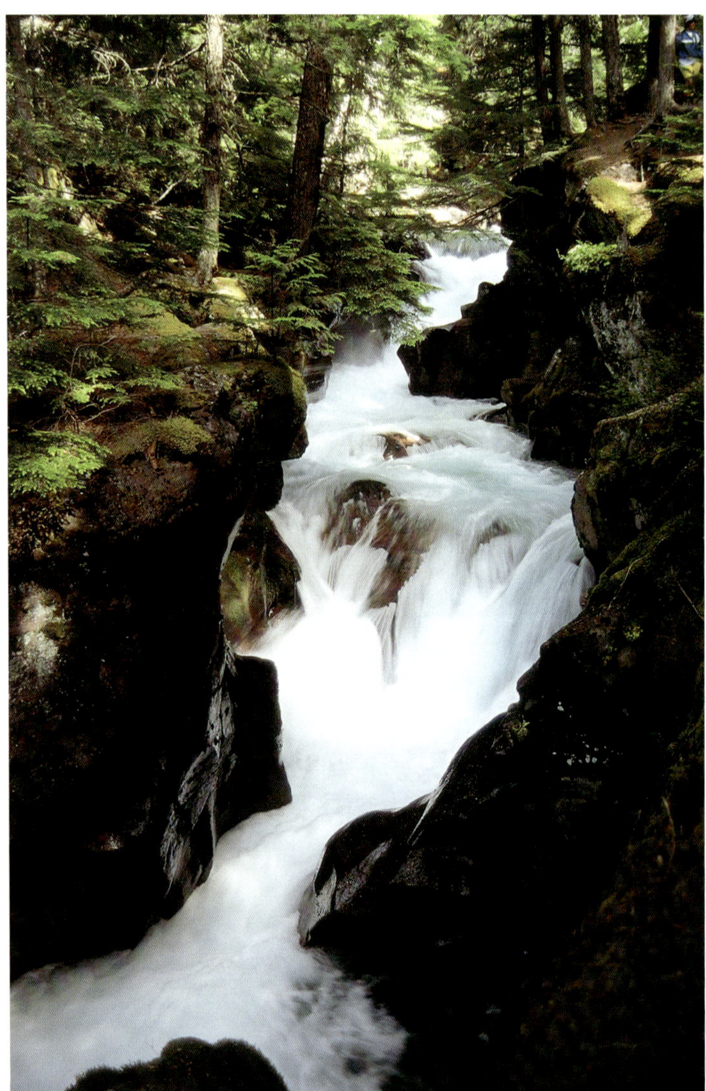

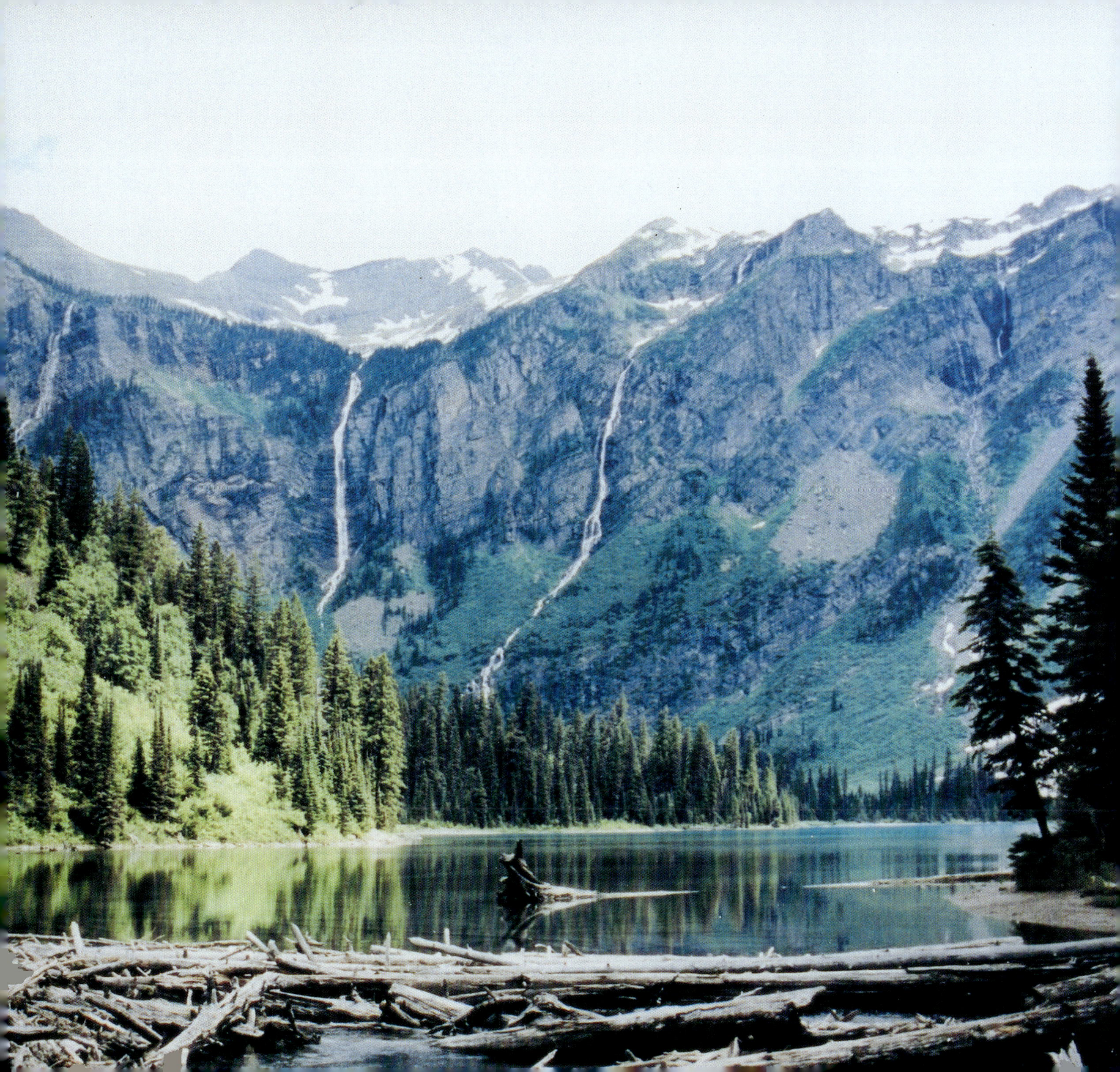

RIGHT: ***Mile 15.7.*** Look back to your left to see an expansive view of Mount Vaught, which is stunning when it is bright with the yellows and reds of fall. Be sure to include the small stream in the foreground of the picture.

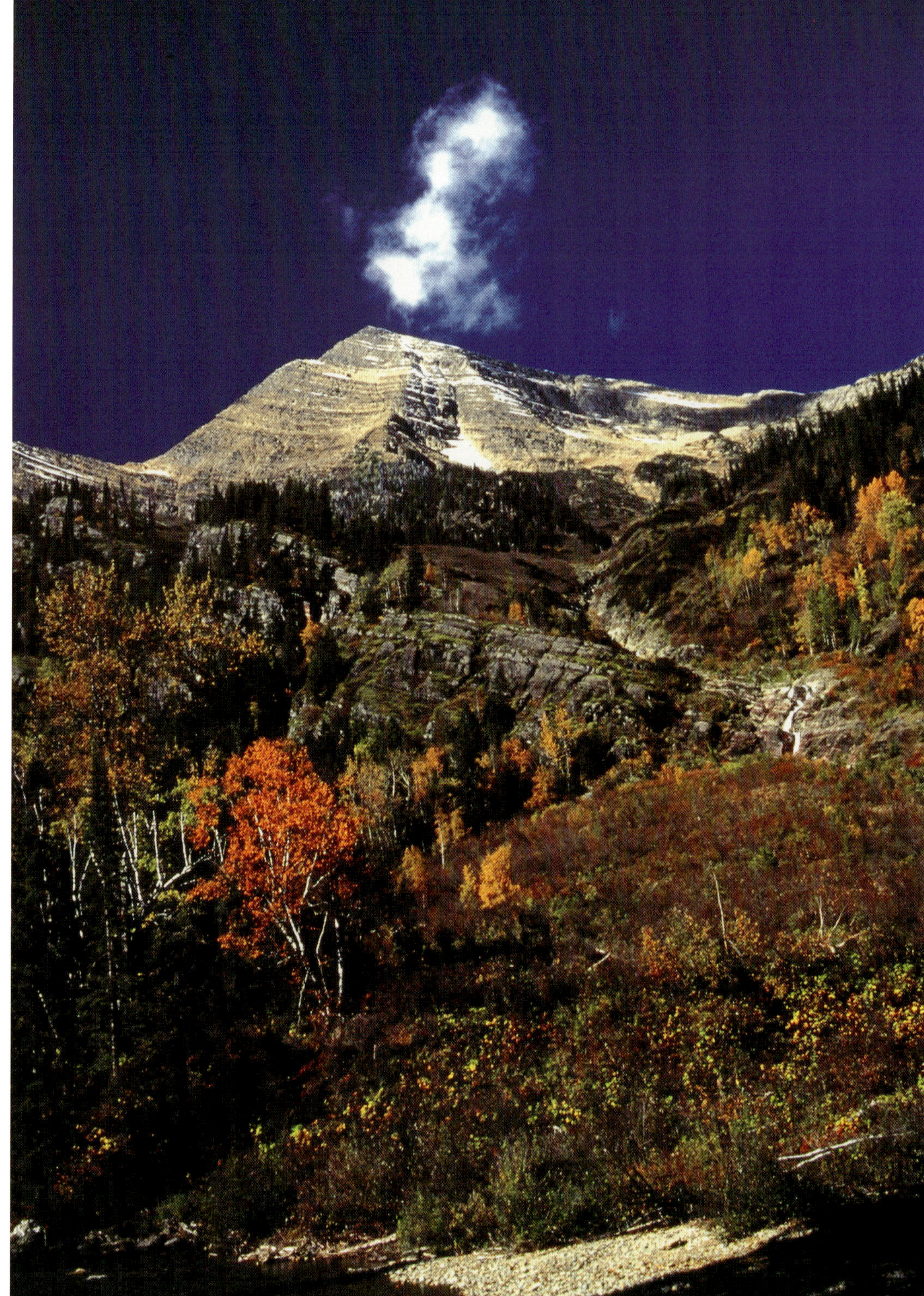

BELOW: ***Mile 16.4.*** From the gravel bar on the left, you can take an enticing shot of the Garden Wall. I call this "Artist's Point," because so many local artists set up their easels here. If you stop to take photographs, you will often hear a chorus of birds, including mountain bluebirds, black-capped chickadees, and killdeer. There are also many good shots of the forest here, featuring the blue spruce and Douglas fir trees. In the springtime, the Garden Wall is often colored a mossy green.

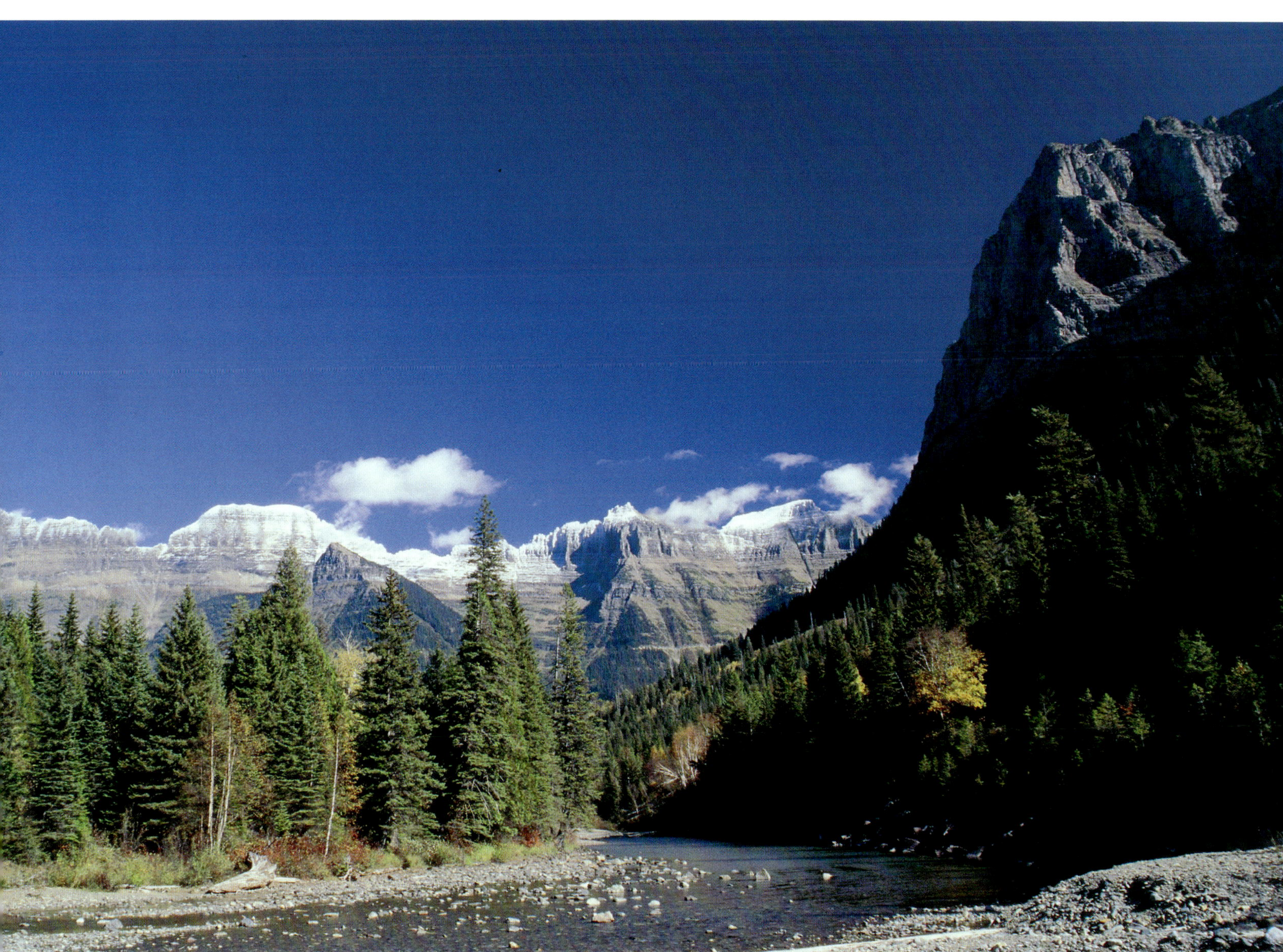

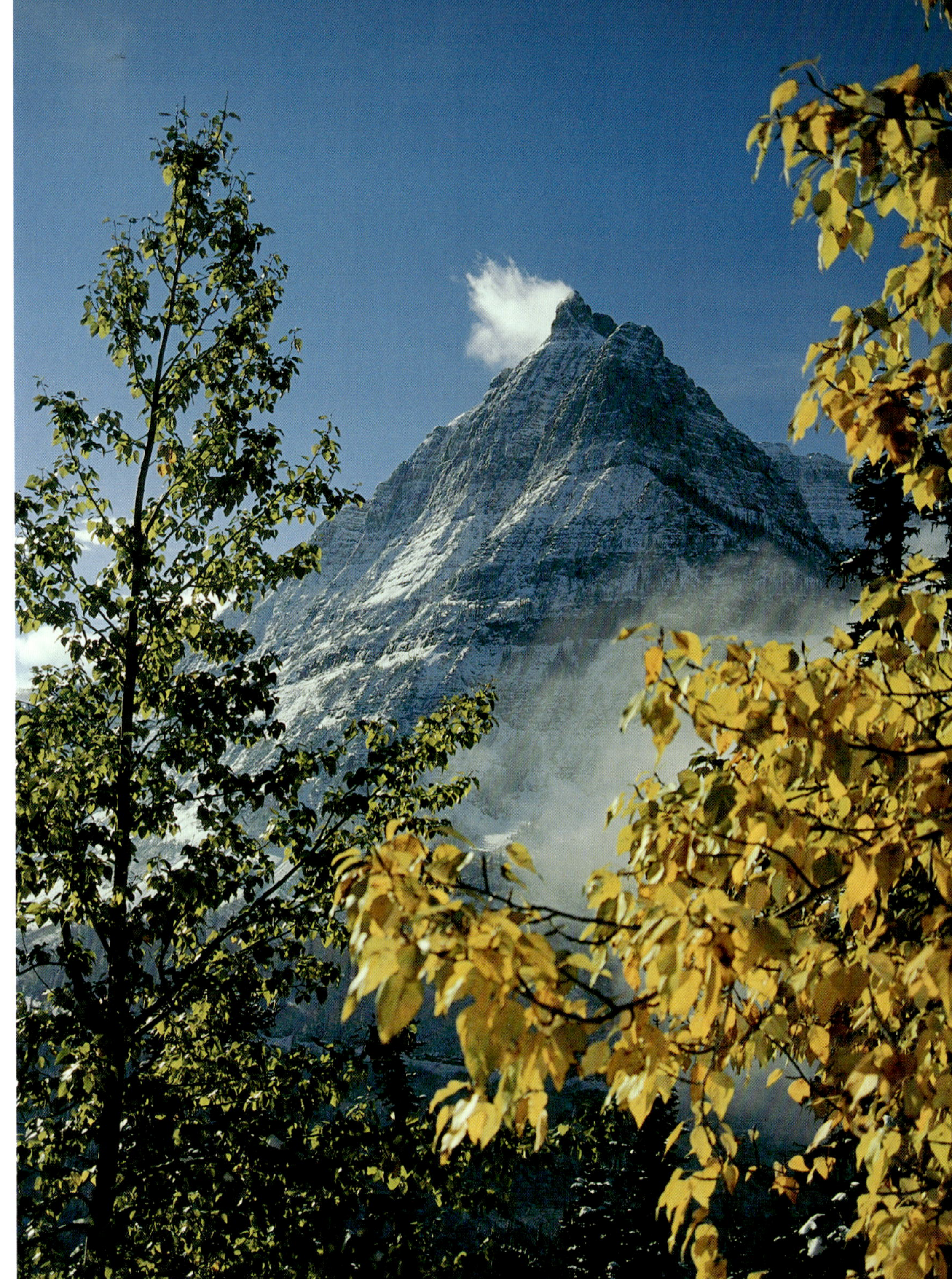

RIGHT: ***Mile 16.4.*** From here, look up to see a superb view of 8,180-foot Mount Oberlin.

BELOW: A view of Glacier National Park's peaks from U.S. Highway 2 East, outside the park.

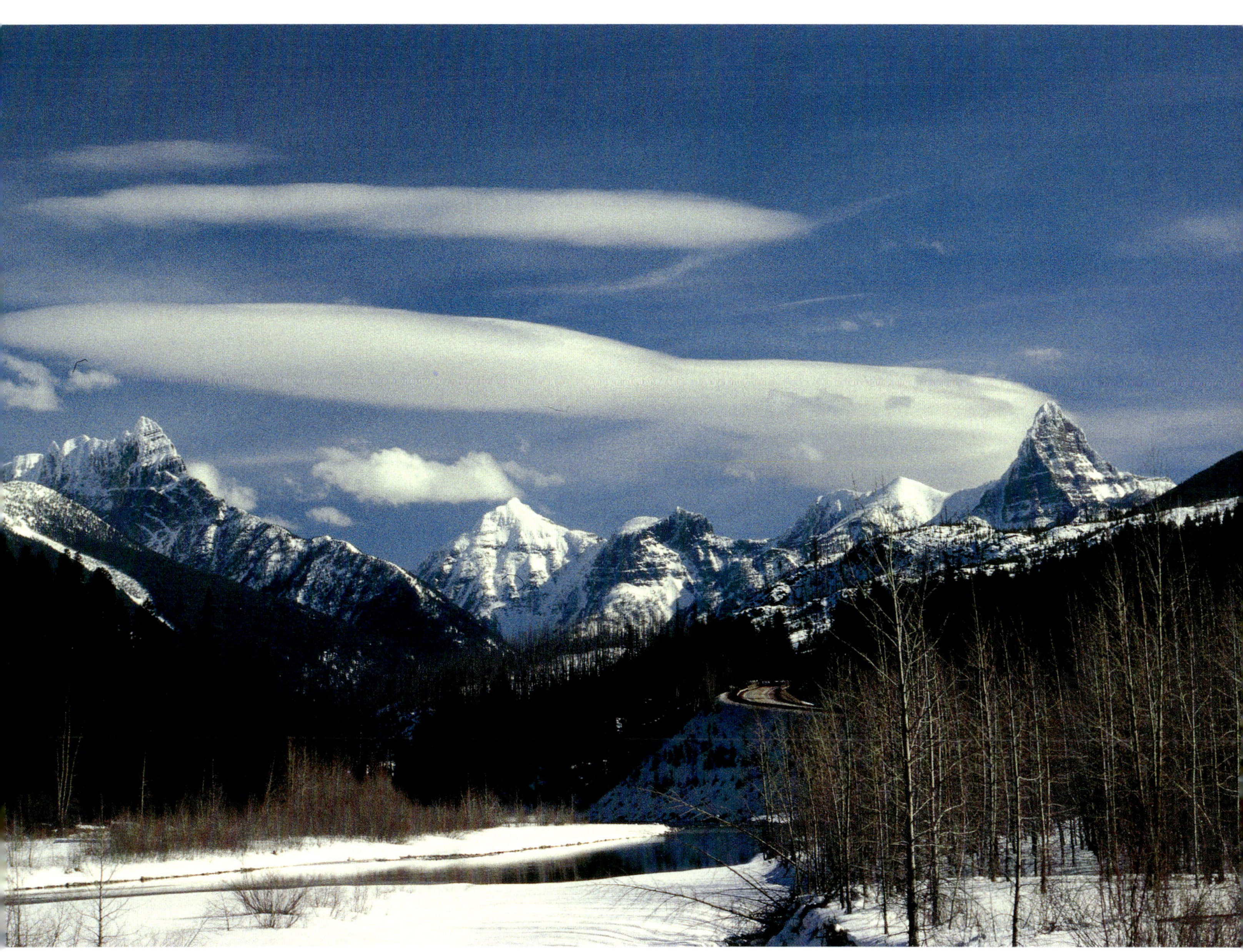

RIGHT: ***Mile 18.4.*** This appealing scene along Logan Creek features Packer's Roost, an old ranger's cabin, with the dramatic 492-foot Bird Woman Falls in the background. Unfortunately there is no real pullout along here, but stopping is worth the trouble. Traffic permitting, park at the side of the road and shoot from the bridge. Early or late-day sun will give you your best light.

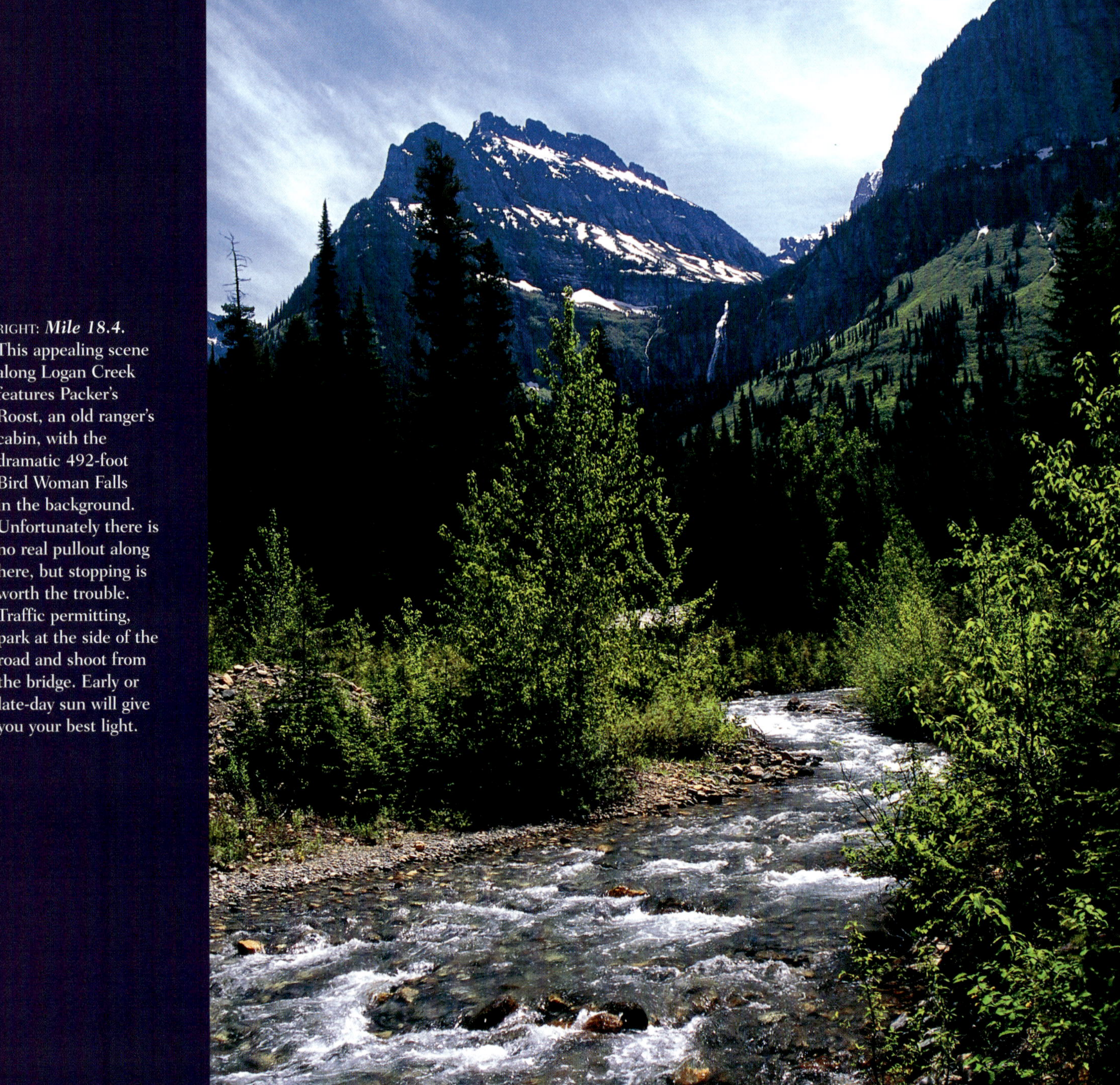

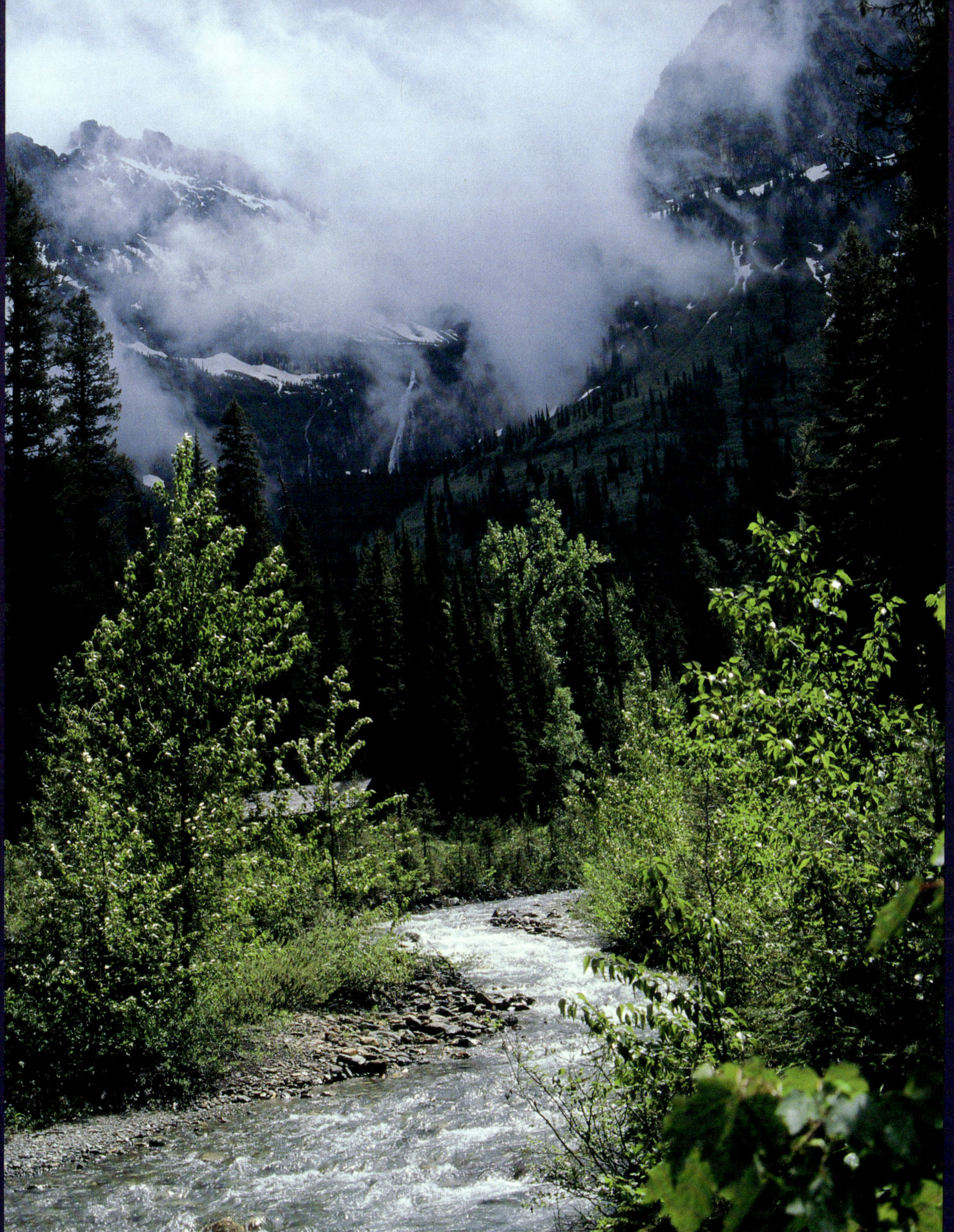

LEFT: ***Mile 18.4.*** Logan Creek with a mist overhead.

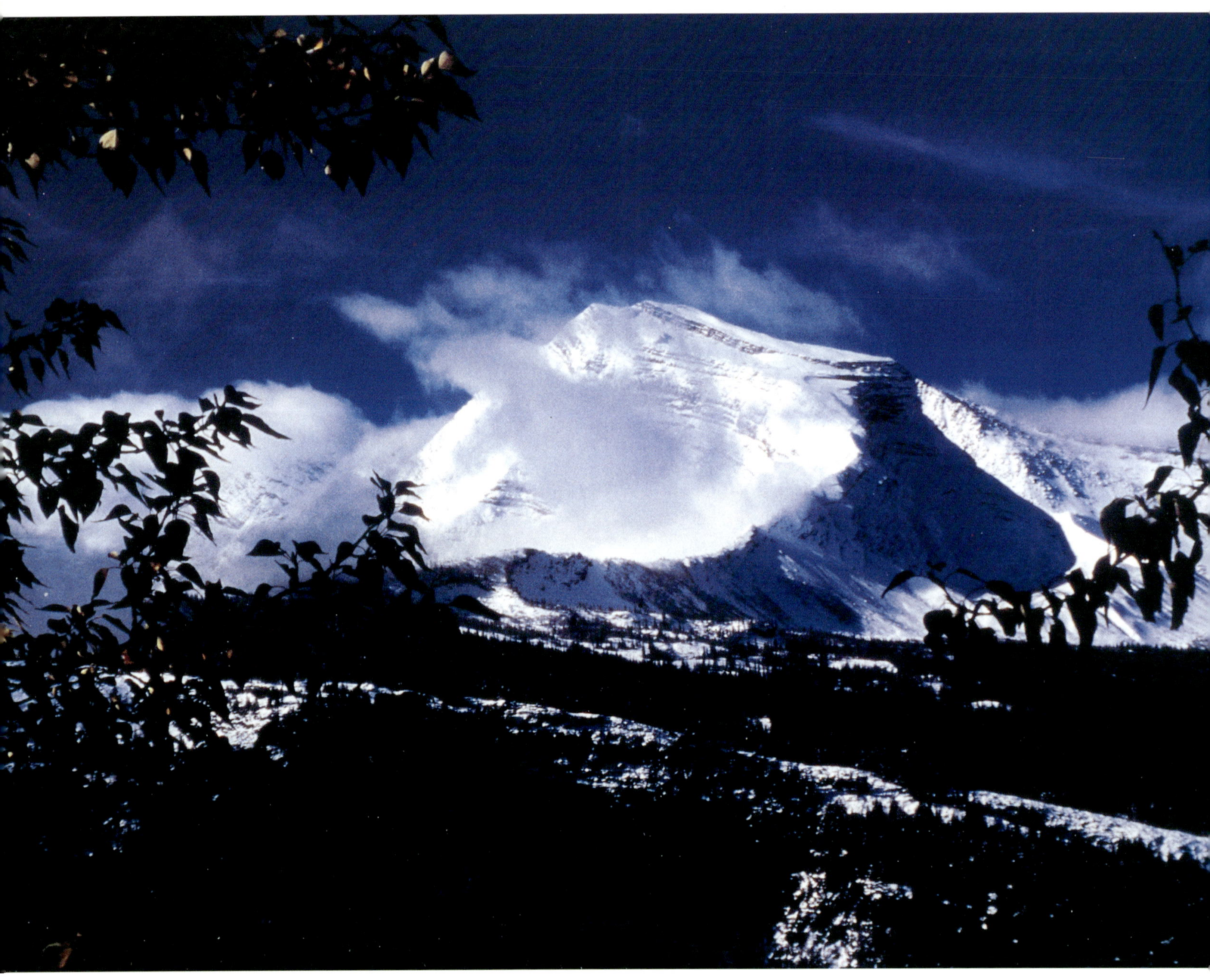

ABOVE: ***Mile 20.8.*** Heaven's Peak at its most glorious! This shot is exquisite when clouds or a late snow flank the 9,000-foot peak. You will see dozens of views of this majestic peak up ahead.

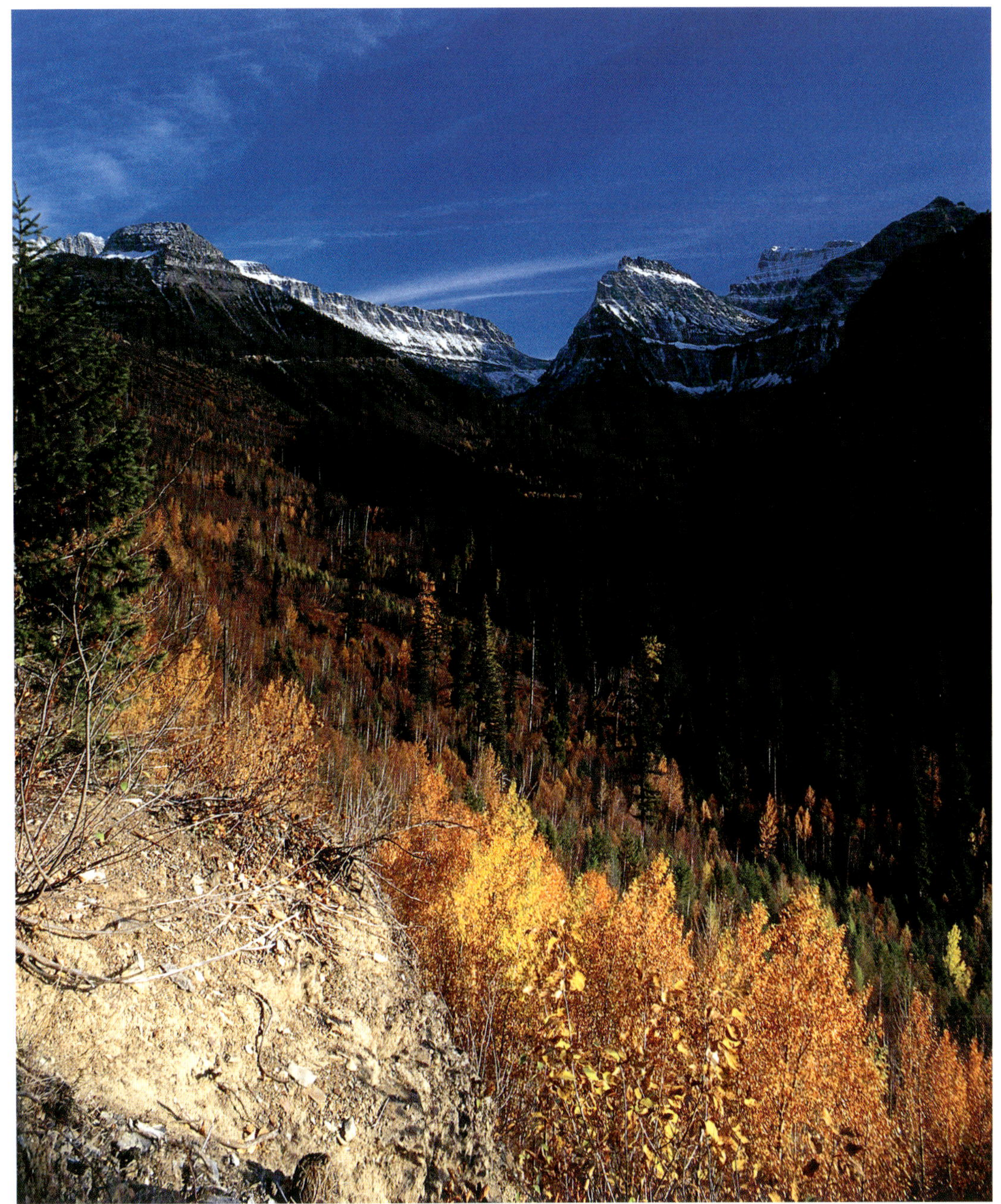

ABOVE: ***Mile 21.8.*** You are now at the Loop, where the road takes a sharp, hairpin turn. This is a significant stop that offers many splendid views, especially in autumn. Here you leave the glacier-carved McDonald Valley, lush with vegetation, and enter the high, dry alpine environment where you are surrounded by massive granite pinnacles as you ascend to Logan Pass.

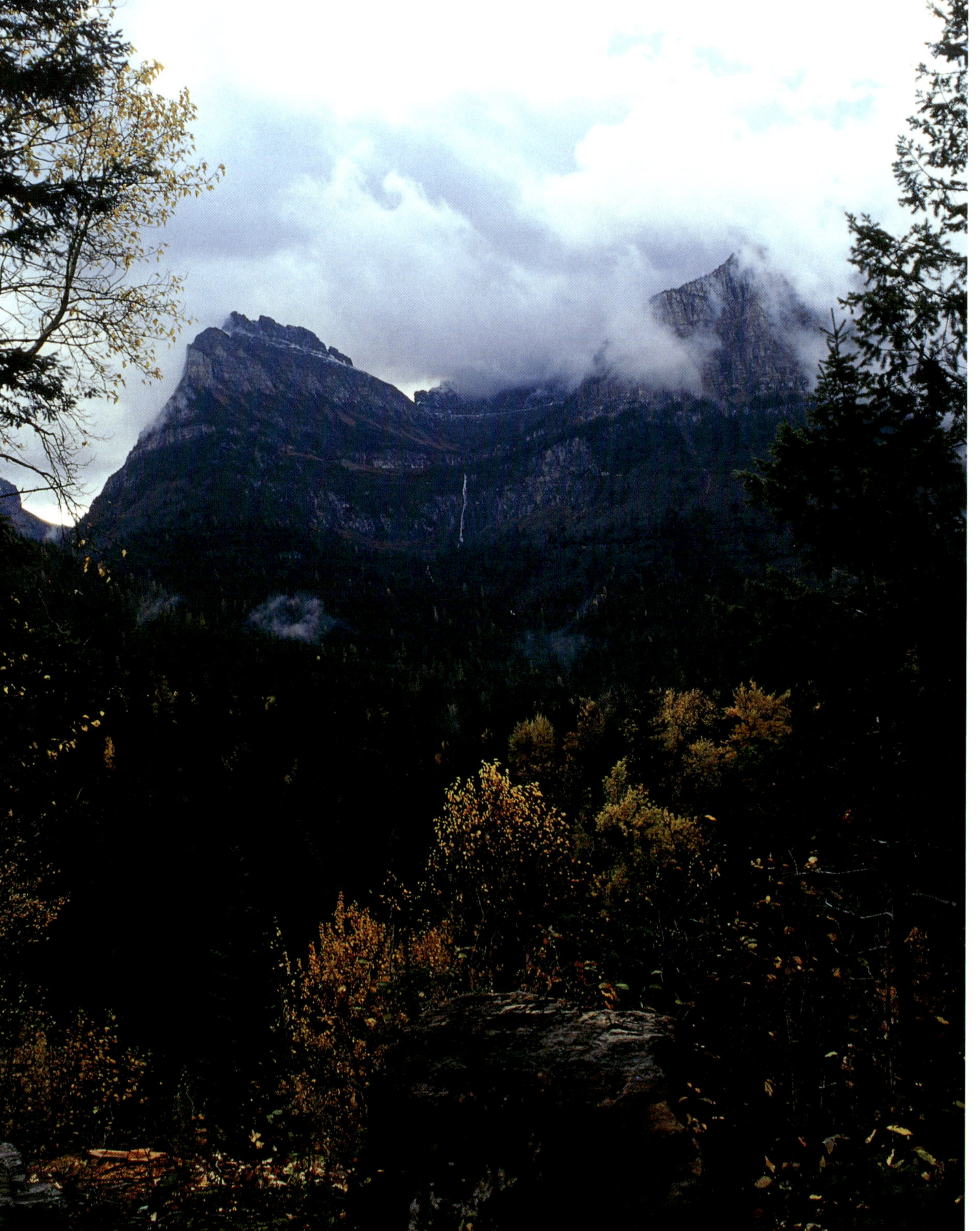

RIGHT: ***Mile 21.8.*** In late September and early October, the season known as Indian summer, the trees put on a show of gold and bronze.

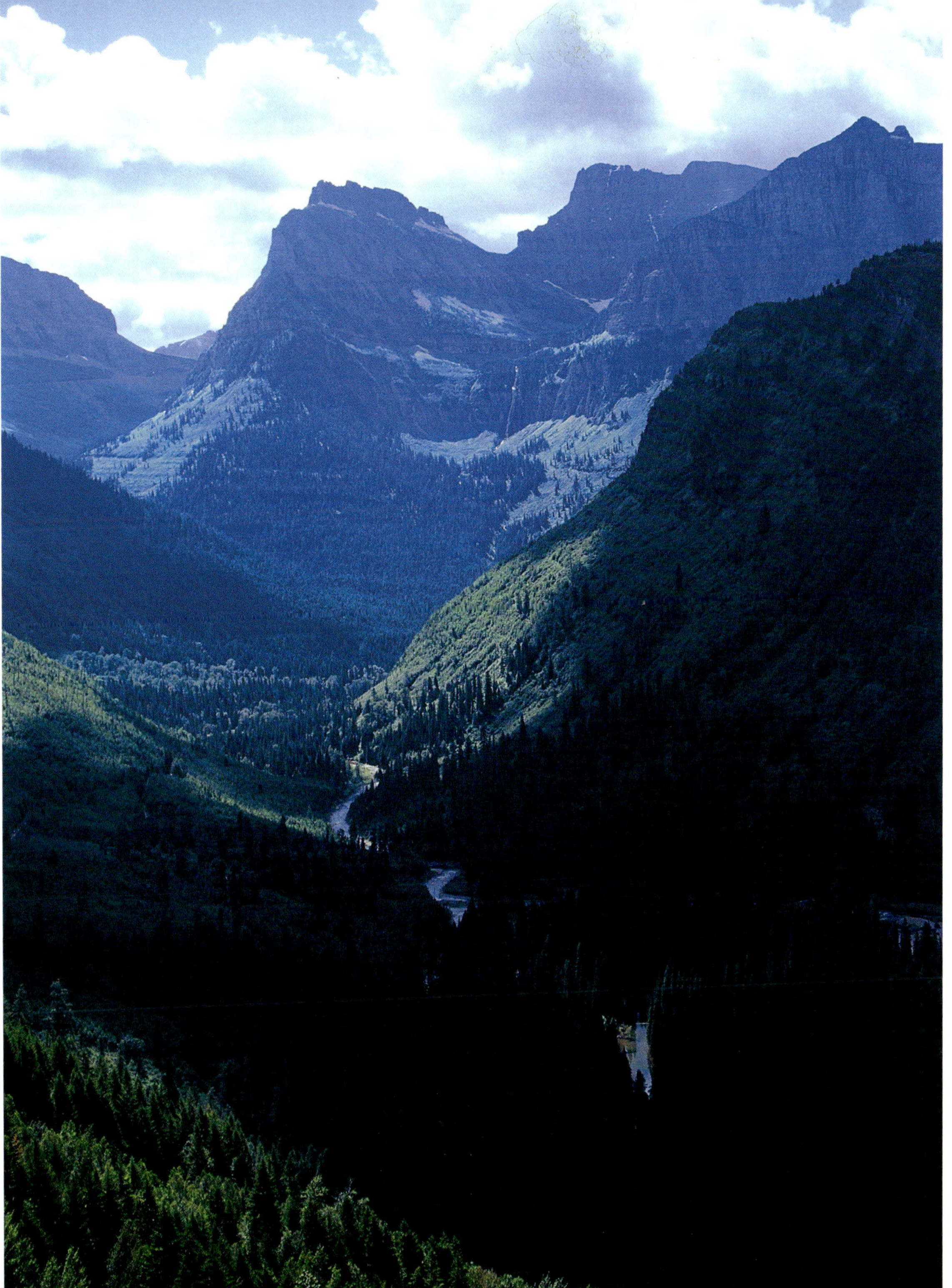

LEFT: ***Mile 21.8.*** At the Loop, the road becomes steeper and narrower, with many smaller, but more numerous pullouts. Magnificent scenery awaits you!

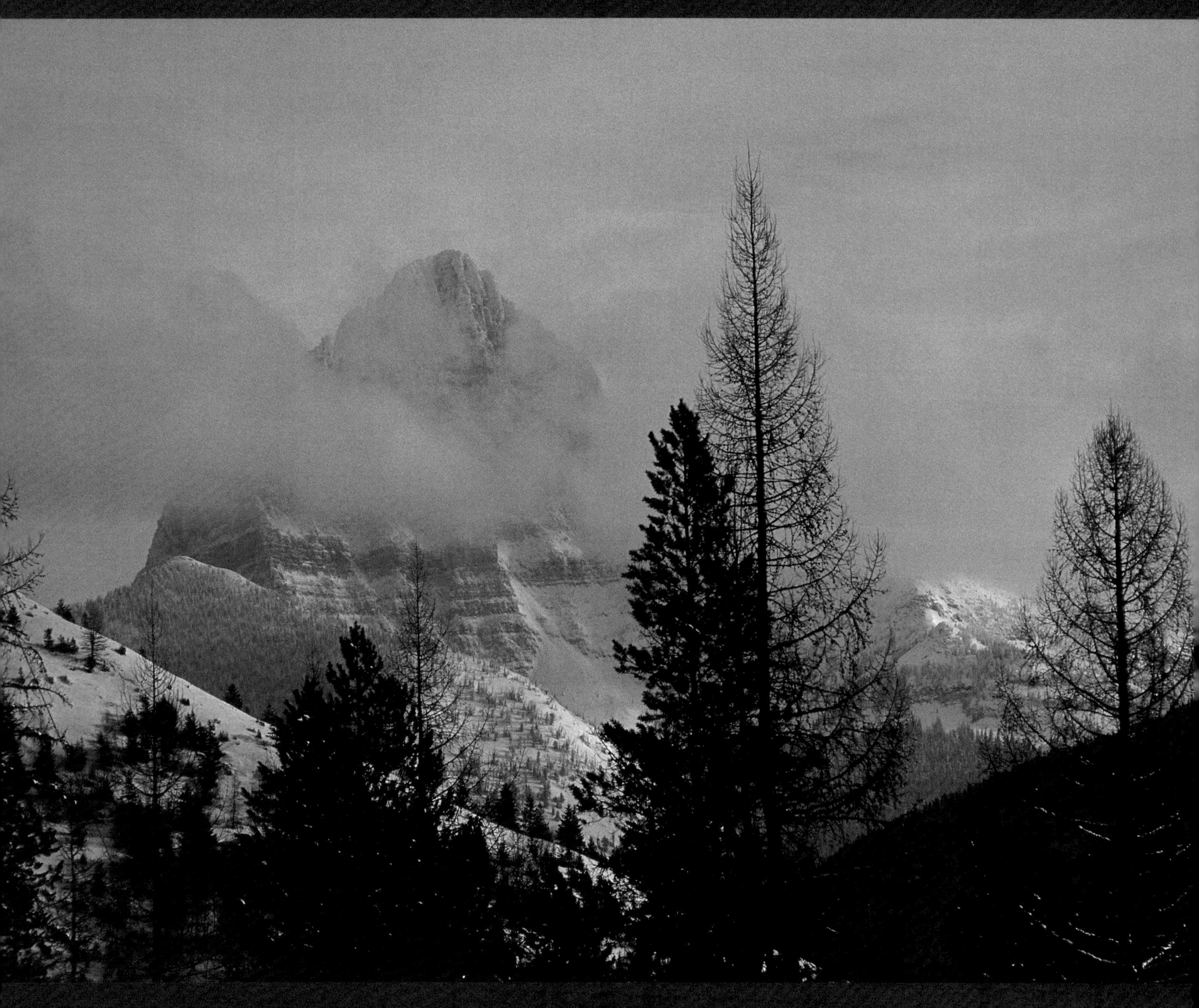

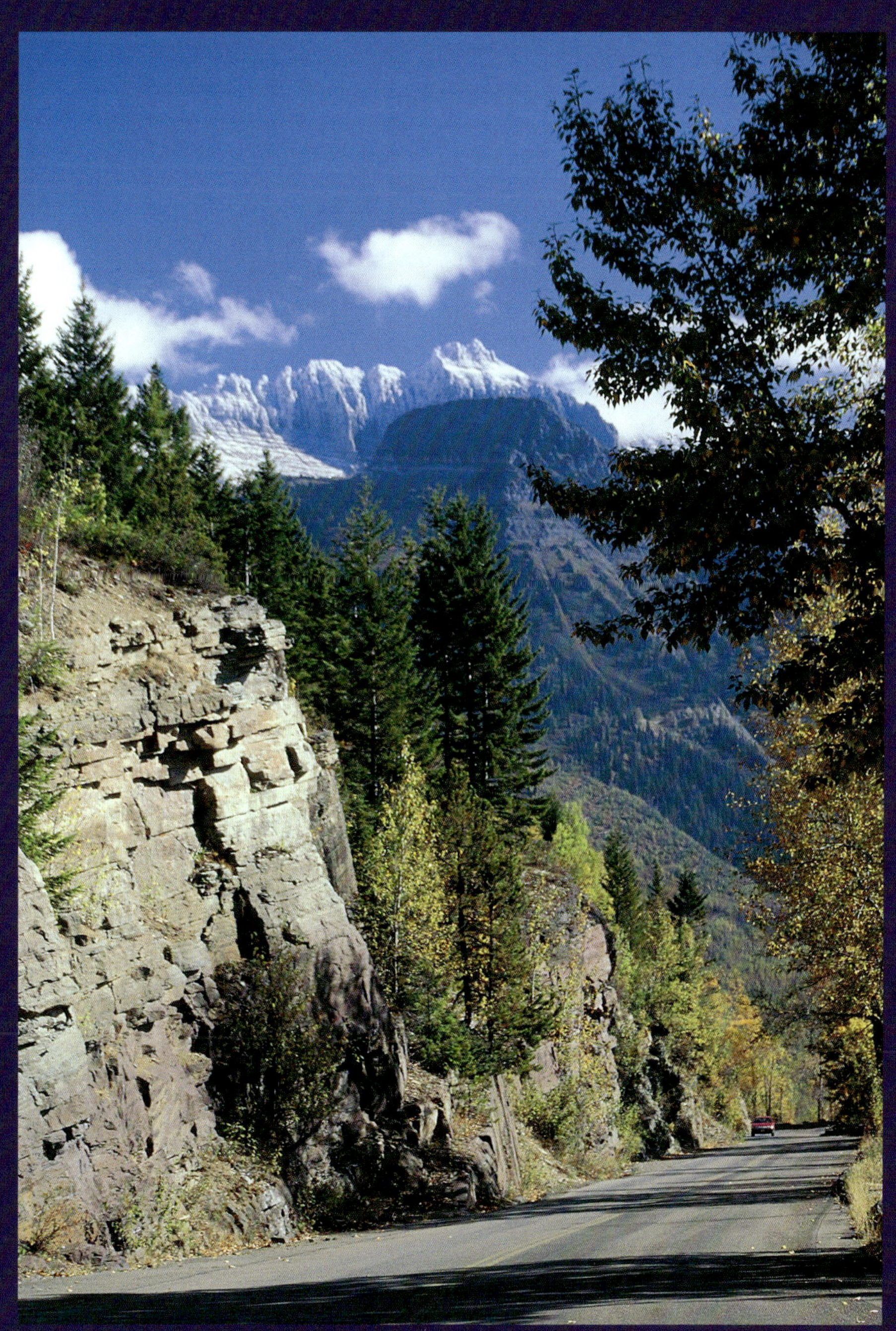

LEFT: ***Mile 21.9.*** The Going-to-the-Sun Road, which was named for a Blackfeet Indian legend, offers innumerable photo opportunities. Notice the red car—it gives you an idea of how large these mountains are.

FACING PAGE: Chilly scenes of winter abound during the snowy season in Glacier National Park.

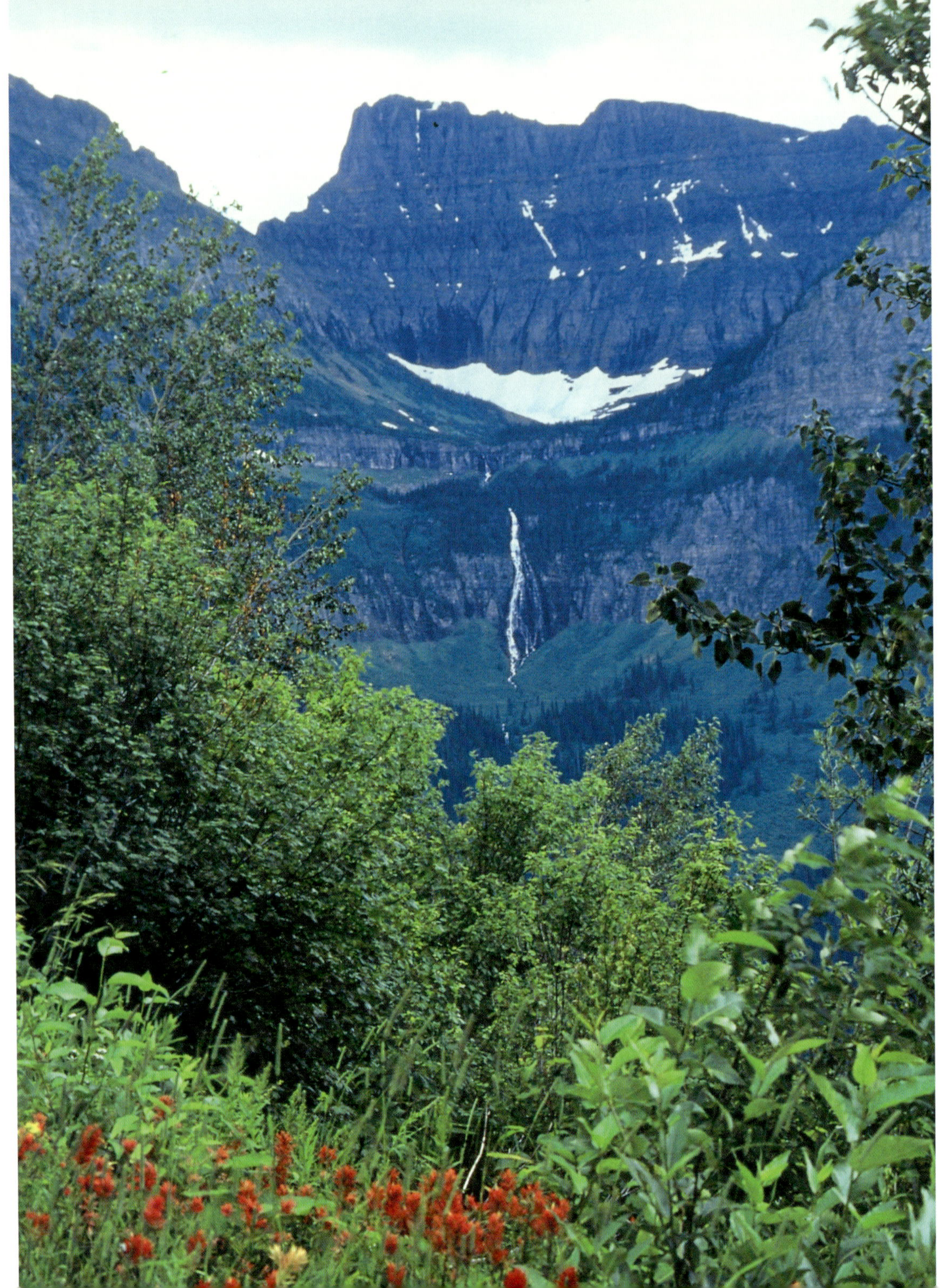

FACING PAGE: ***Mile 22.6.*** Another great vista of Bird Woman Falls, my favorite. I believe these falls are best captured in a vertical format.

BELOW: ***Mile 23.2.*** A delightful panorama of Bird Woman Falls, framed horizontally, captures a very different perspective of this beautiful area. You select your favorite.

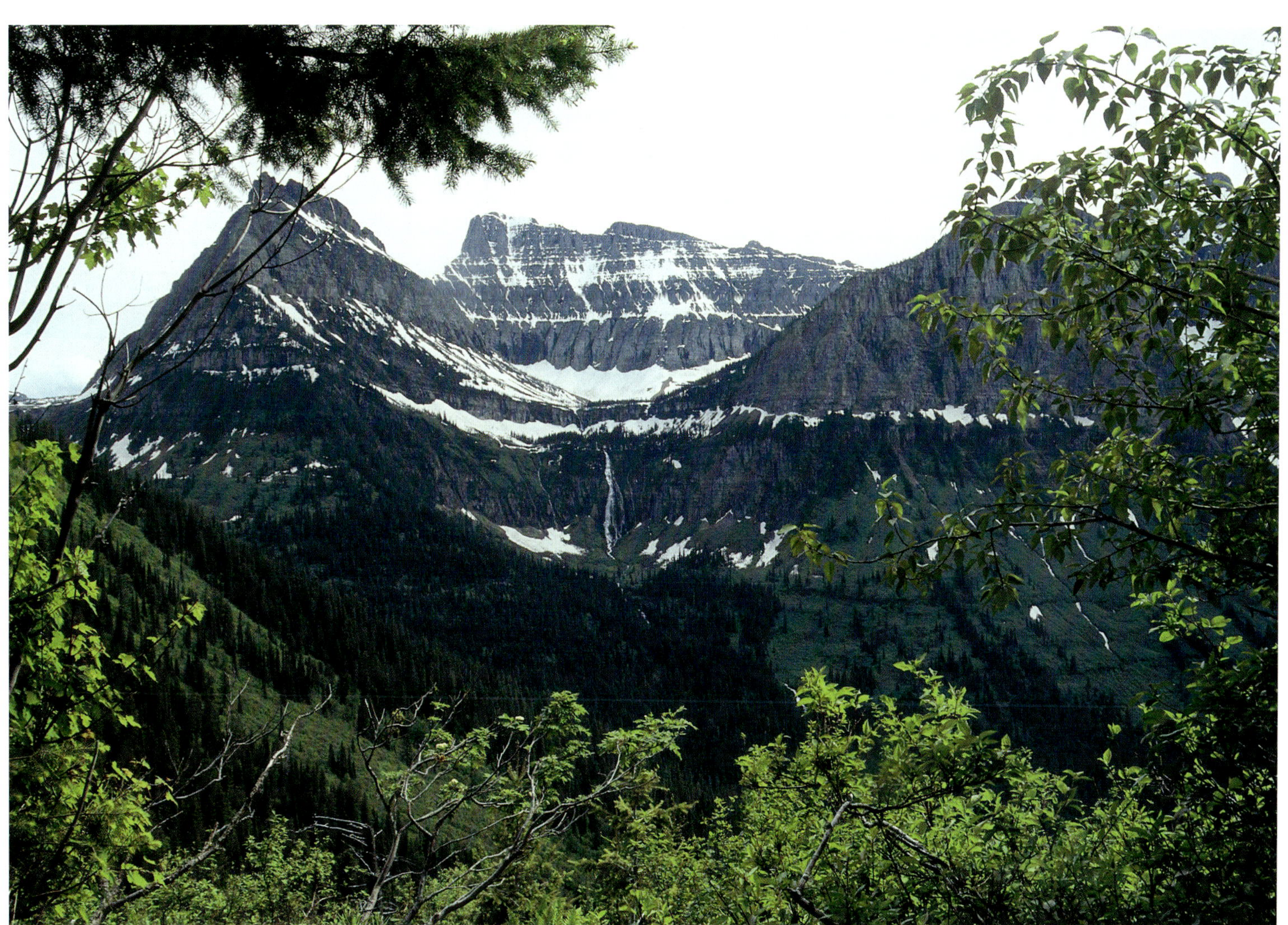

RIGHT: ***Mile 24.6.*** The park keeps its equipment to maintain the Going-to-the-Sun Road at this corner. Because this area receives so much snow, the road is closed each winter and road machinery is needed to open it each spring.

Cross the road and walk down a few steps for some exceptional views, including this one of Haystack Creek, which crosses the road twice as it descends the alpine slopes. Here you can catch your first glimpse of Logan Pass up ahead.

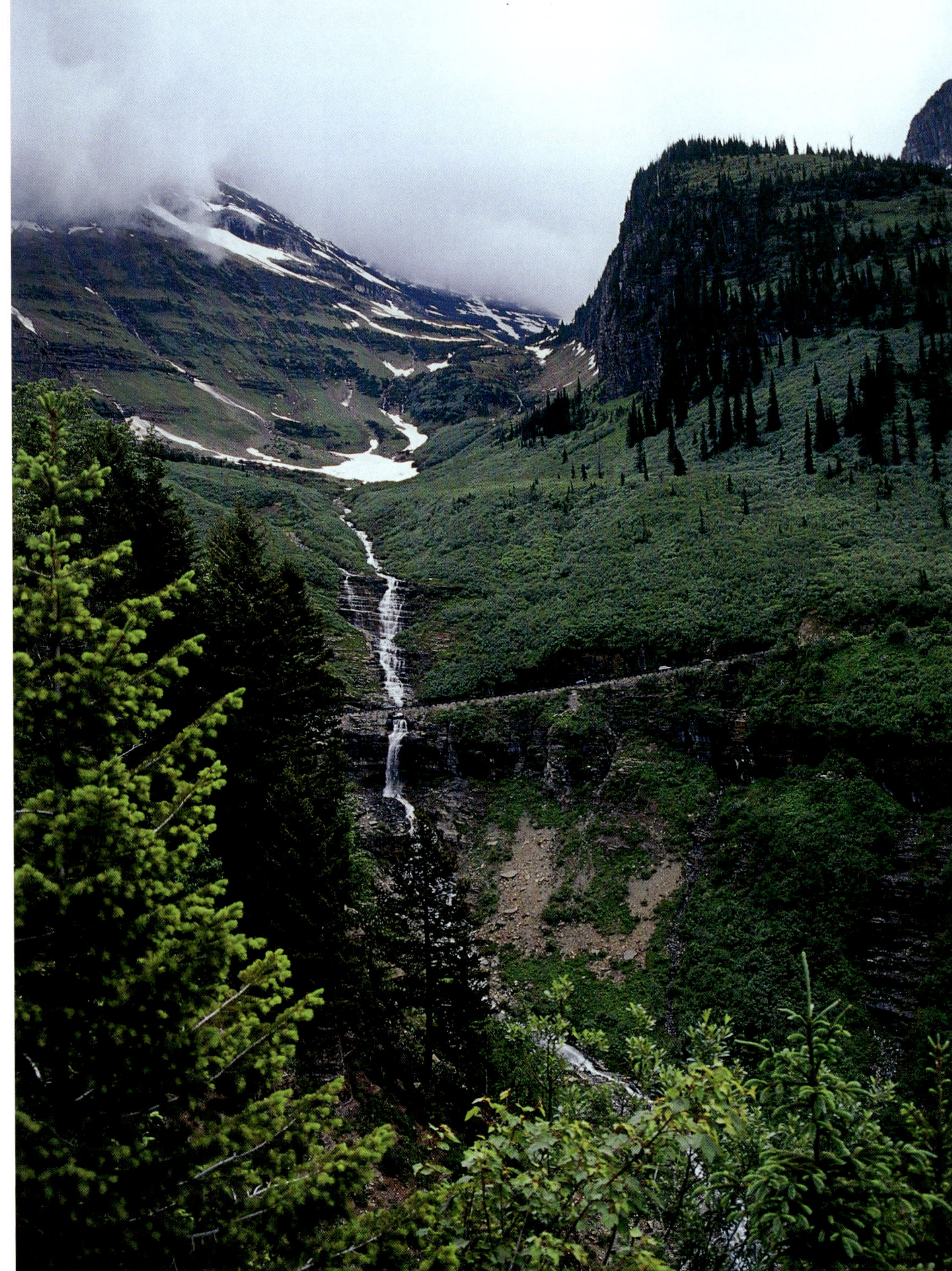

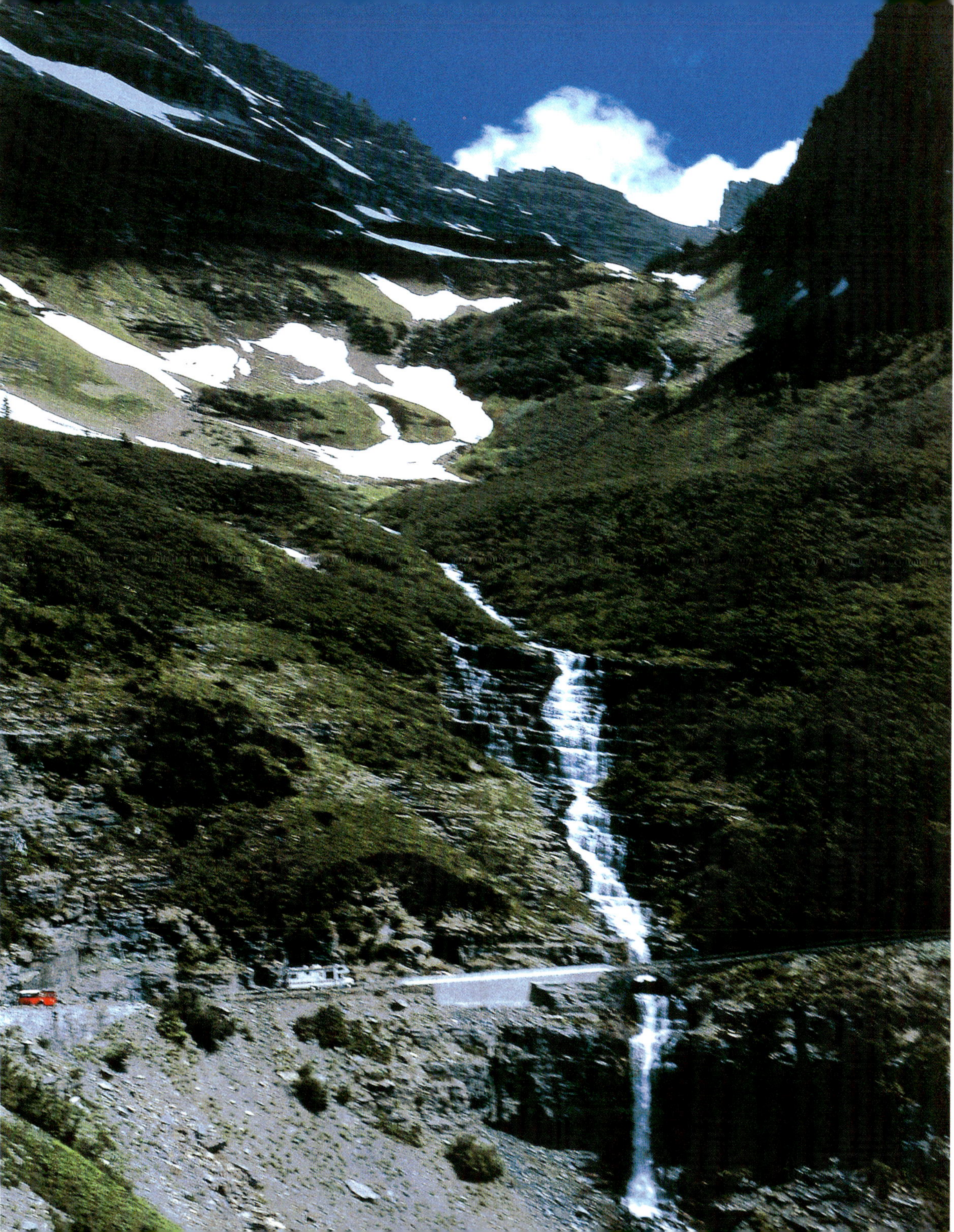

LEFT: ***Mile 24.7.*** An "in-your-face" view of Haystack Creek, which tumbles down the mountain in a series of steps and passes under a bridge on the Going-to-the-Sun Road. As you drive up to 6,646-foot Logan Pass, you will see a number of waterfalls course down the side of the mountain and under the road.

RIGHT: ***Mile 25.5.*** This stop features an interpretive exhibit as well as impressive views across McDonald Valley, from whence you have come. In the shadow of Mount Gould, this is the beginning of the large curve in the road known as The Big Bend.

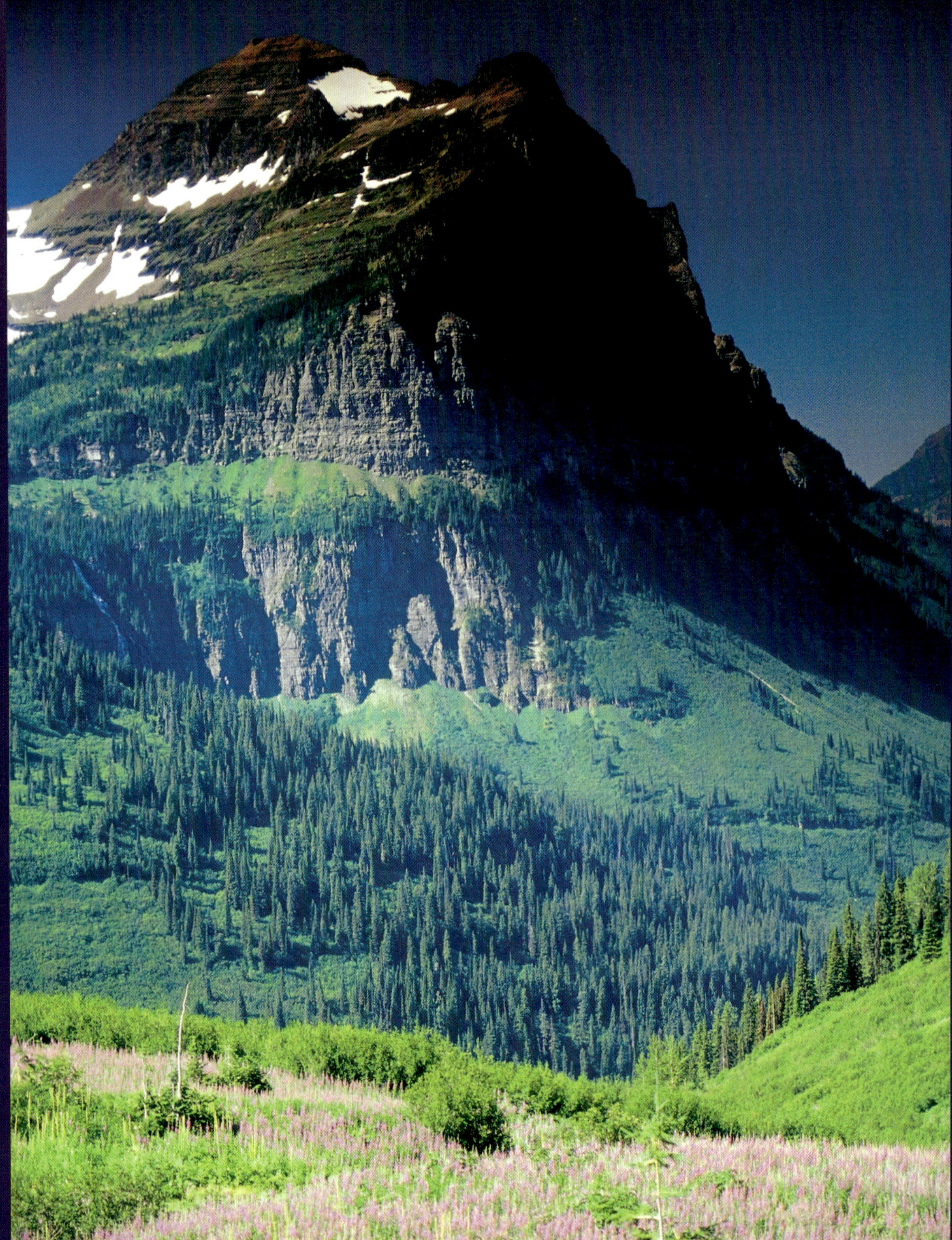

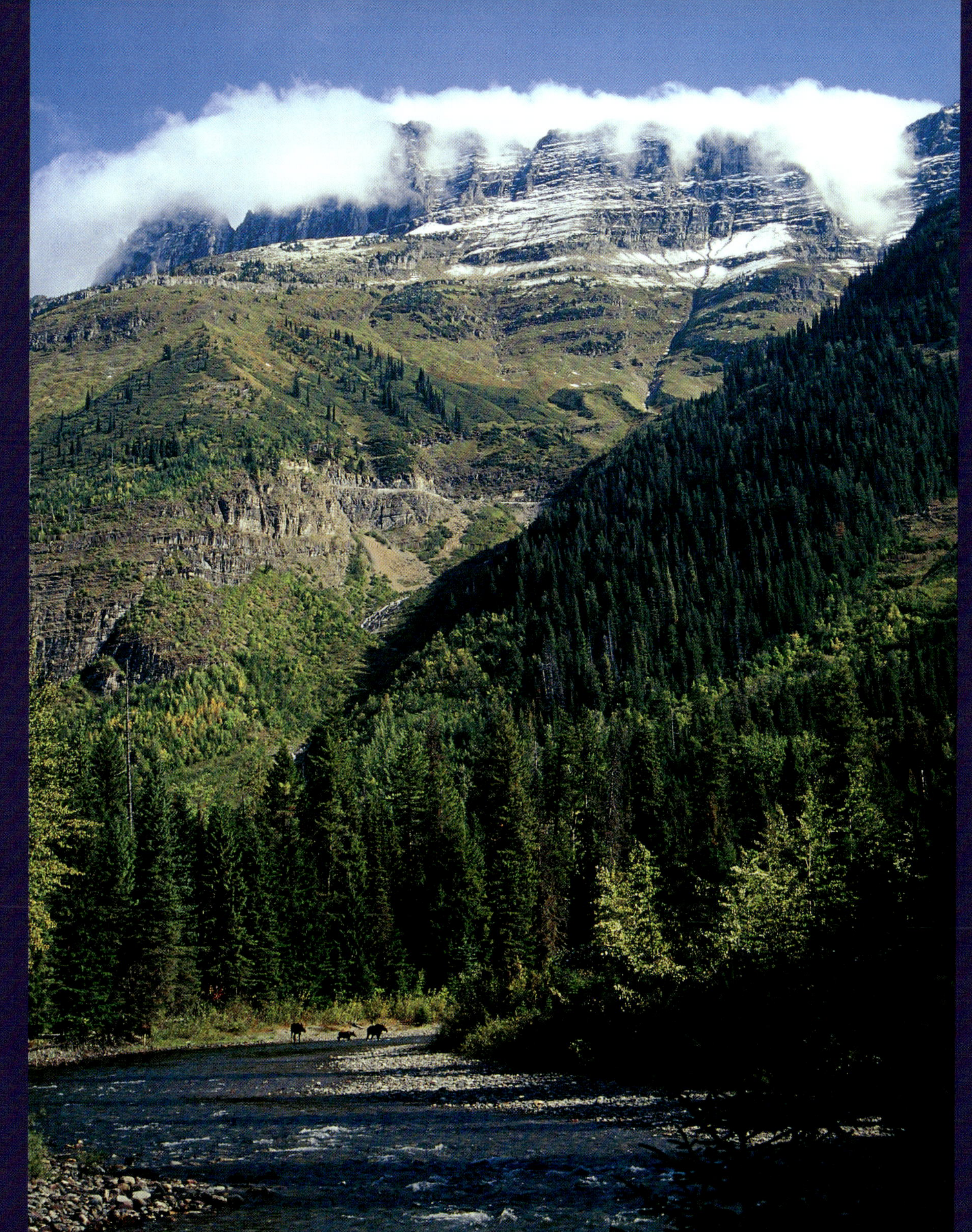

RIGHT: ***Mile 26.8.*** The amount of "weeping" at the Weeping Wall varies from a trail of tears to a torrent, depending on the snow levels above it.

BELOW: Glacier flowers with morning dew.

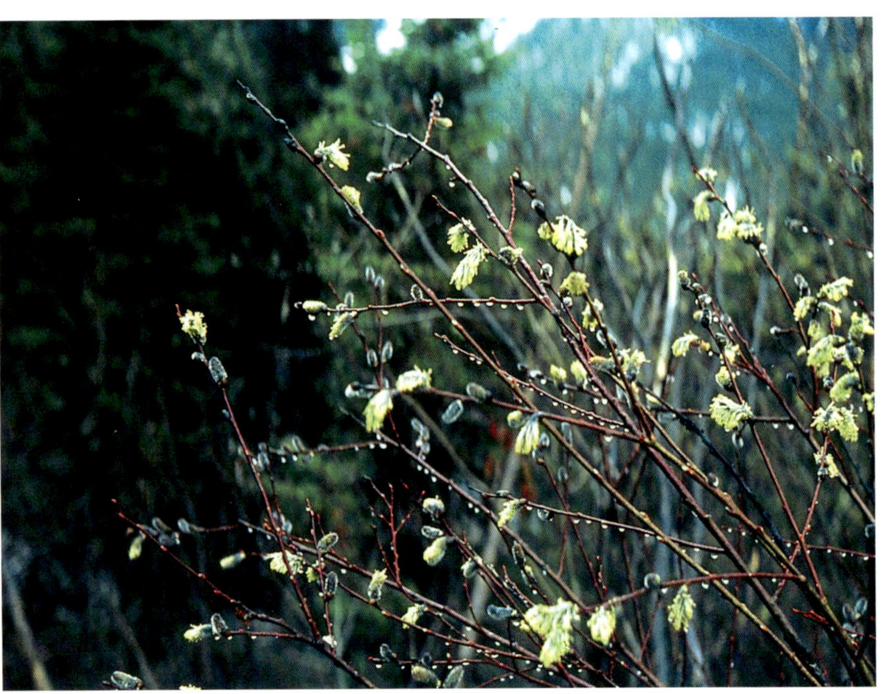

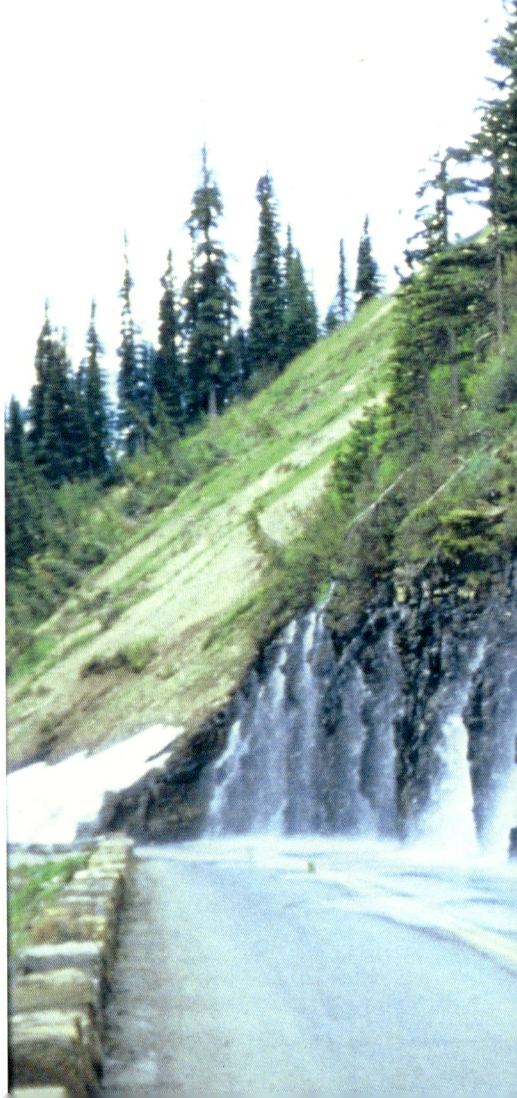

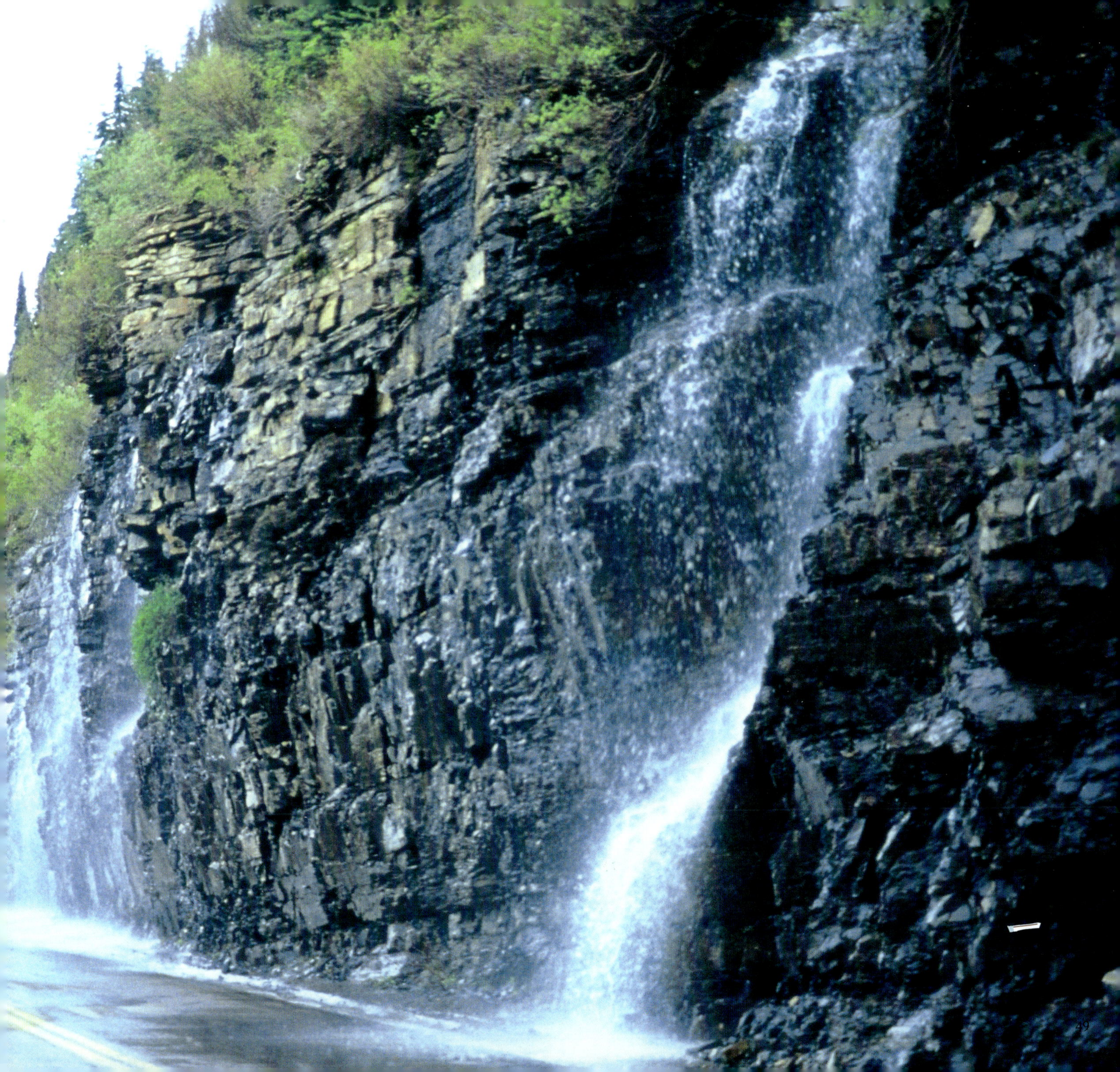

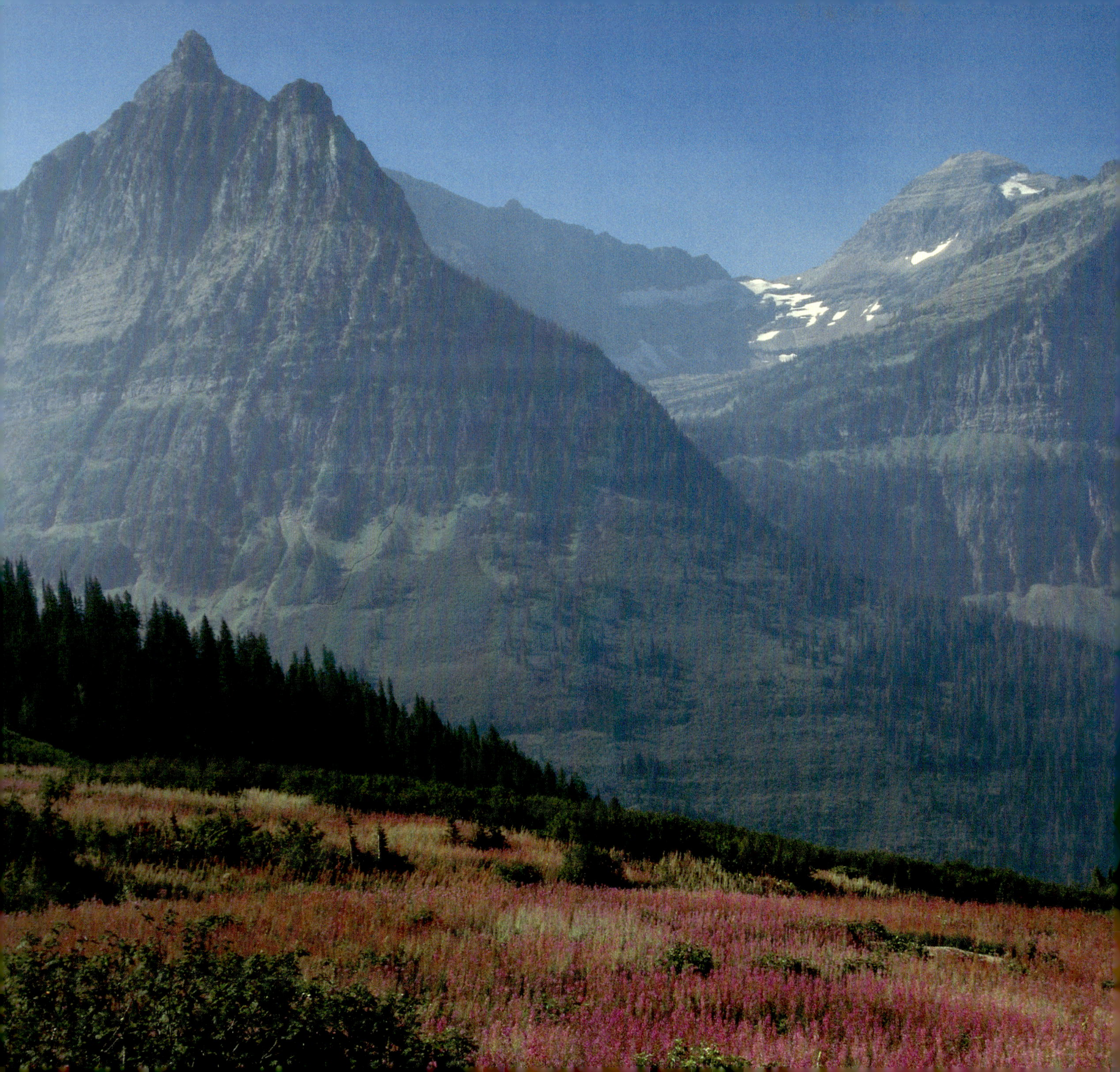

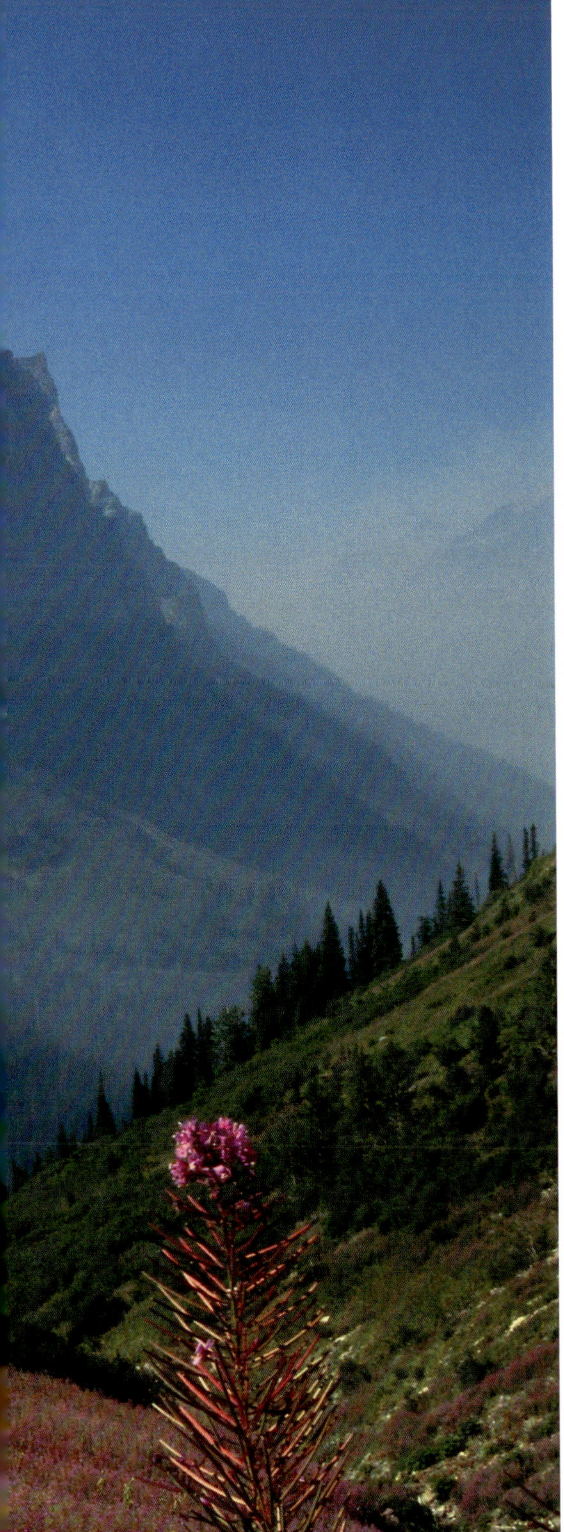

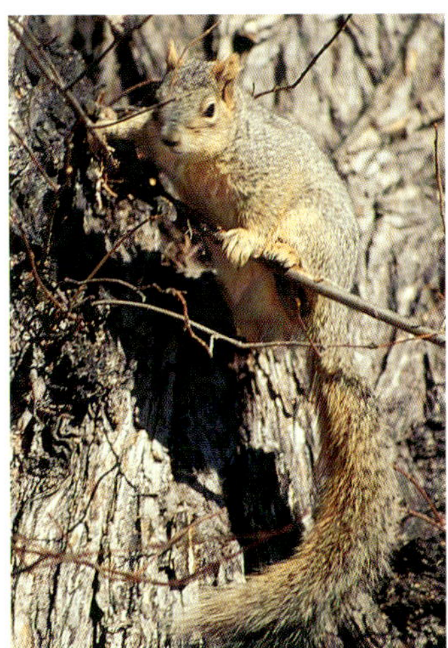

ABOVE: A squirrel pauses for the photographer.

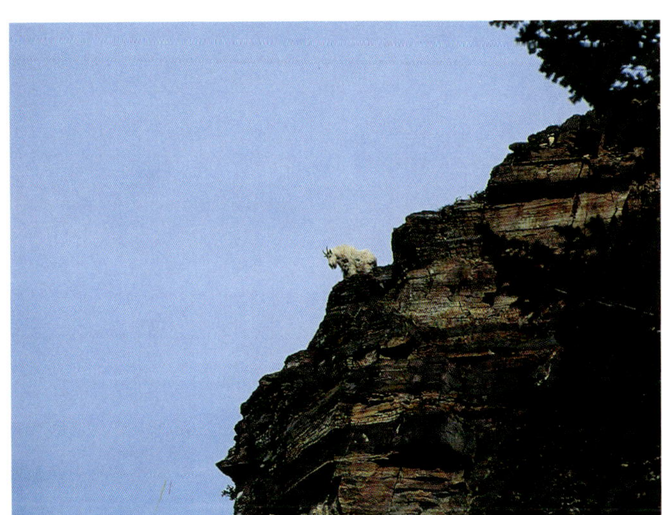

ABOVE: A mountain goat perched on a rocky cliff.

LEFT: ***Mile 26.9.*** Also located within the Big Bend, this pullout features two National Park Service interpretive exhibits. Depending on the season, there are often patches of snow or beautiful summer wildflowers. Mountain goats can be seen grazing in the cliffs above. This stop also offers another view of Bird Woman Falls, which drops down from the classic hanging valley surrounded by Mounts Oberlin, Clements, and Cannon.

Caution: Do not stop underneath the large rock faces ahead on your left.

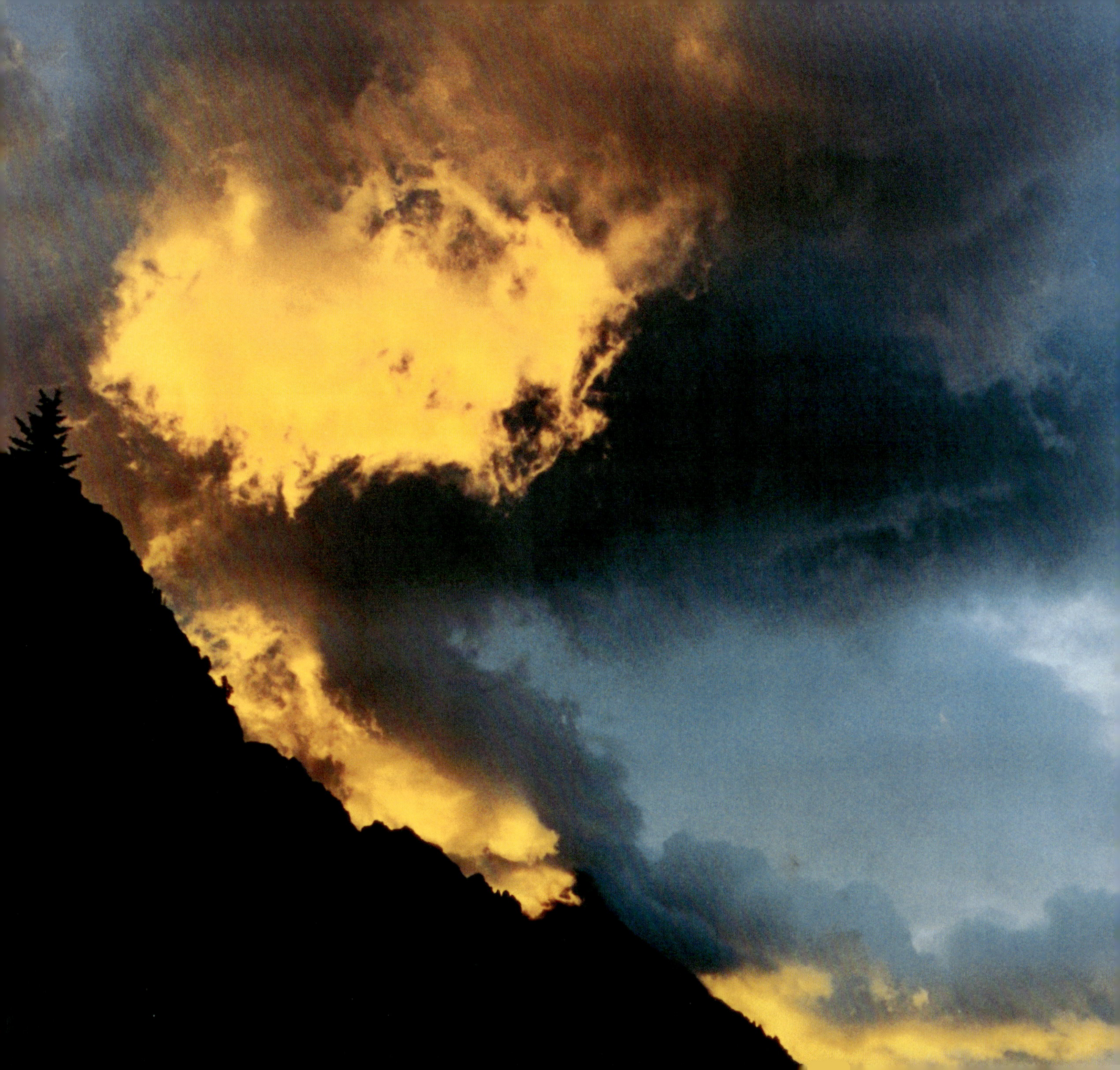

LEFT: ***Mile 27.9.*** I call this shot on the Going-to-the-Sun Road "Almost There." It appears that you literally are almost to the sun itself. This image, which seems to be a forest fire but is a sunrise, was taken in mid-July about 4:30 A.M., while I was in a class with the late Galen Rowell. I submit this photo as a remembrance in his honor.

BELOW: ***Mile 29.0.*** The pleasant little brook on your left is often surrounded by wildflowers in season. These brooks are called rills.

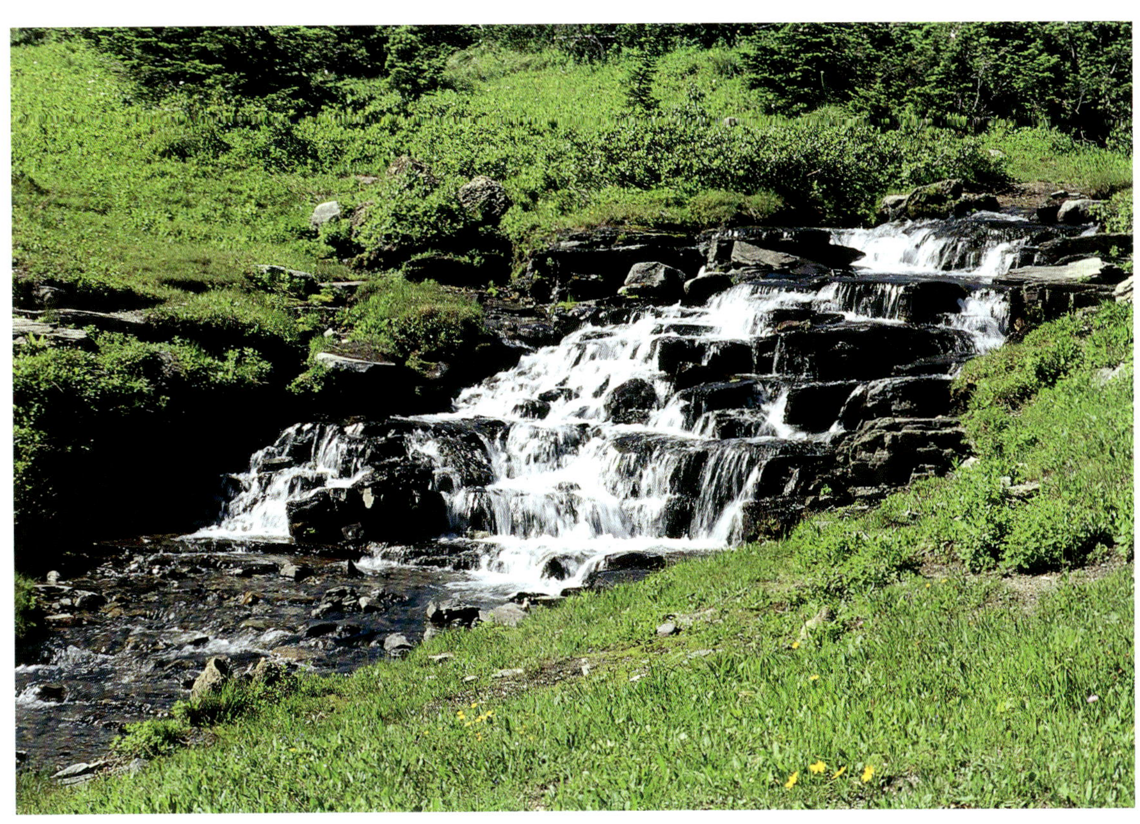

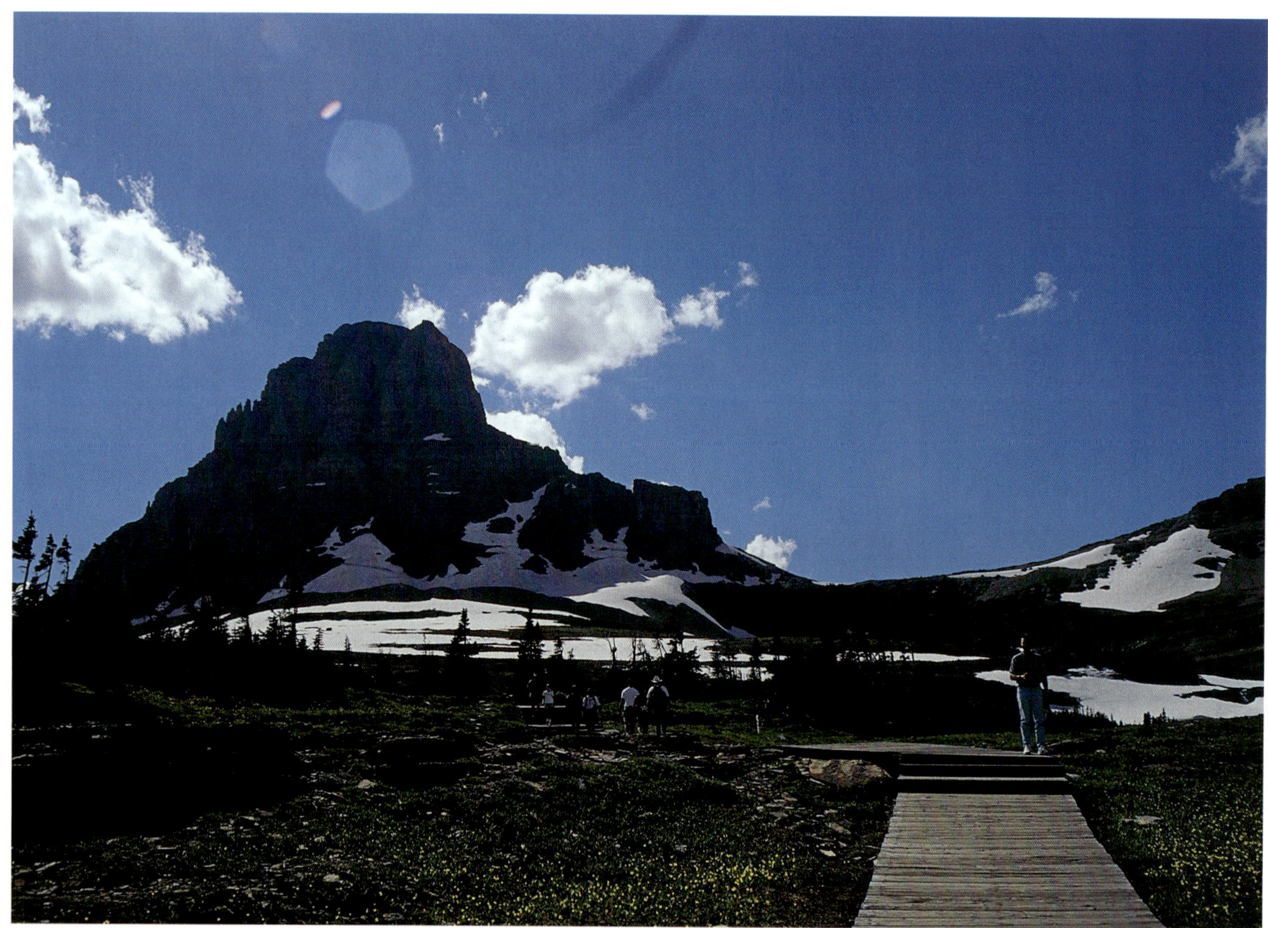

ABOVE: ***Mile 29.5/Mile 0.*** This is Logan Pass, at 6,646 feet. The extensive Logan Pass Visitor Center has displays on park history, geology, flora, and fauna and a bookstore that features titles specific to Glacier National Park. Take time to enjoy this site, which has a boardwalk to protect the extremely fragile terrain.

The highest point on the Going-to-the-Sun Road, the pass also offers you a grand opportunity to see the six prominent mountains pictured on the following pages. These photographs were taken from the parking lot at the Logan Pass Visitor Center. Mount Reynolds rises majestically behind the visitor center. Mount Oberlin and Mount Clements flank Bird Woman Falls on the right. Heavy Runner Mountain is the elongated mountain to your left. The Garden Wall is on your right, extending to the north. As you leave the lower exit of the parking area, you will see Going-to-the-Sun Mountain, which parallels the road as it descends on the east side.

***Note:* At Logan Pass, reset your odometer to zero.**

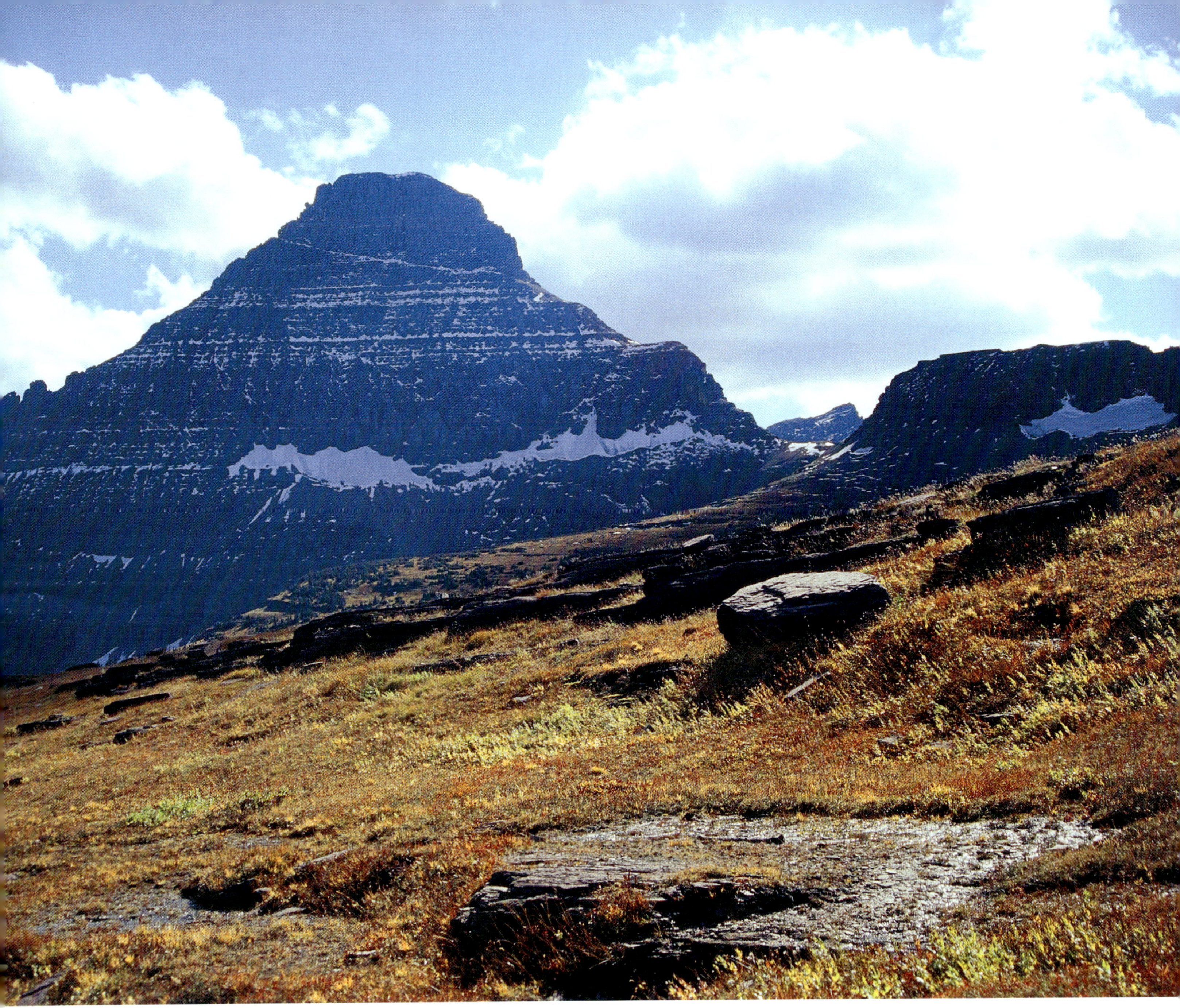

ABOVE: ***Mile 29.5/Mile 0.*** The 9,125-foot Mount Reynolds was named for Charles R. Reynolds, an editor of *Field and Stream* magazine.

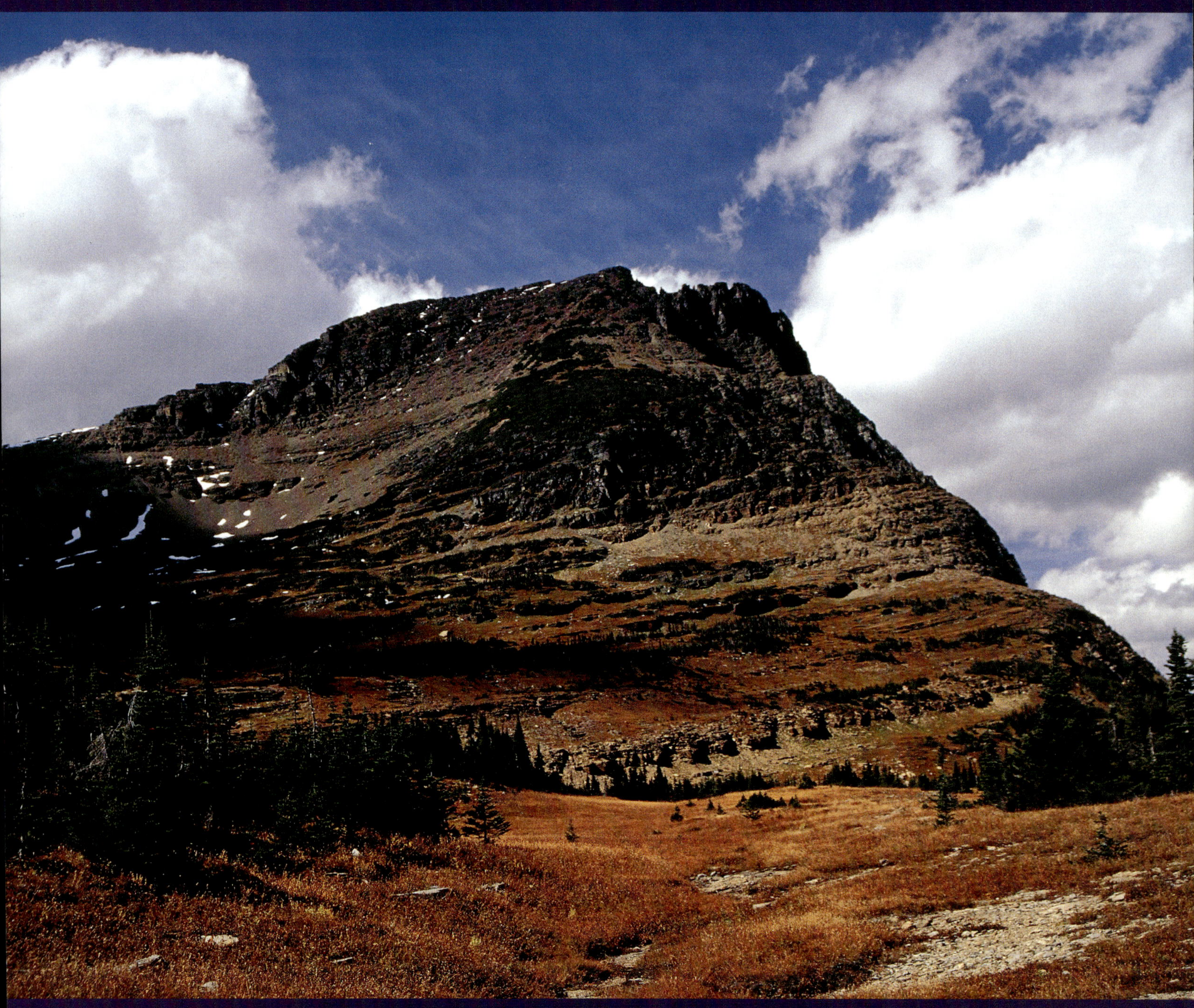

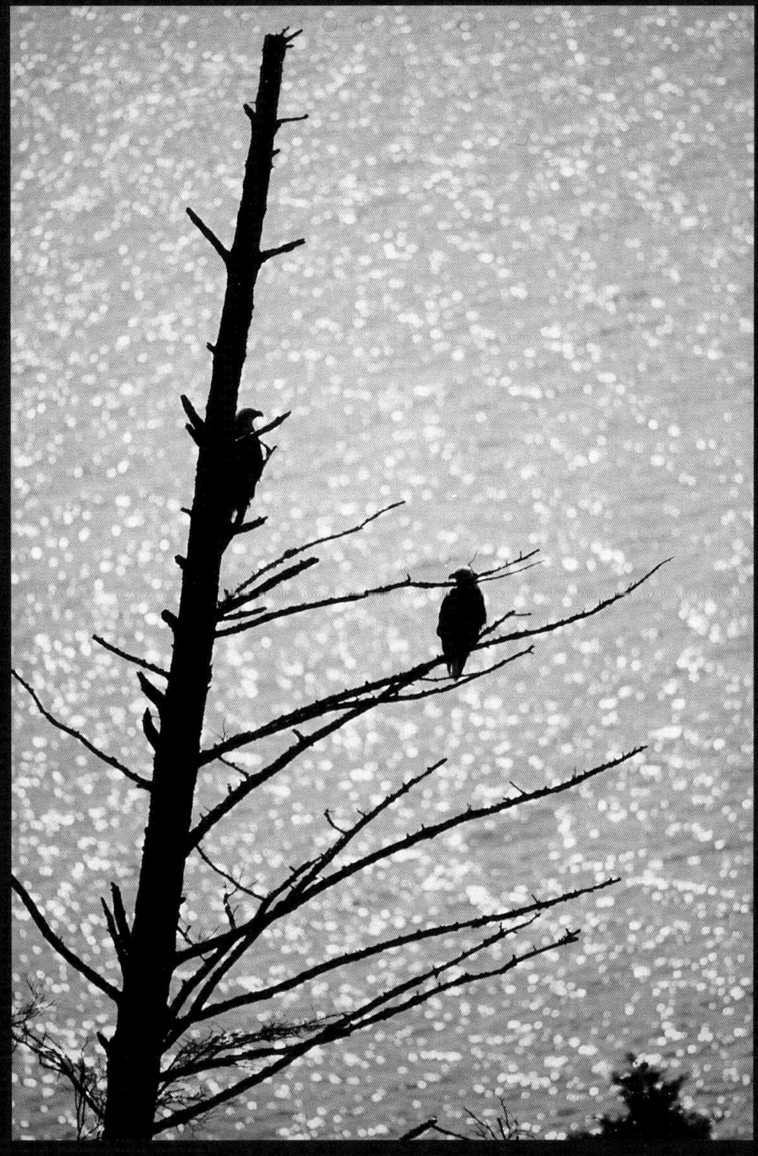

ABOVE: Two eagles scan the water below for fish.

LEFT: ***Mile 29.5/Mile 0.*** The 8,760-foot Mount Clements was named for Walter Clements, who negotiated the treaty between the Blackfeet Indians and the United States to buy the eastern half of Glacier National Park.

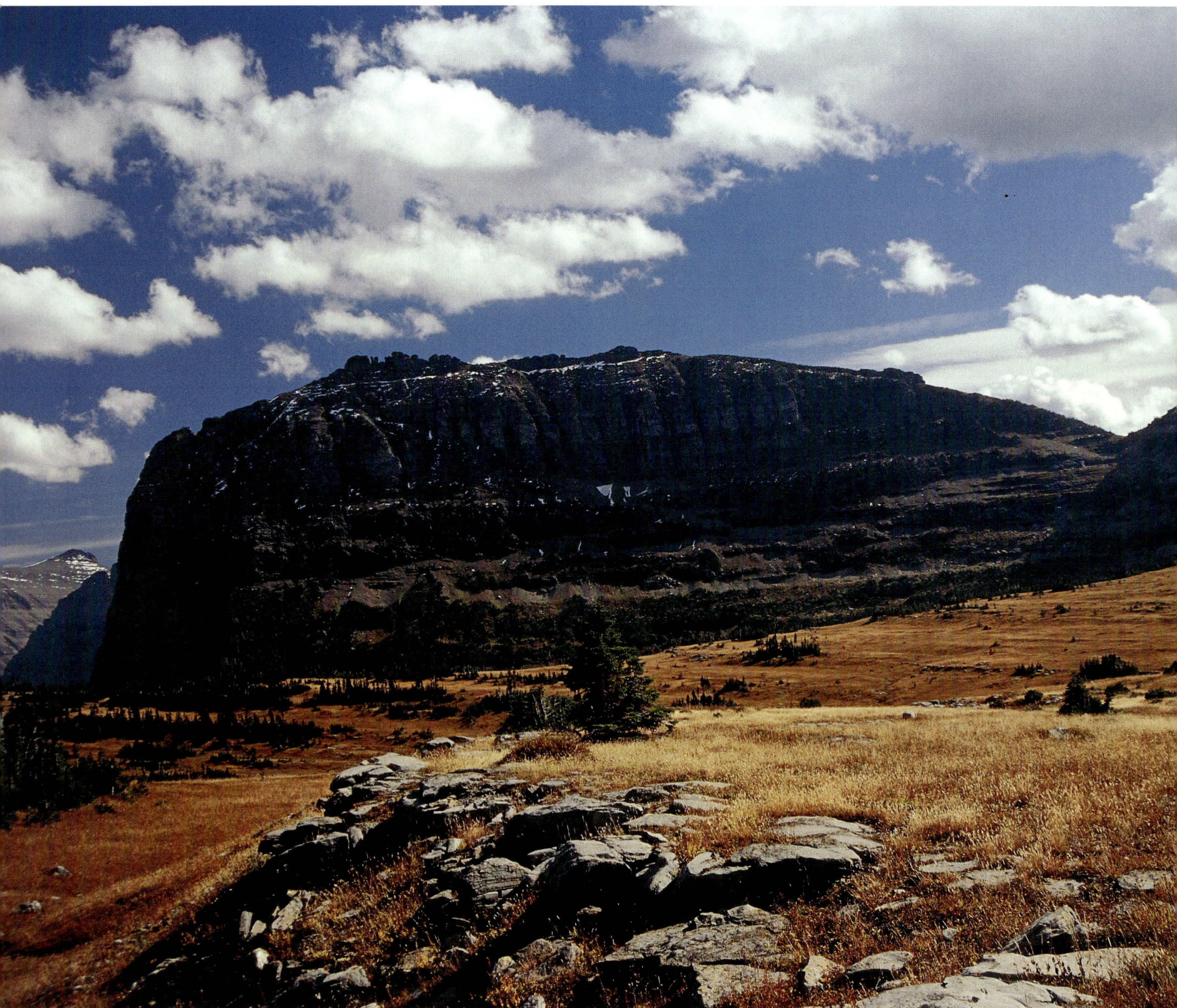

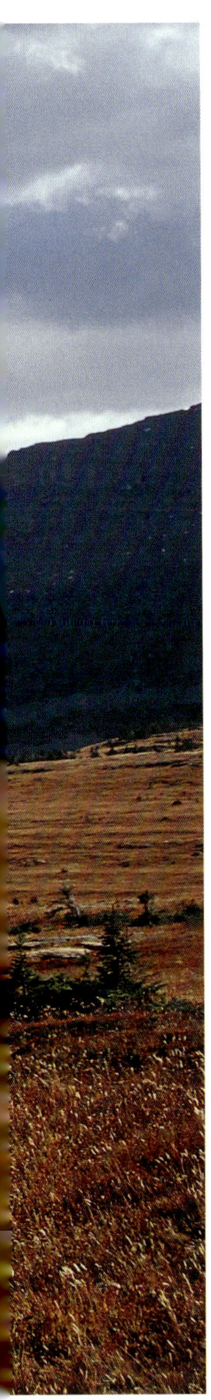

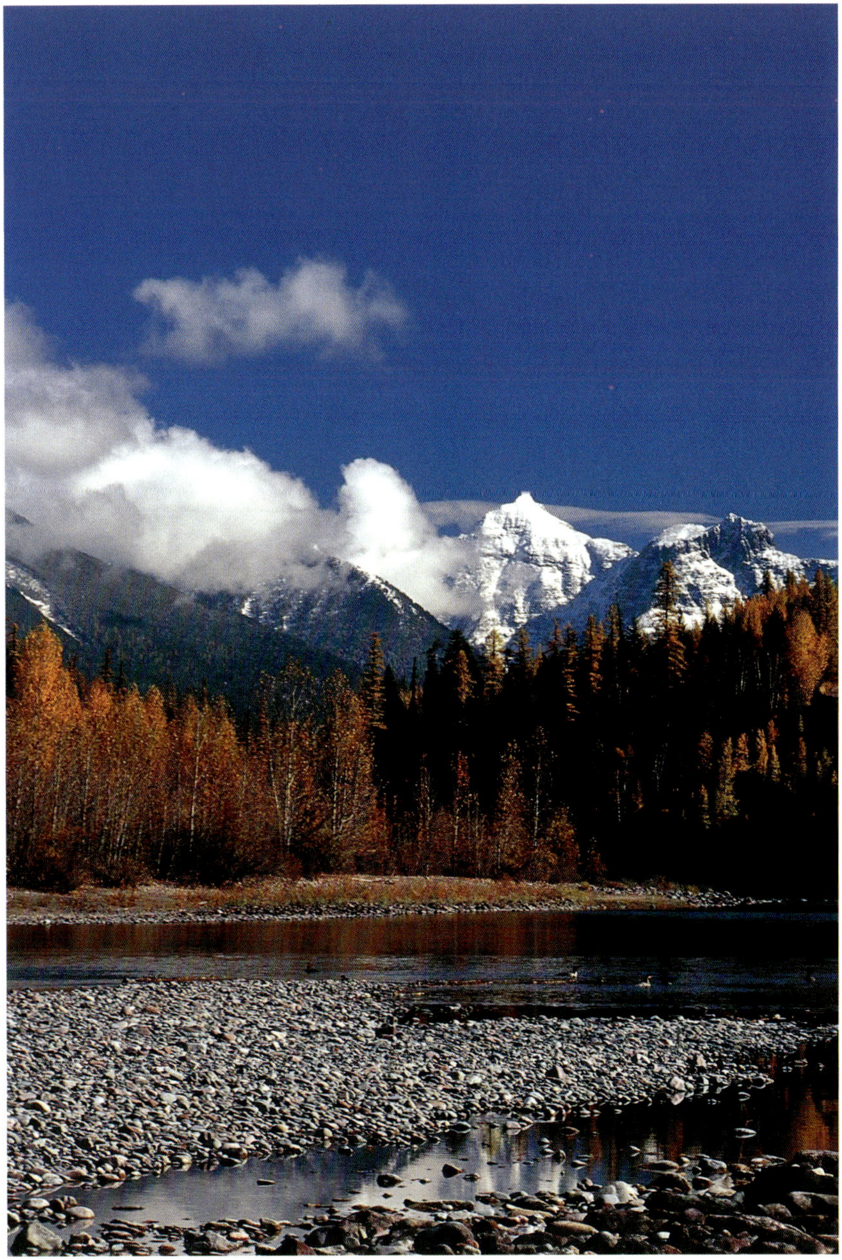

LEFT: A view of snow-covered peaks in Glacier National Park from U.S. Highway 2.

FAR LEFT: ***Mile 29.5/Mile 0.*** The 8,016-foot Heavy Runner Mountain was named for a Blackfeet tribal chief.

RIGHT: ***Mile 29.5/Mile 0.*** The Garden Wall is the park's most famous example of an arête, a knife-edged ridge. It stretches along the Continental Divide and is flanked by Mount Gould at 9,553 feet.

BELOW: ***Mile 29.5/Mile 0.*** The 9,642-foot Going-to-the-Sun Mountain was the mountain that, according to a Blackfeet legend, the mythical trickster figure of Napi used to climb up in order to get back to his home in the sun after he had come down to earth to help the Blackfeet people.

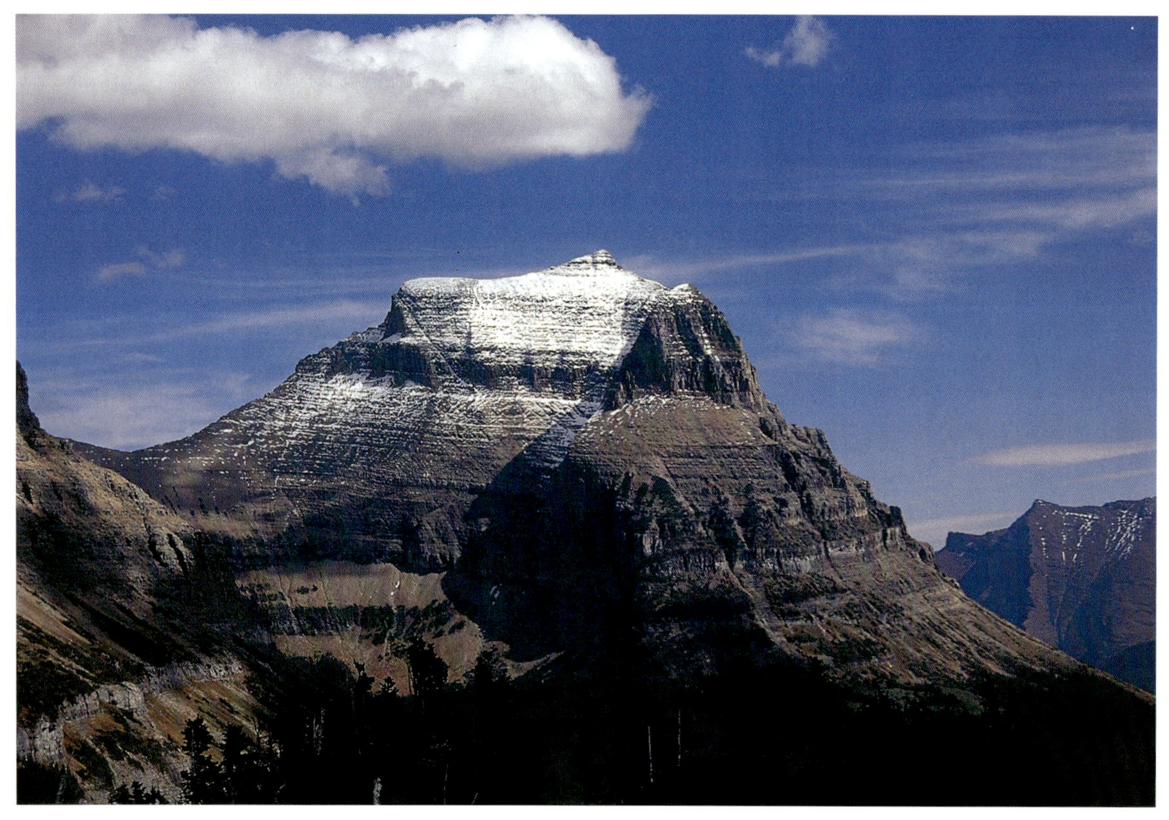

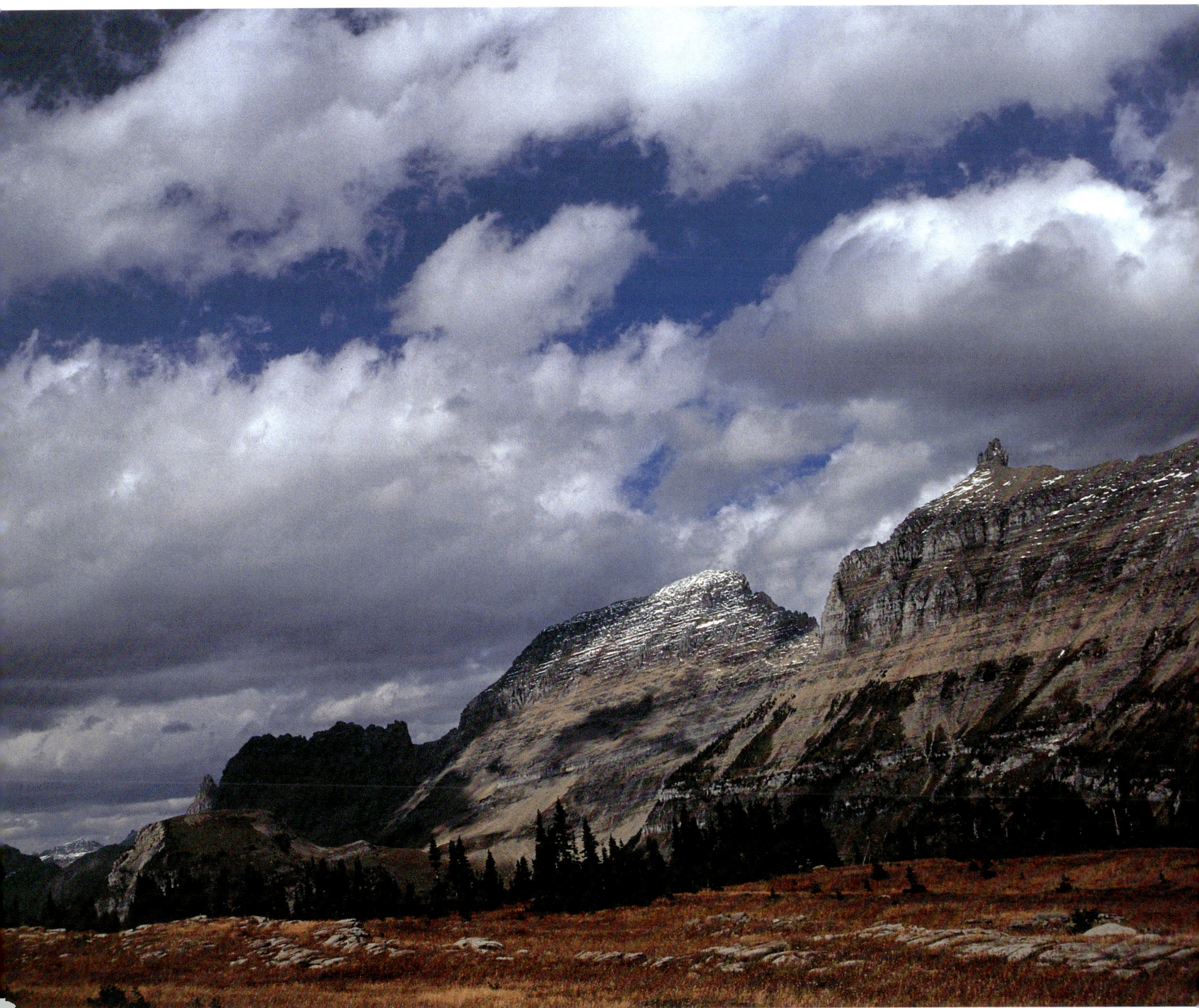

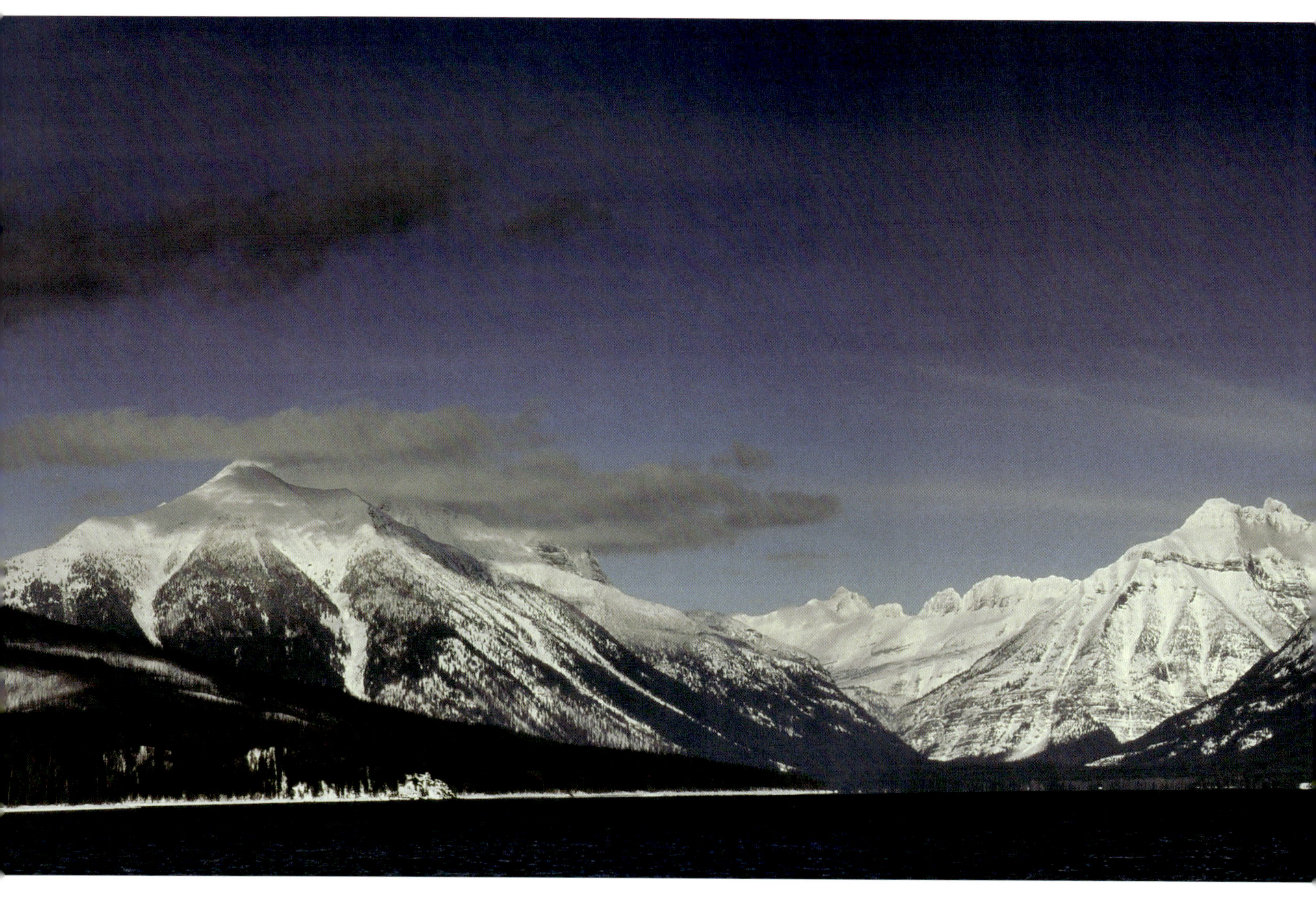

ABOVE: A panorama of mountains surrounding Lake McDonald. From the left, they are Stanton Mountain, Mount Vaught, Garden Wall, Mount Cannon, Mount Brown, Snyder Ridge, Edwards Mountain, and Gunsight Mountain, with the Little Matterhorn Mountain in the background.

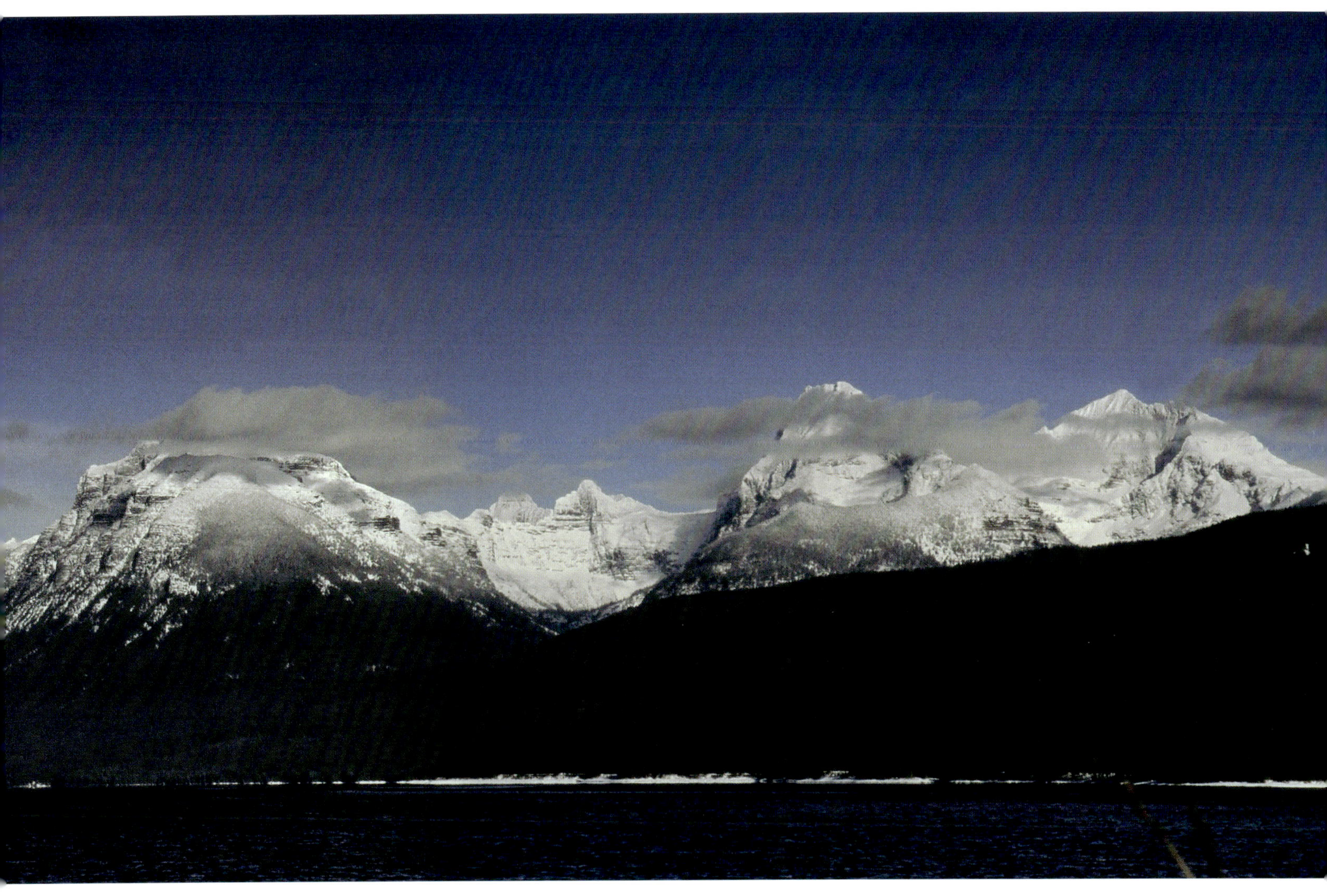

Lunch Creek to Saint Mary

***Note*: As you exit the Logan Pass Visitor Center to continue your journey down the east side of the Going-to-the-Sun Road, reset your odometer to zero.**

The next three shots illustrate Lunch Creek at three different perspectives.

RIGHT: ***Mile 0.6.*** There is a small alpine rivulet on your left called Lunch Creek. Often there is a profusion of spring wildflowers on its banks.

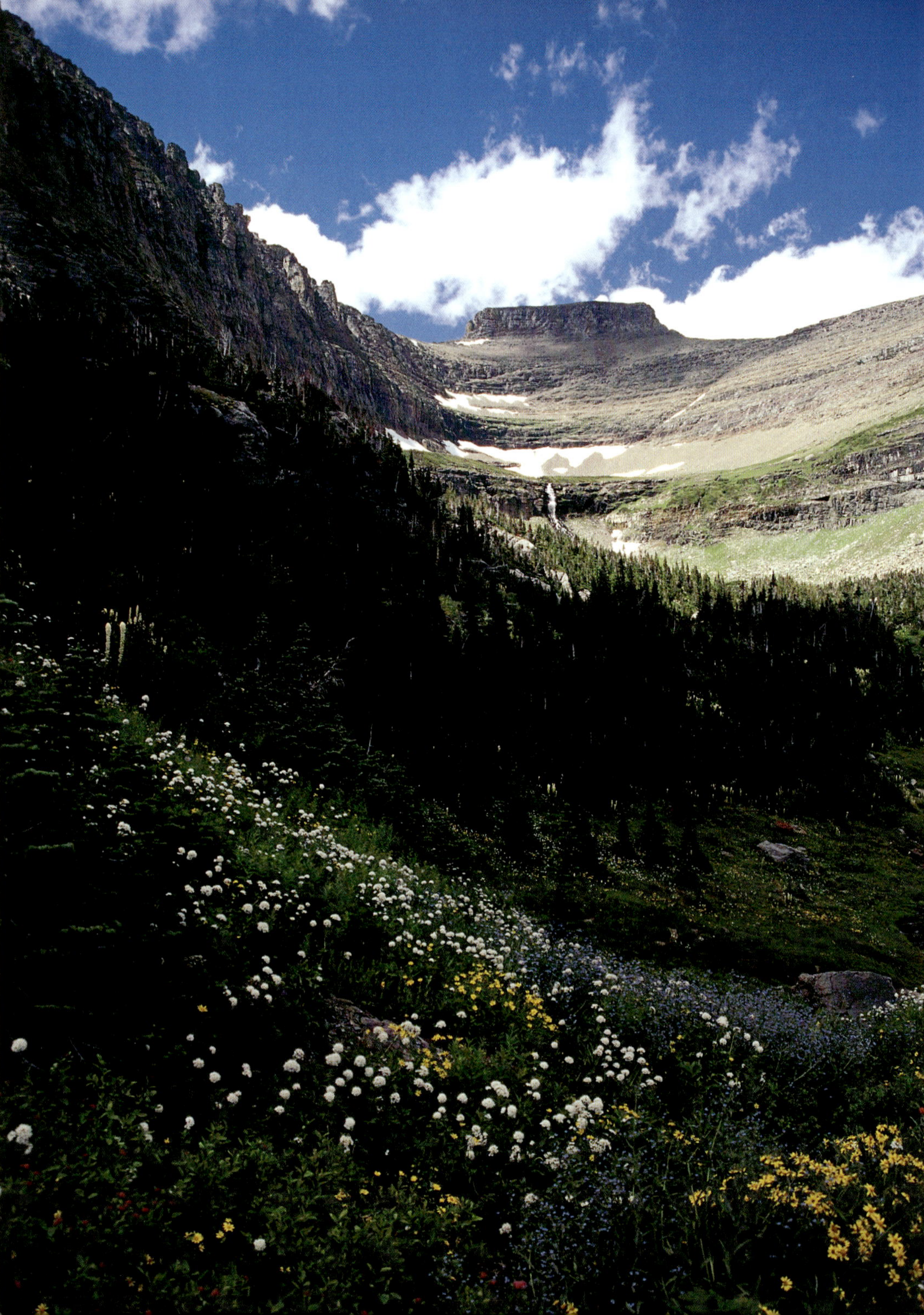

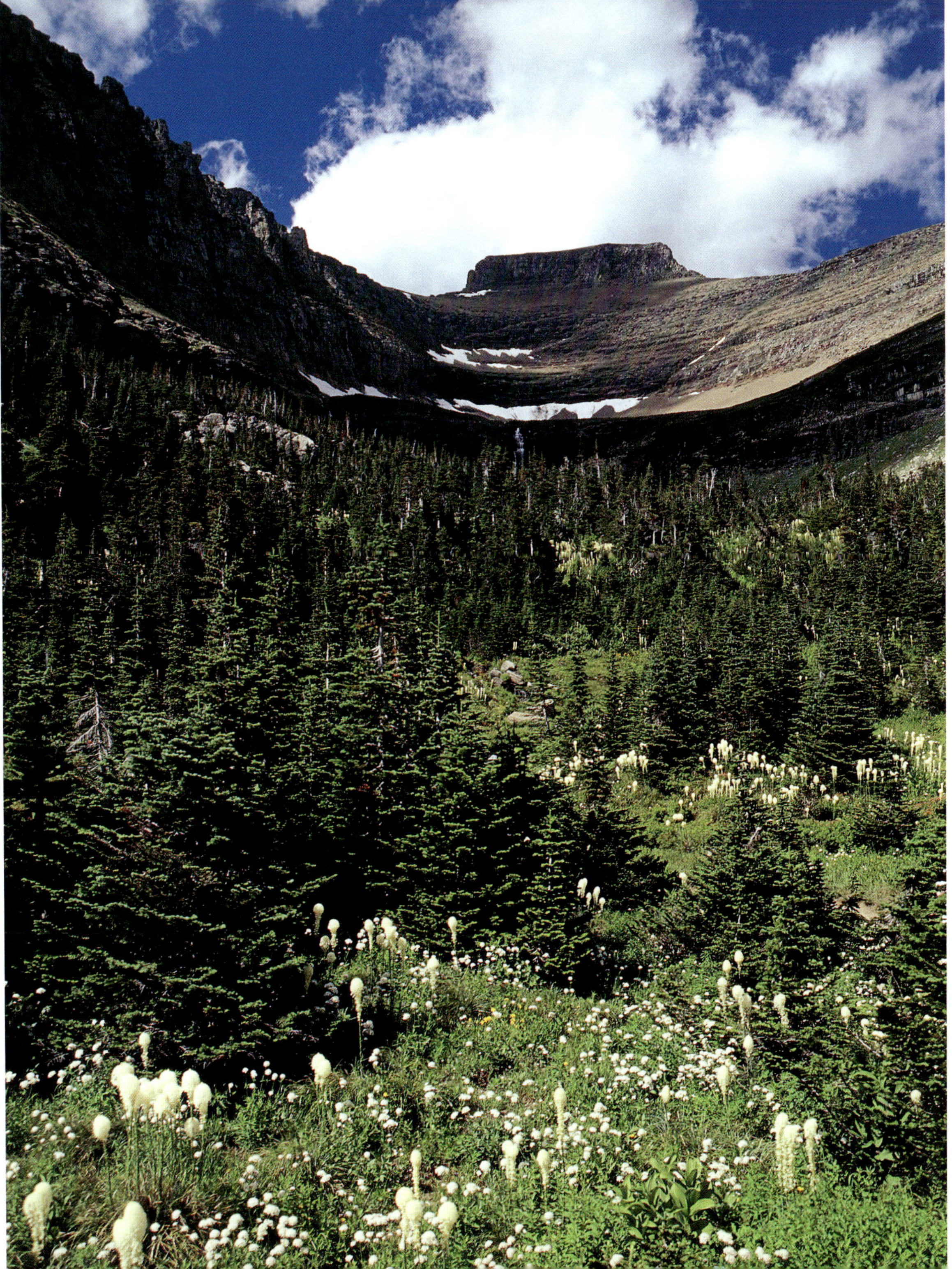

LEFT: ***Mile 0.6.*** Lunch Creek with tall stalks of bear grass in the foreground. Bear grass is a lily native to Glacier National Park that blooms in moist areas and shows up on its own timetable in the summer.

RIGHT: ***Mile 0.6.*** Lunch Creek swells with a powerful spring runoff.

FAR RIGHT: A black bear looks for food in a summer snow drift.

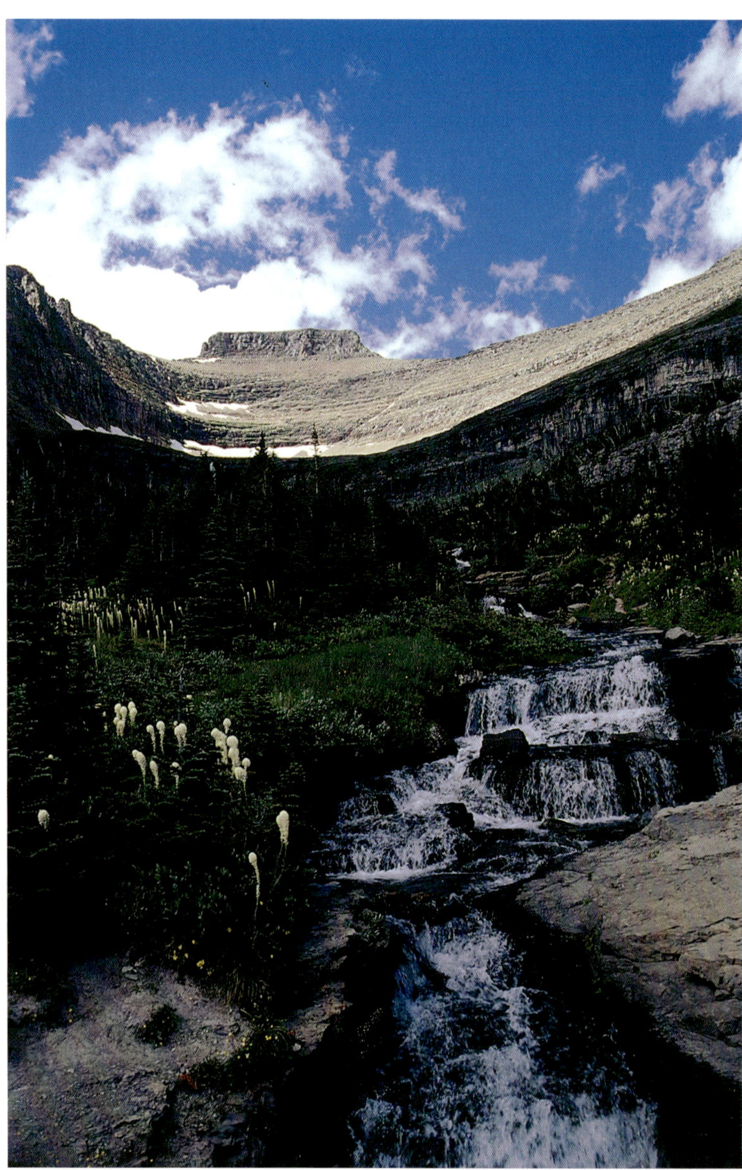

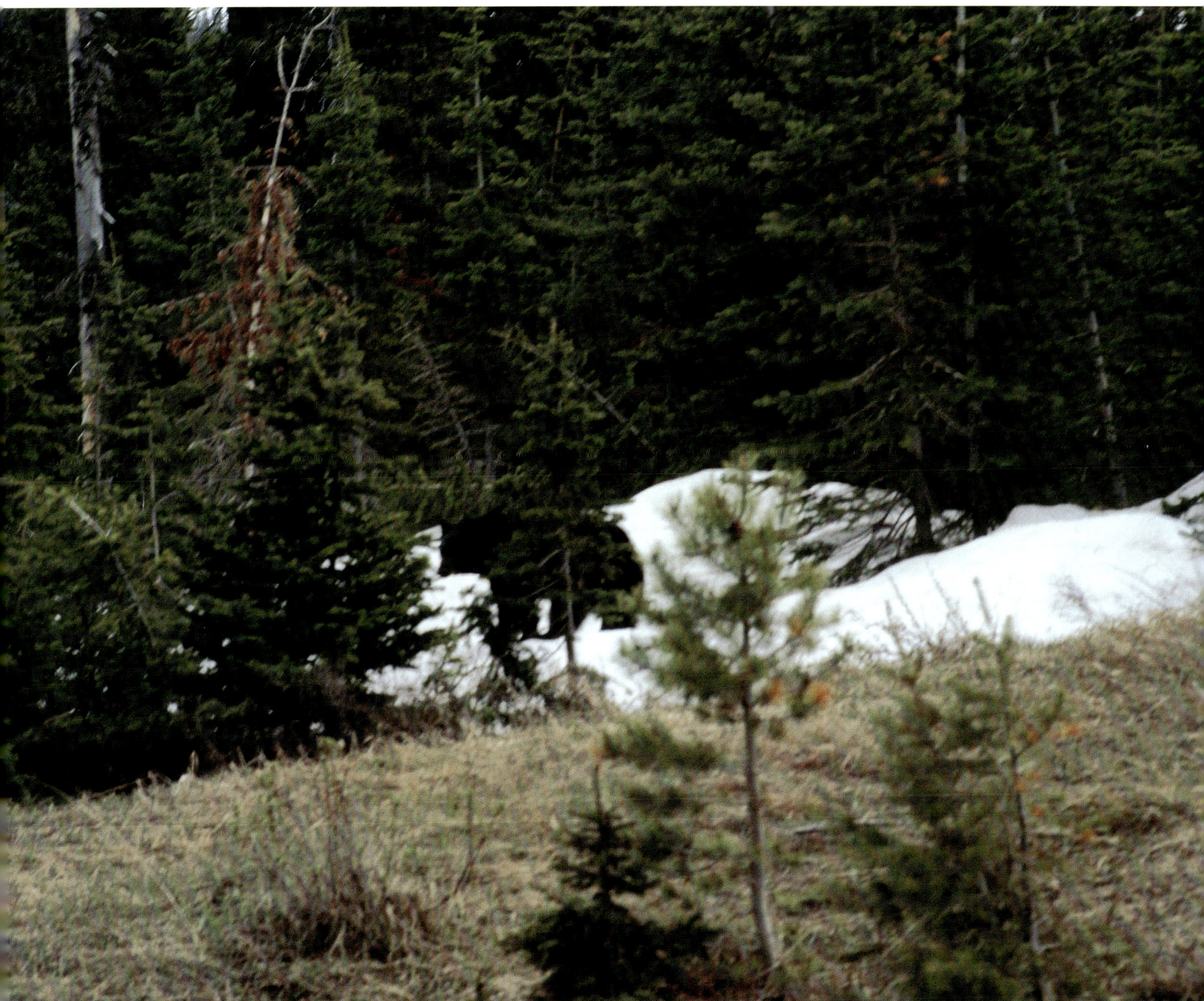

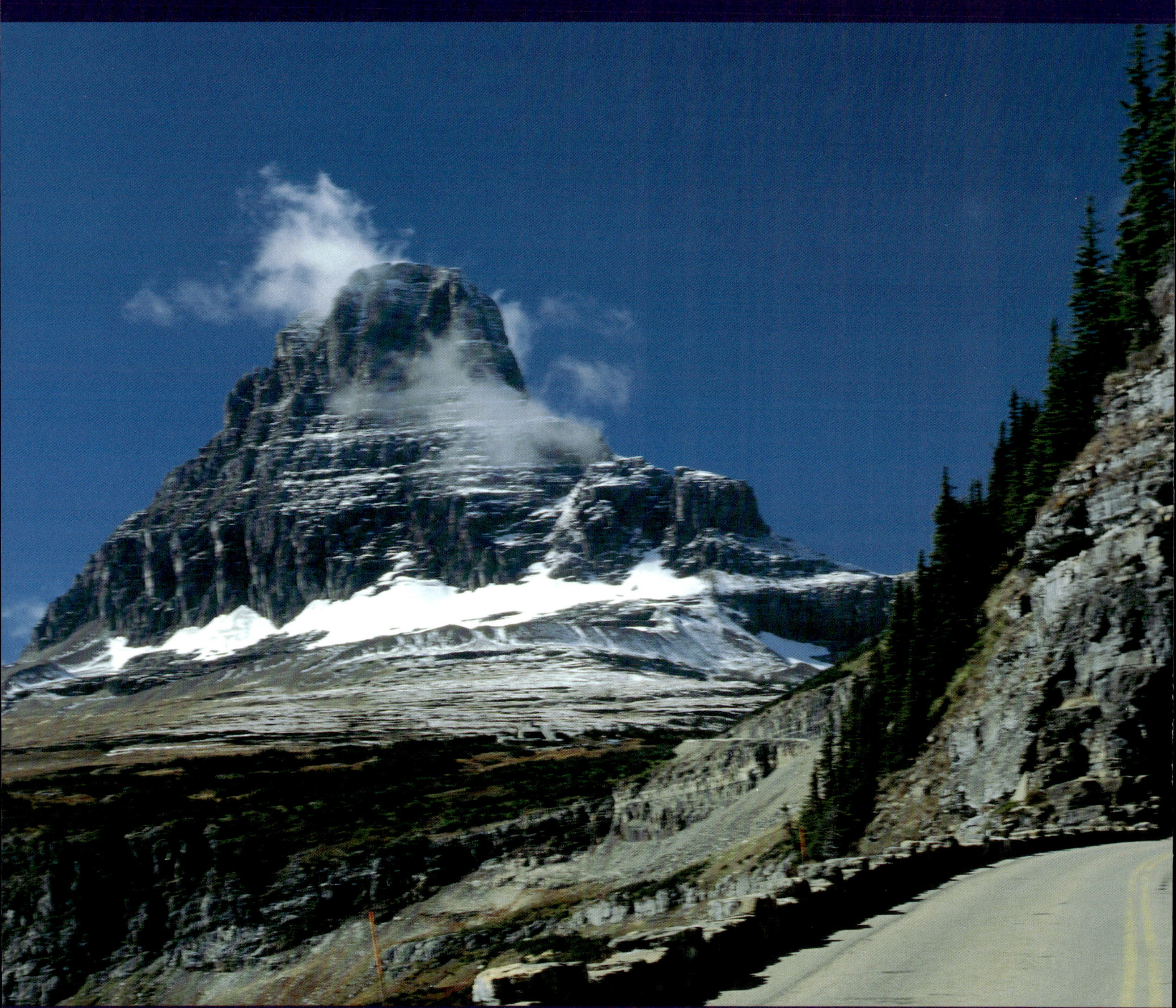

They say good things come in threes—and sometimes, so do good landscape shots! The following three great scenic shots are from the east side of the park, just below Logan Pass. Be prepared to stop right after you travel through the tunnel.

LEFT: ***Mile 1.2.*** I like to call this photograph of this east side tunnel the "Great Tunnel Shot," with Mount Reynolds in the background.

BELOW: Deer graze along the Going-to-the-Sun Road.

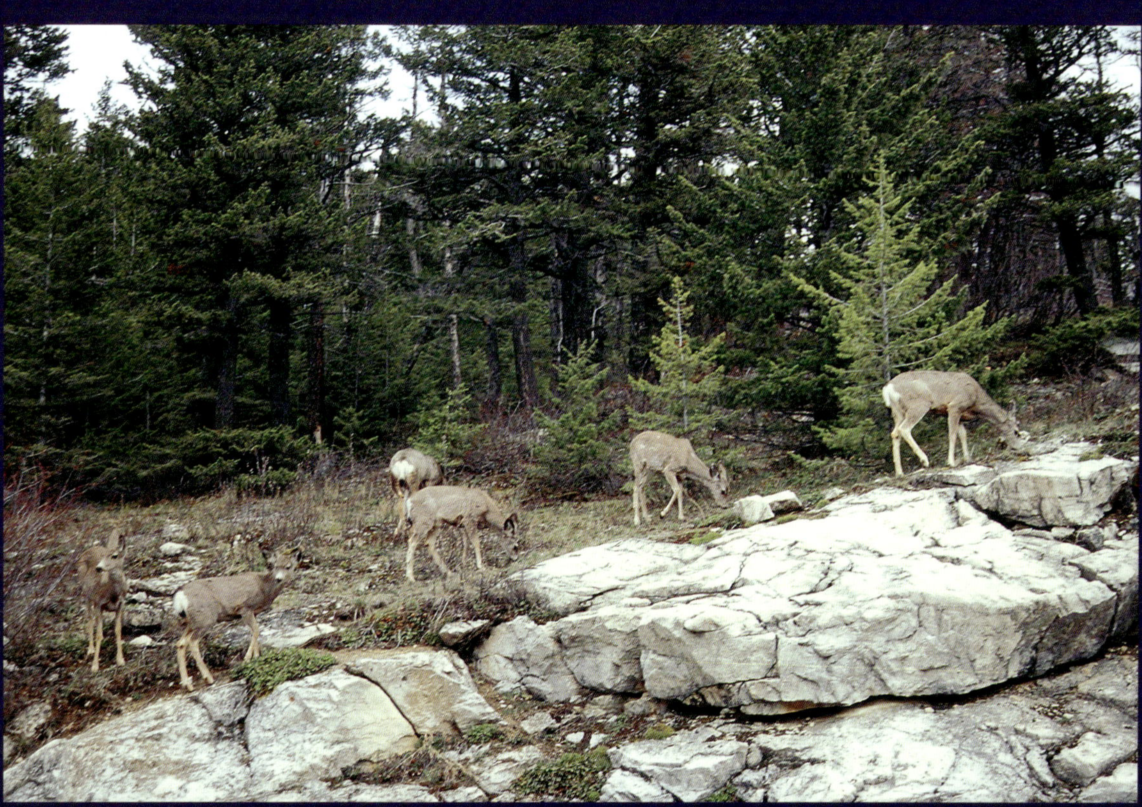

RIGHT: ***Mile 1.3.*** Logan Pass with spiky bear grass in the foreground.

FAR RIGHT: ***Mile 1.35.*** From a bit farther down the road, you can take this great scenic shot that includes Mount Reynolds and Mount Heavy Runner.

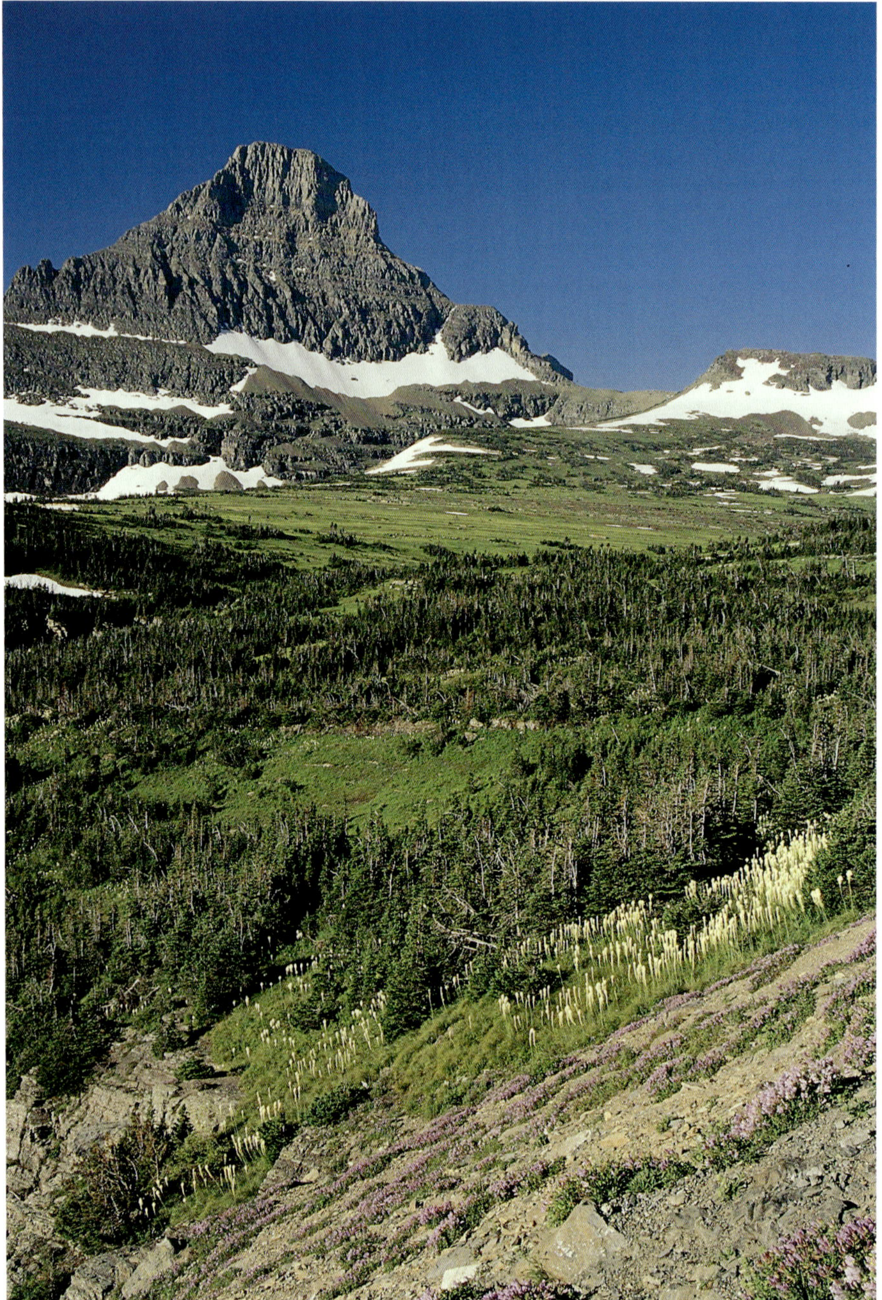

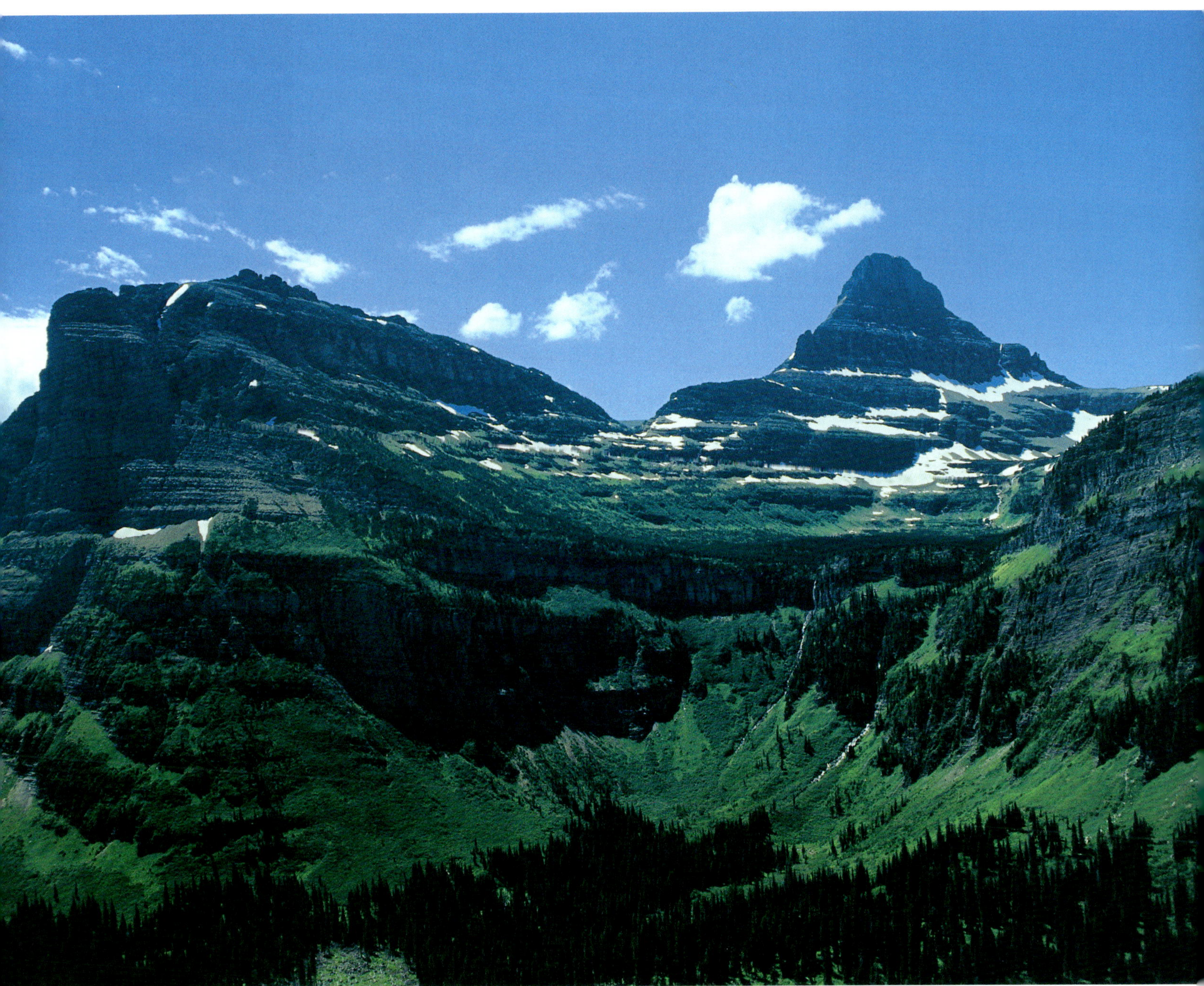

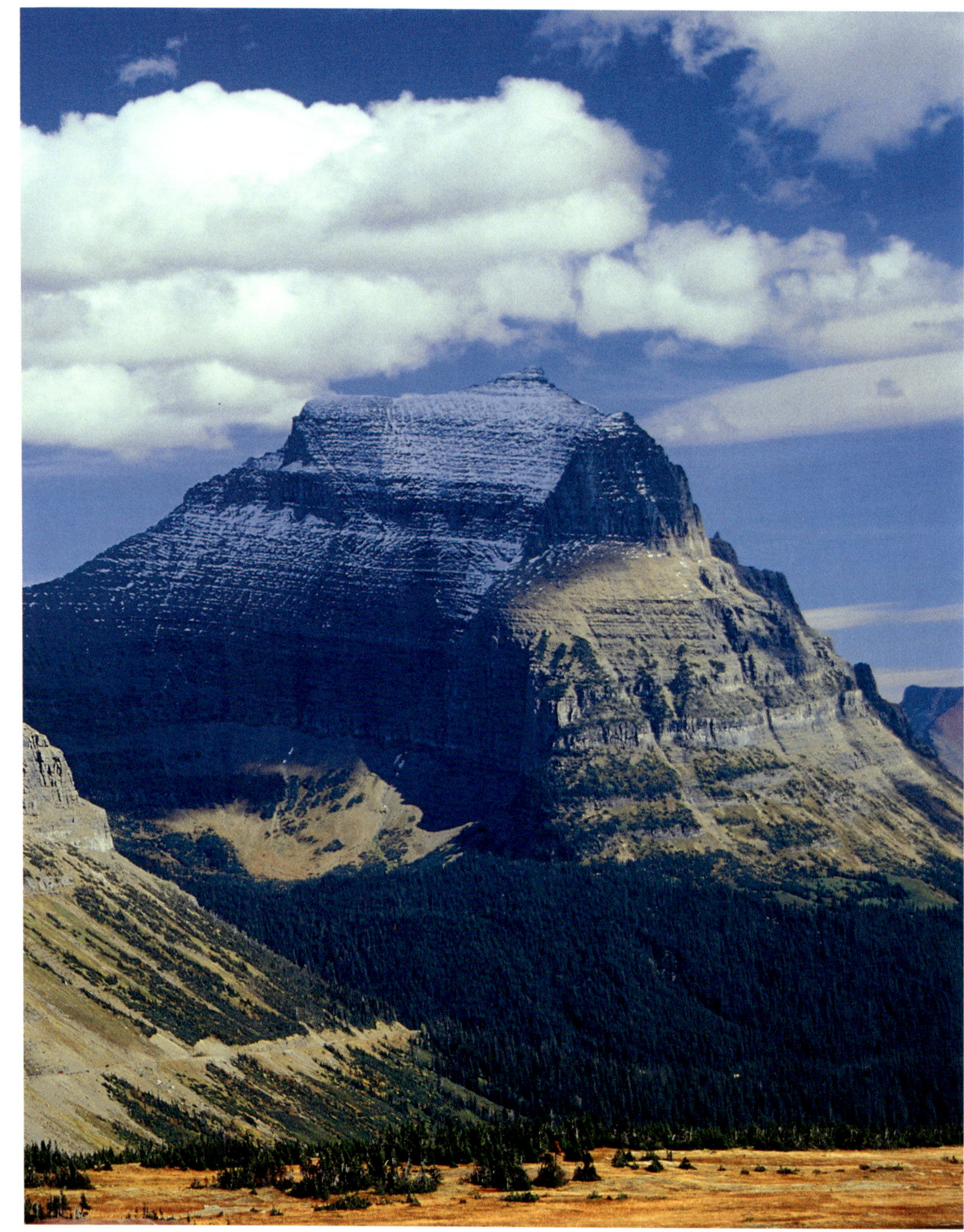

FACING PAGE: ***Mile 1.4.*** From this location on Lunch Creek, there is a good opportunity to take a spectacular shot of Going-to-the-Sun Mountain. It can be very dramatic in midday, if the heavens contribute to what I call "Kodachrome skies."

Note: Just past this spot is an exhibit for Jackson Glacier Overlook that explains how the glacier has shrunk from its mid-nineteenth-century size and overshadows forests of Engelmann spruce and subalpine fir, the dominant tree species on the park's east side. The overlook, however, is not that impressive a photograph.

BELOW: ***Mile 4.5.*** Just 0.1 miles down the road, you will find a much better view of the glorious Jackson Peak, home of the Jackson Glacier. Take your picture at this spot, as I did.

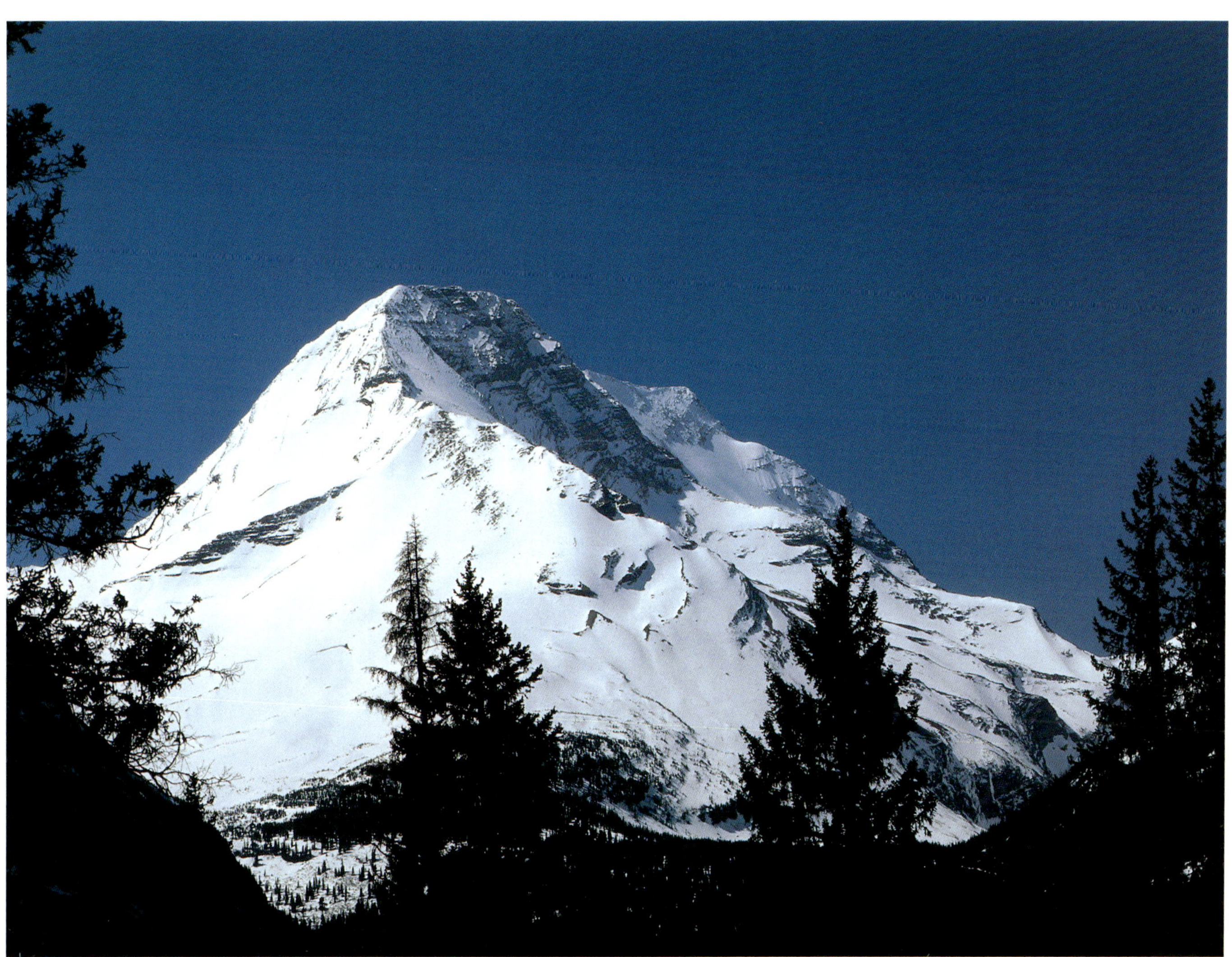

RIGHT: ***Mile* 7.5.** Two picturesque lakes were formed as glaciers scraped a trough in the area that eventually became Saint Mary and Lower Saint Mary Lakes. Near the beginning of Saint Mary Lake, the narrow Sunrift Gorge was created by a small fault in the earth.

FAR RIGHT: ***Mile* 8.5.** Sun Point features a self-guided, 1-mile hiking trail that offers wonderful views along the shores of Saint Mary Lake.

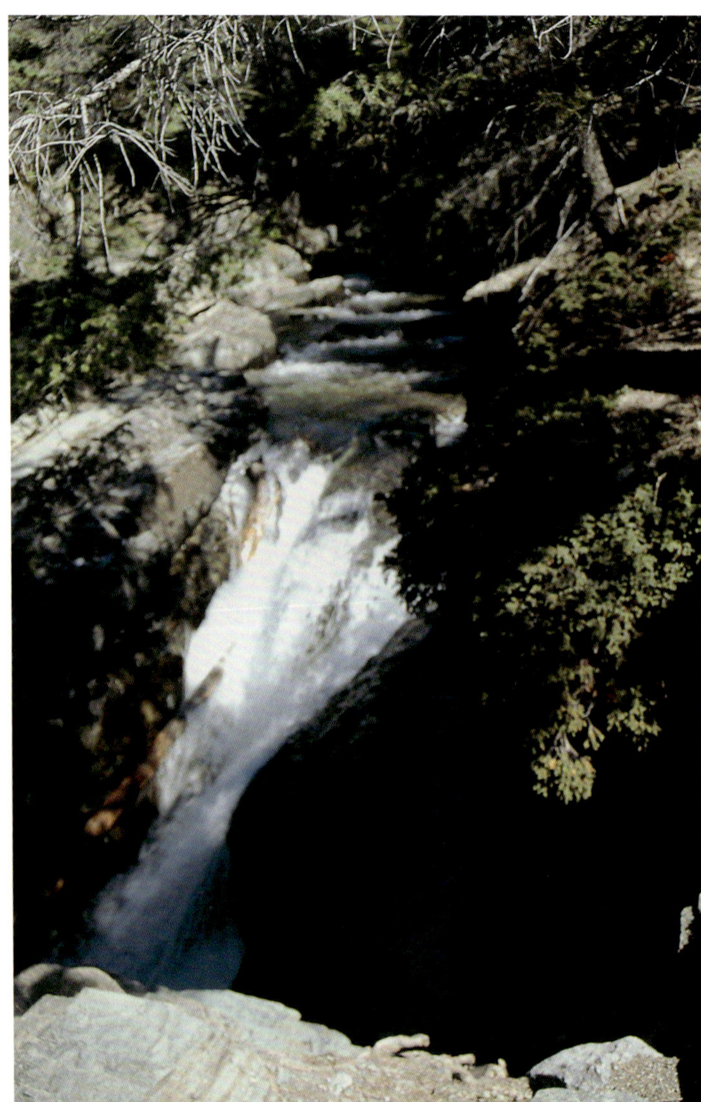

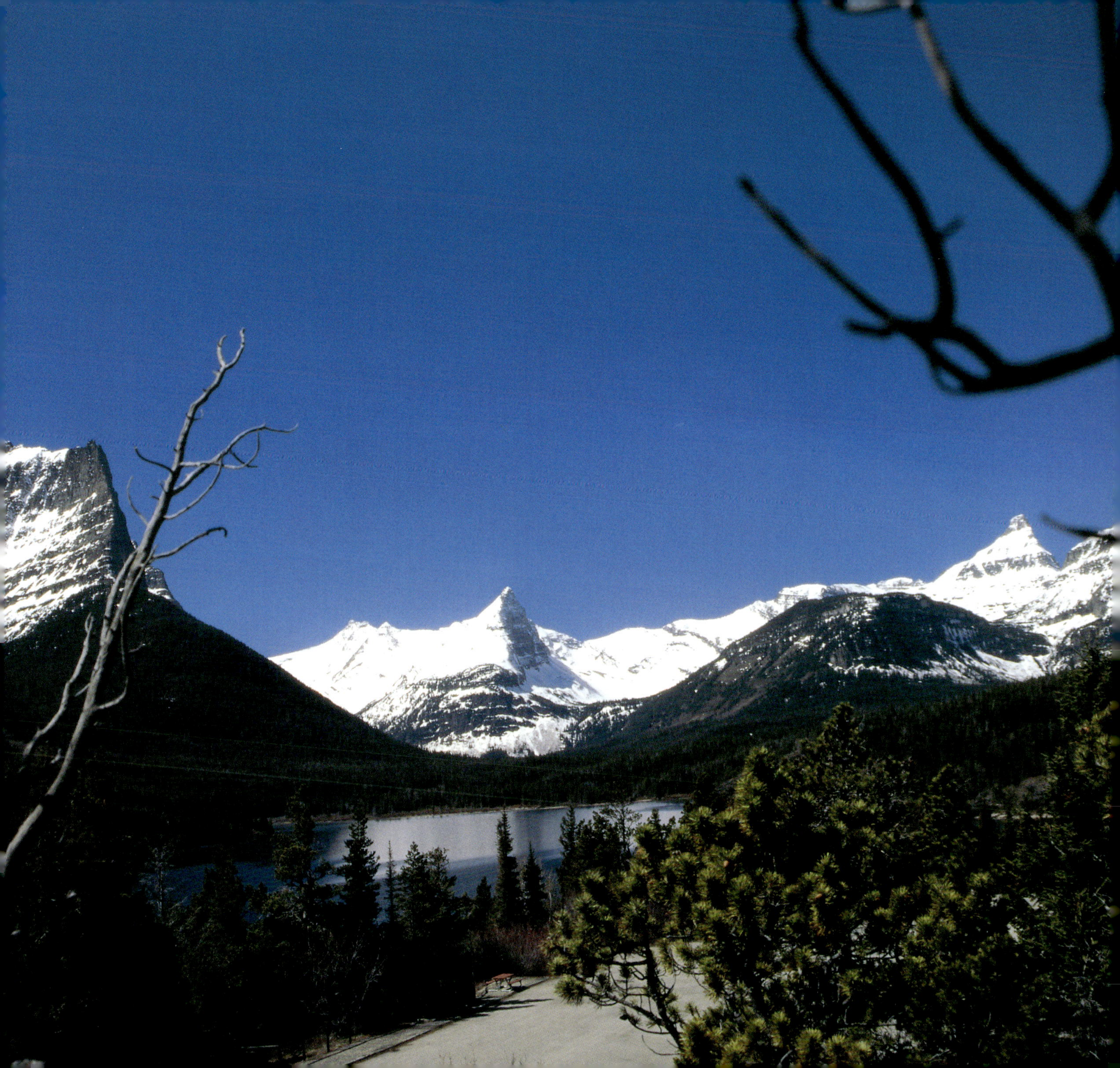

RIGHT: ***Mile 8.5.*** Sun Point, as photographed from a turnout along the shores of Saint Mary Lake.

BELOW: Red berries are bright against the white snow.

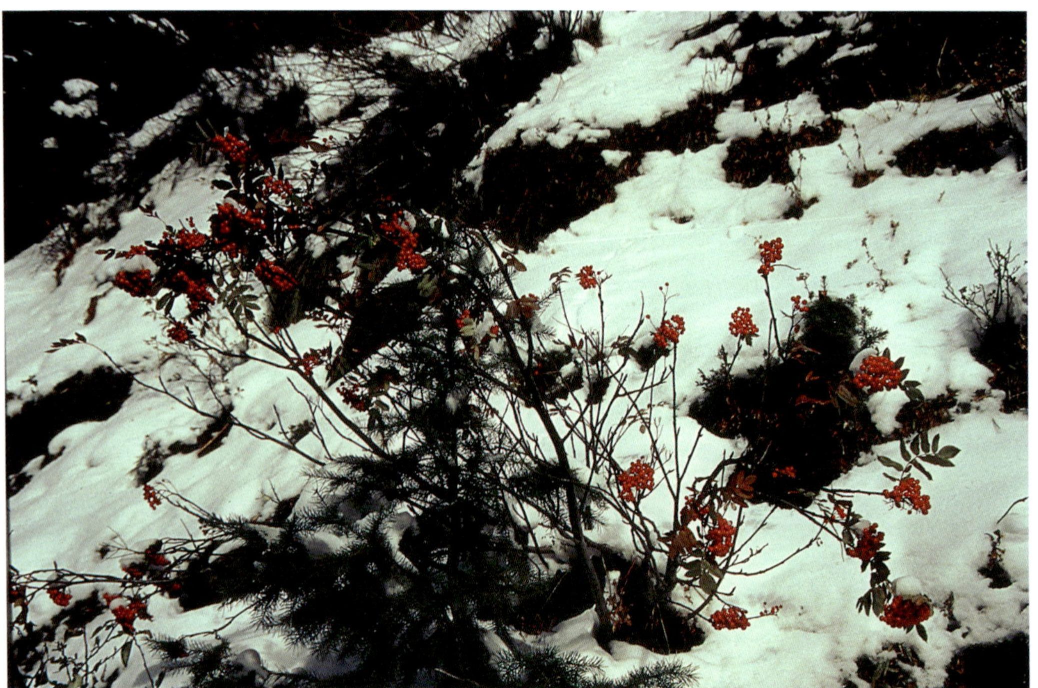

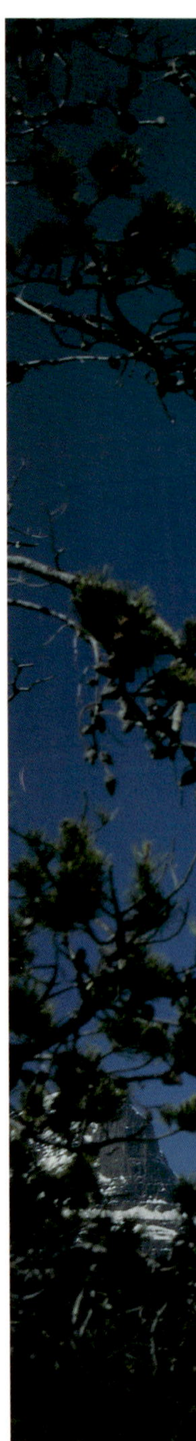

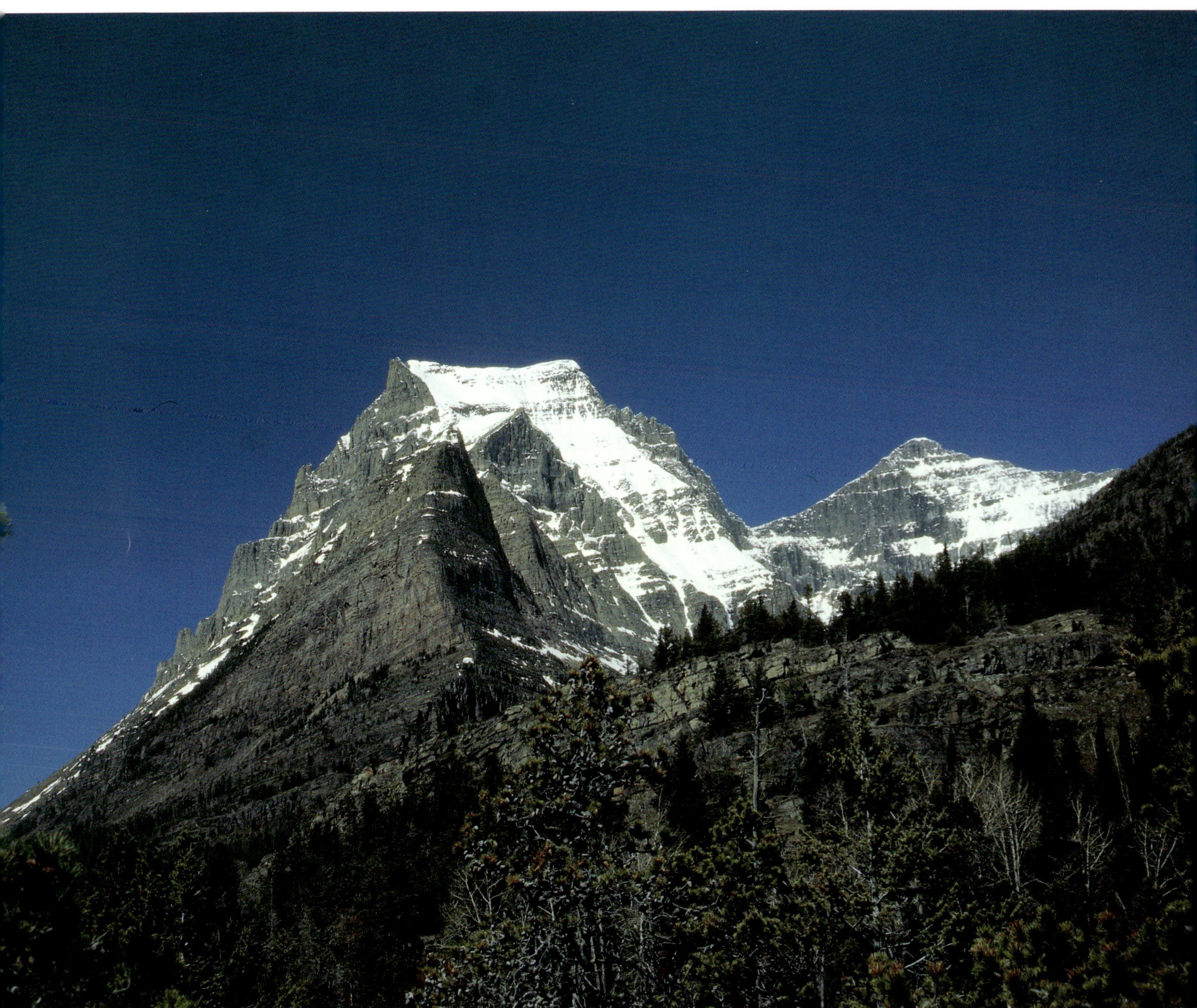

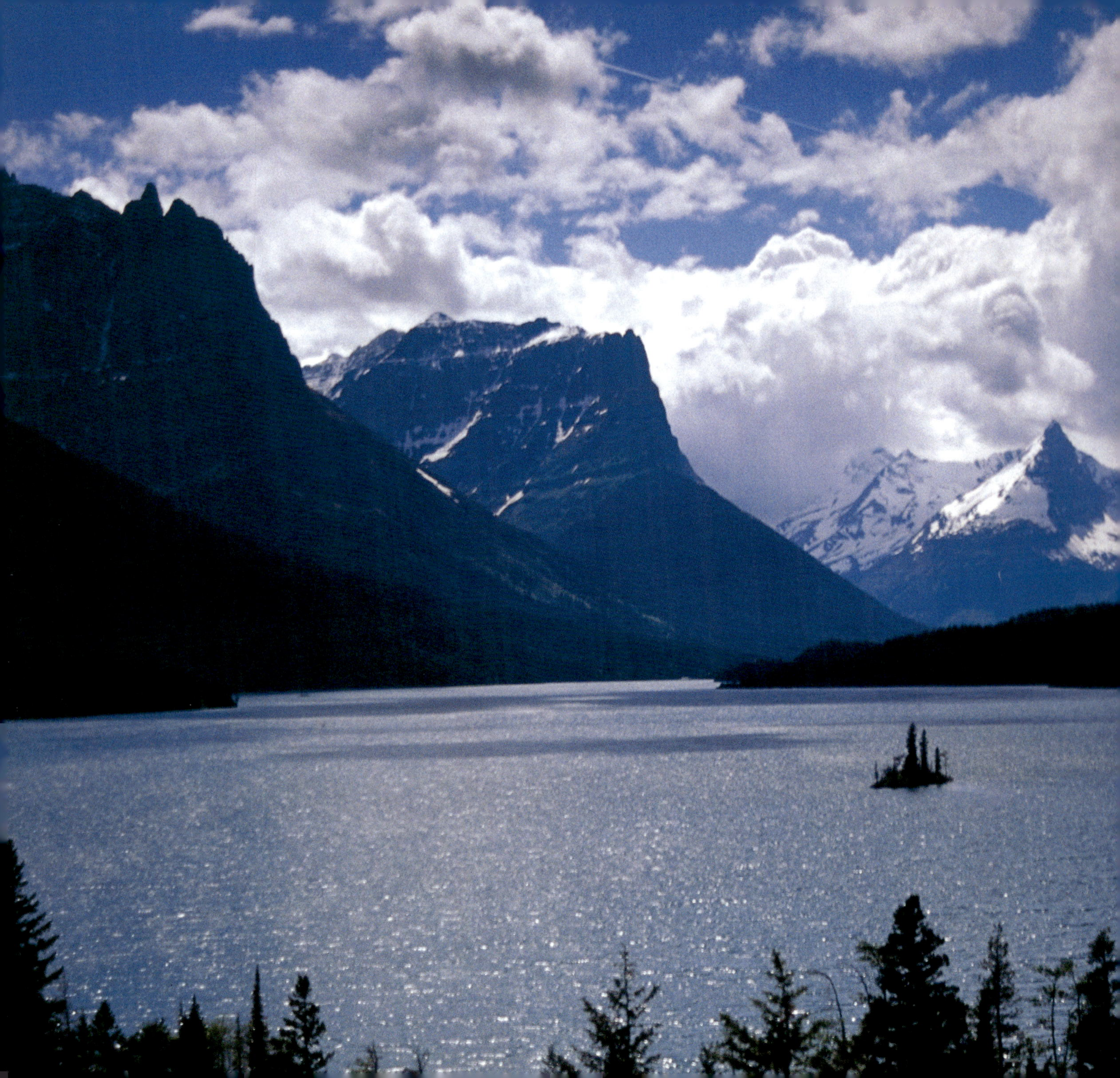

LEFT: ***Mile 11.7.*** This is the most photographed site in Glacier National Park—and with reason! Here you see an exceptional view of the picturesque Wild Goose Island in the foreground of the glacier-carved Saint Mary Lake. Absolutely, don't miss this!

BELOW: ***Mile 11.7.*** The waters of Saint Mary Lake and craggy granite peaks surround romantic Wild Goose Island.

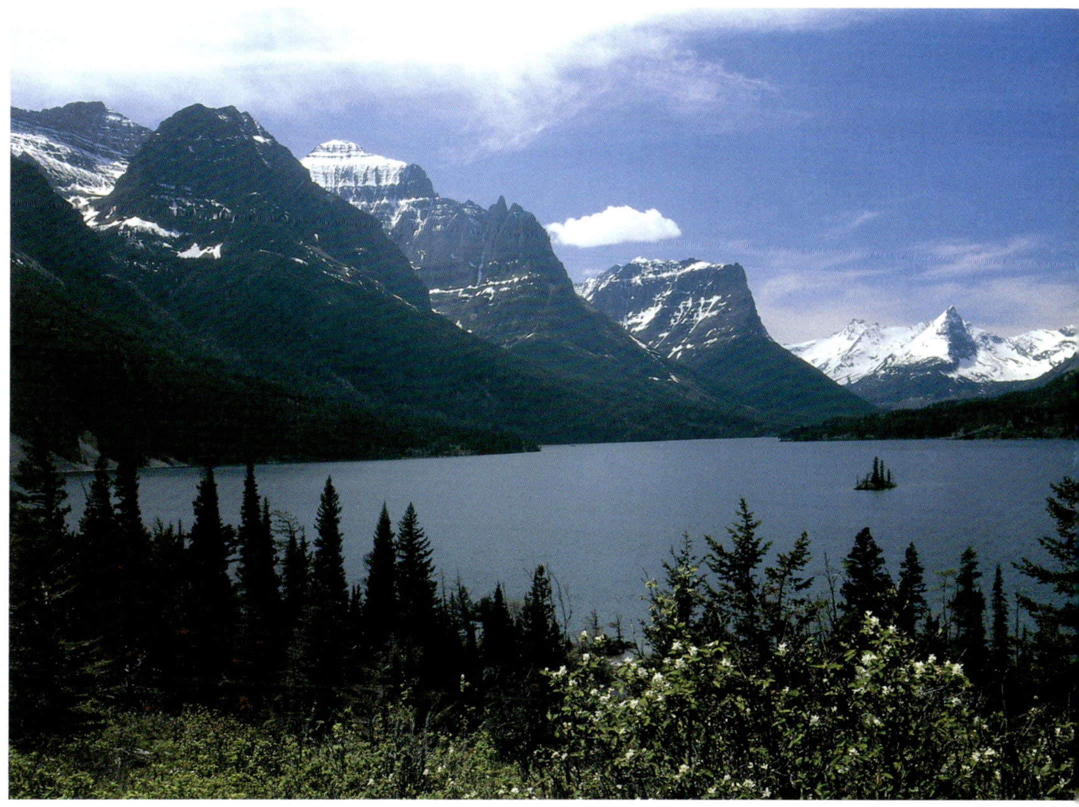

RIGHT: Saint Mary Lake with a profusion of wildflowers in the foreground.

BELOW: A mountain in Glacier National Park is shrouded in fog on a cool, autumn morning.

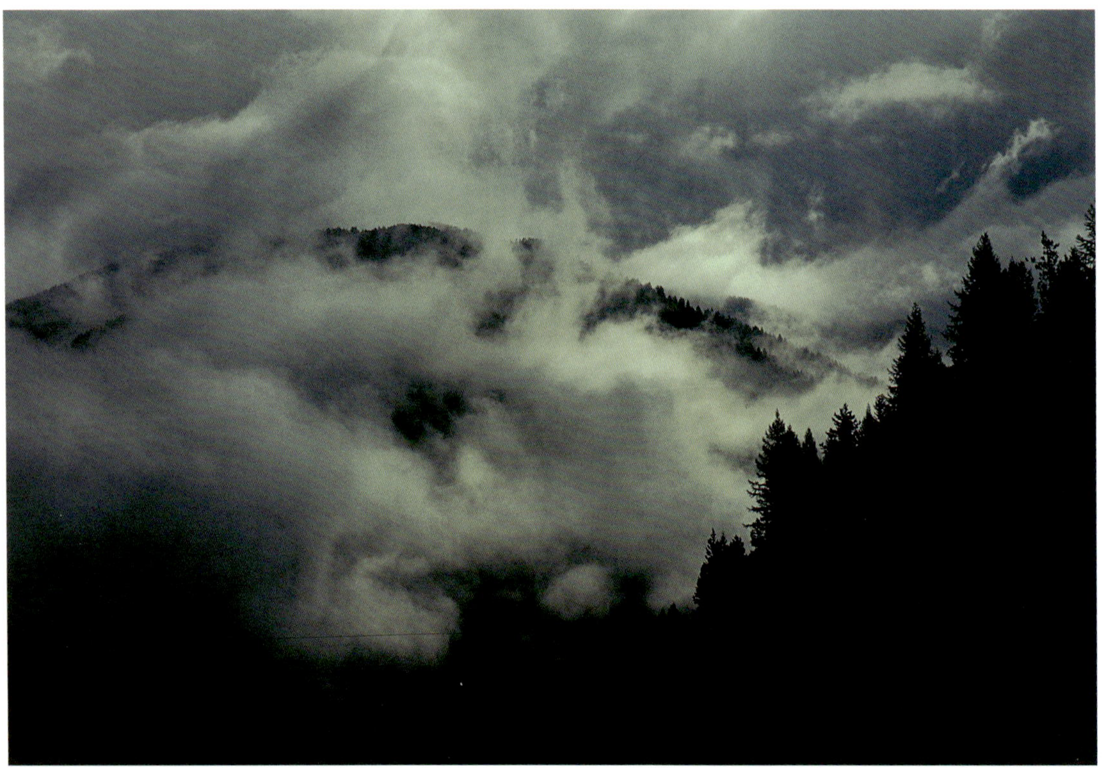

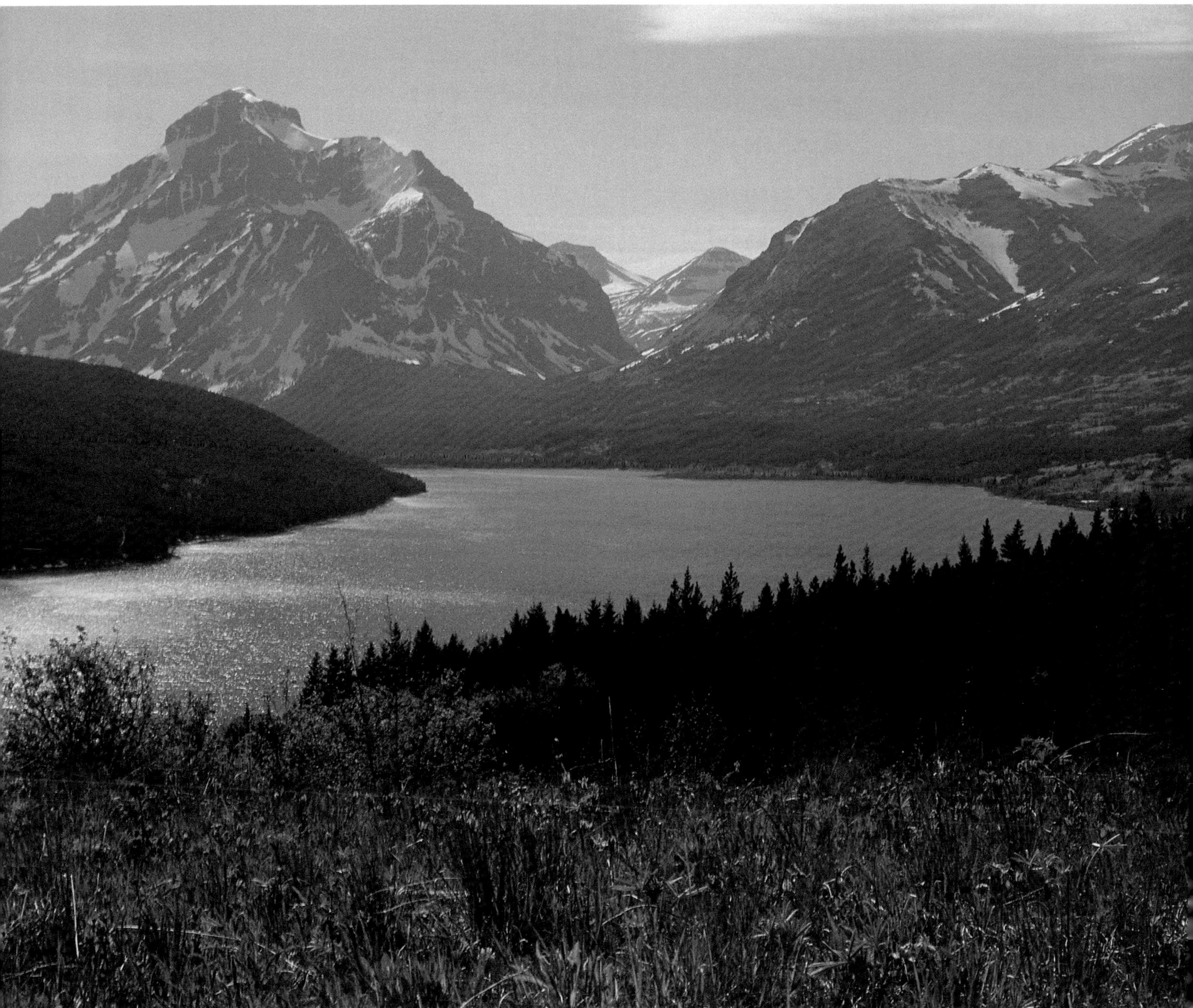

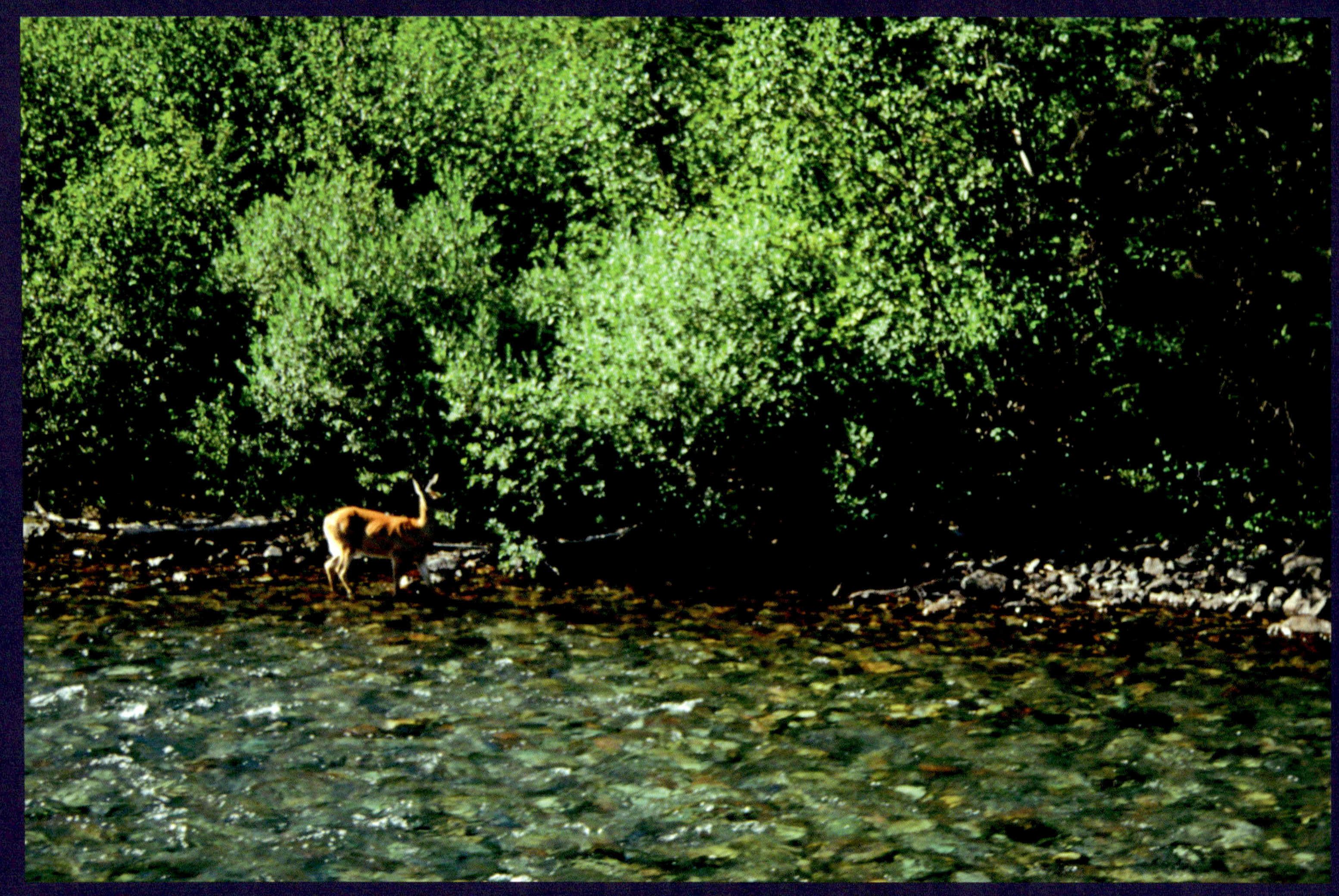

ABOVE: A deer forages in the thick brush along a jade-colored stream.

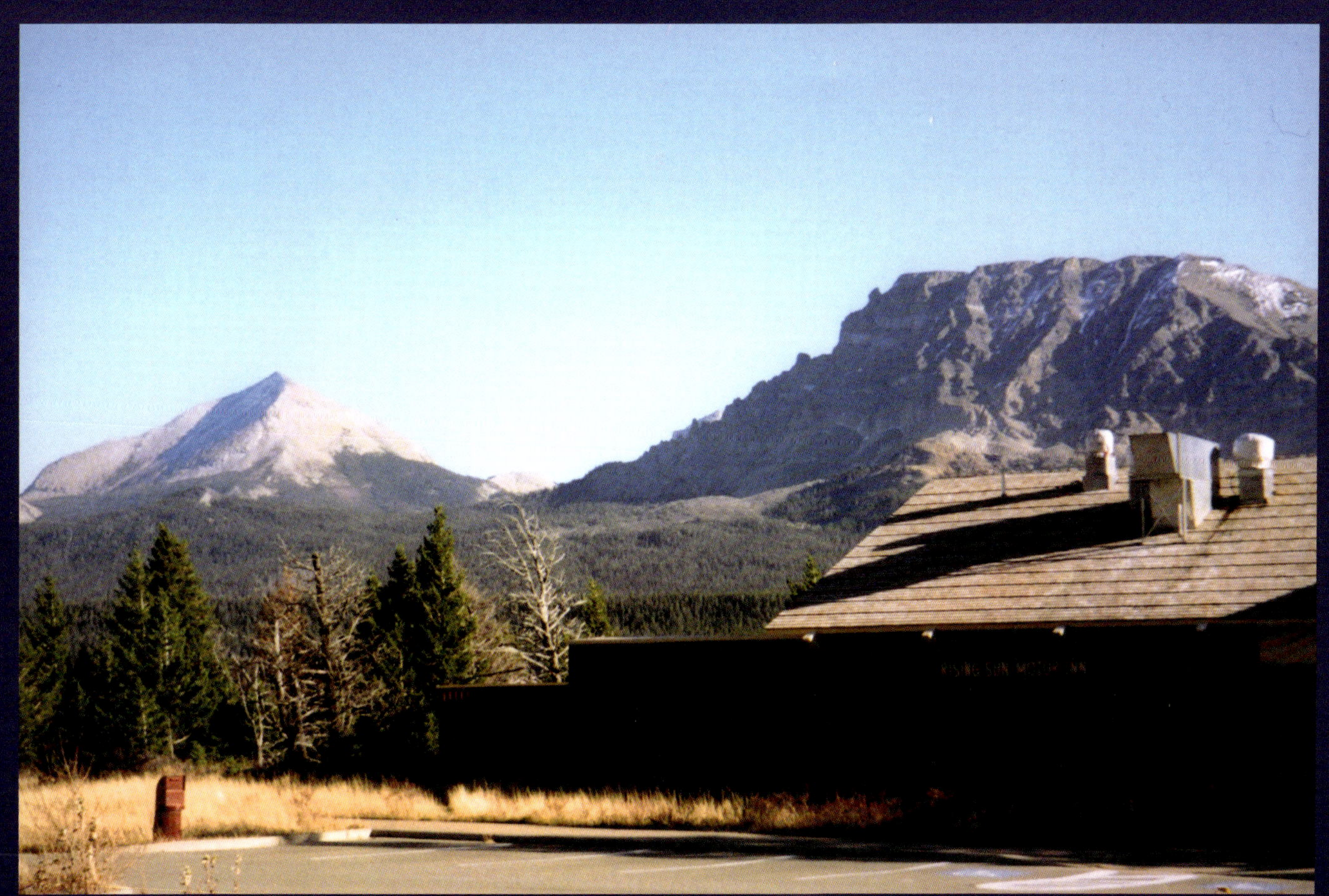

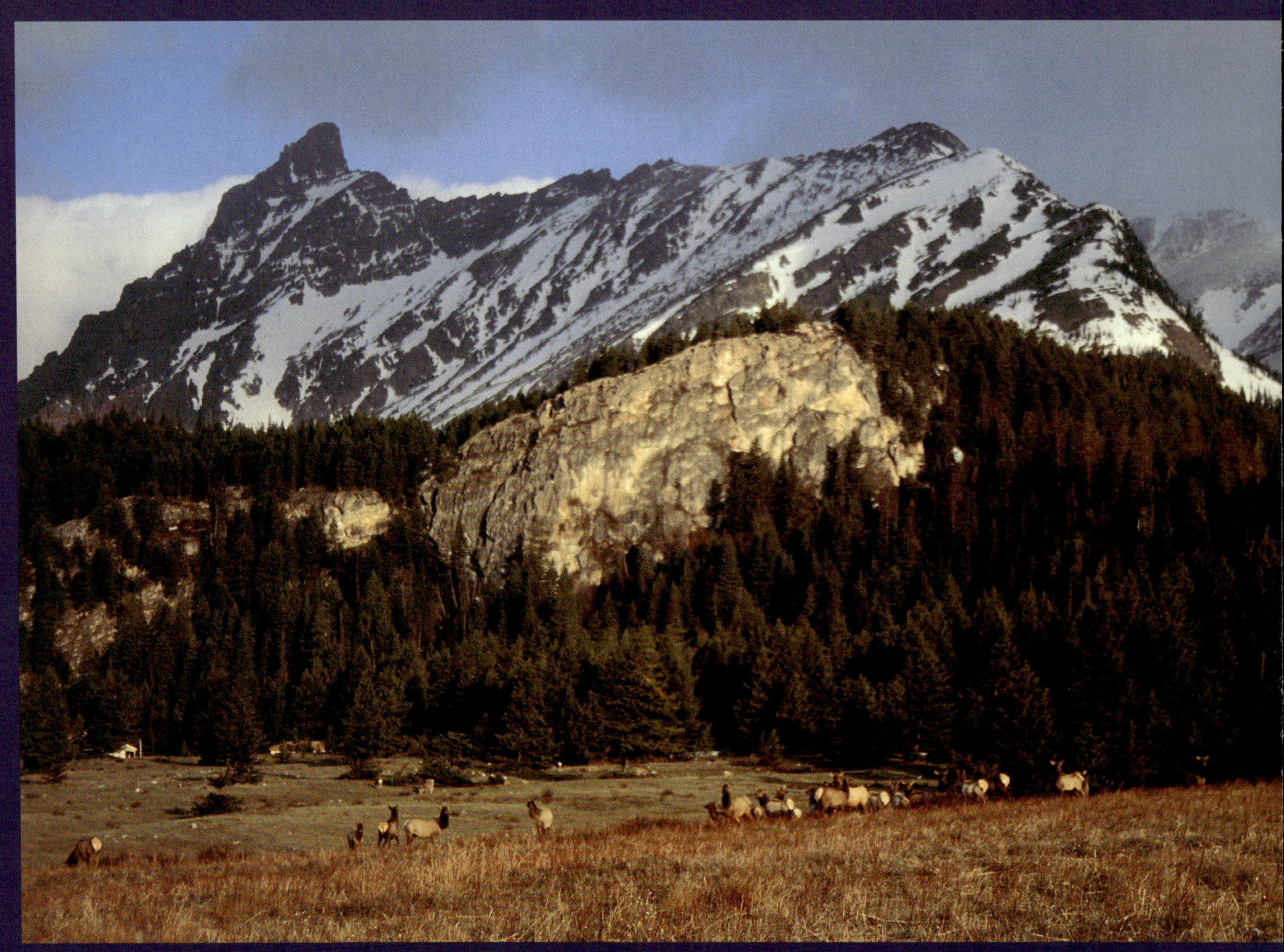

ABOVE: ***Mile 15.7.*** As you continue your trip along the northwest side of Saint Mary Lake, the valley widens into an area called Two Dog Flats. A sizeable elk herd prospers here, and the animals are often out grazing in this open area early and late in the day.

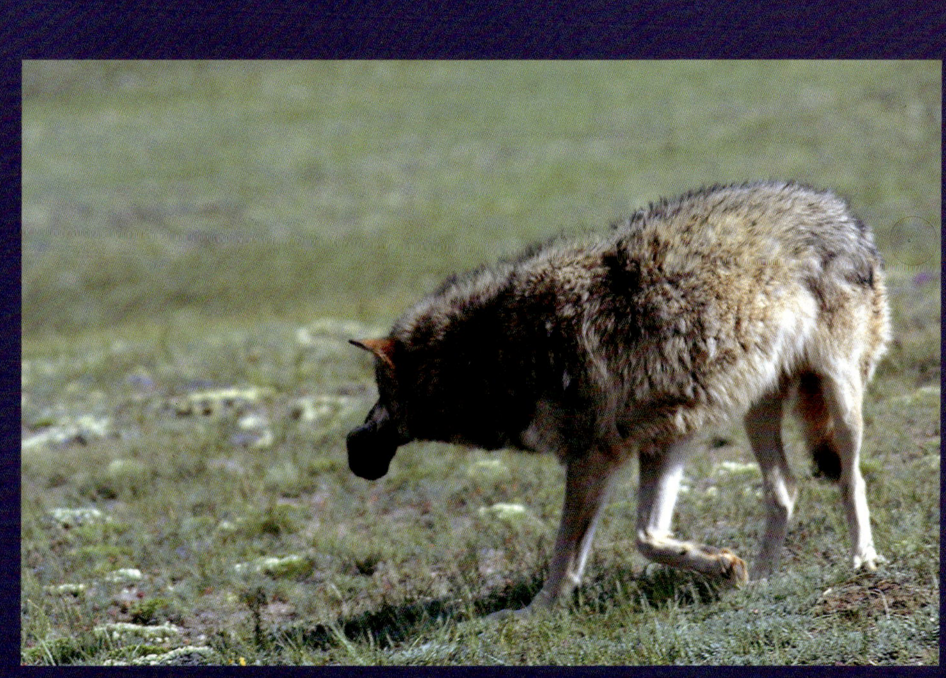

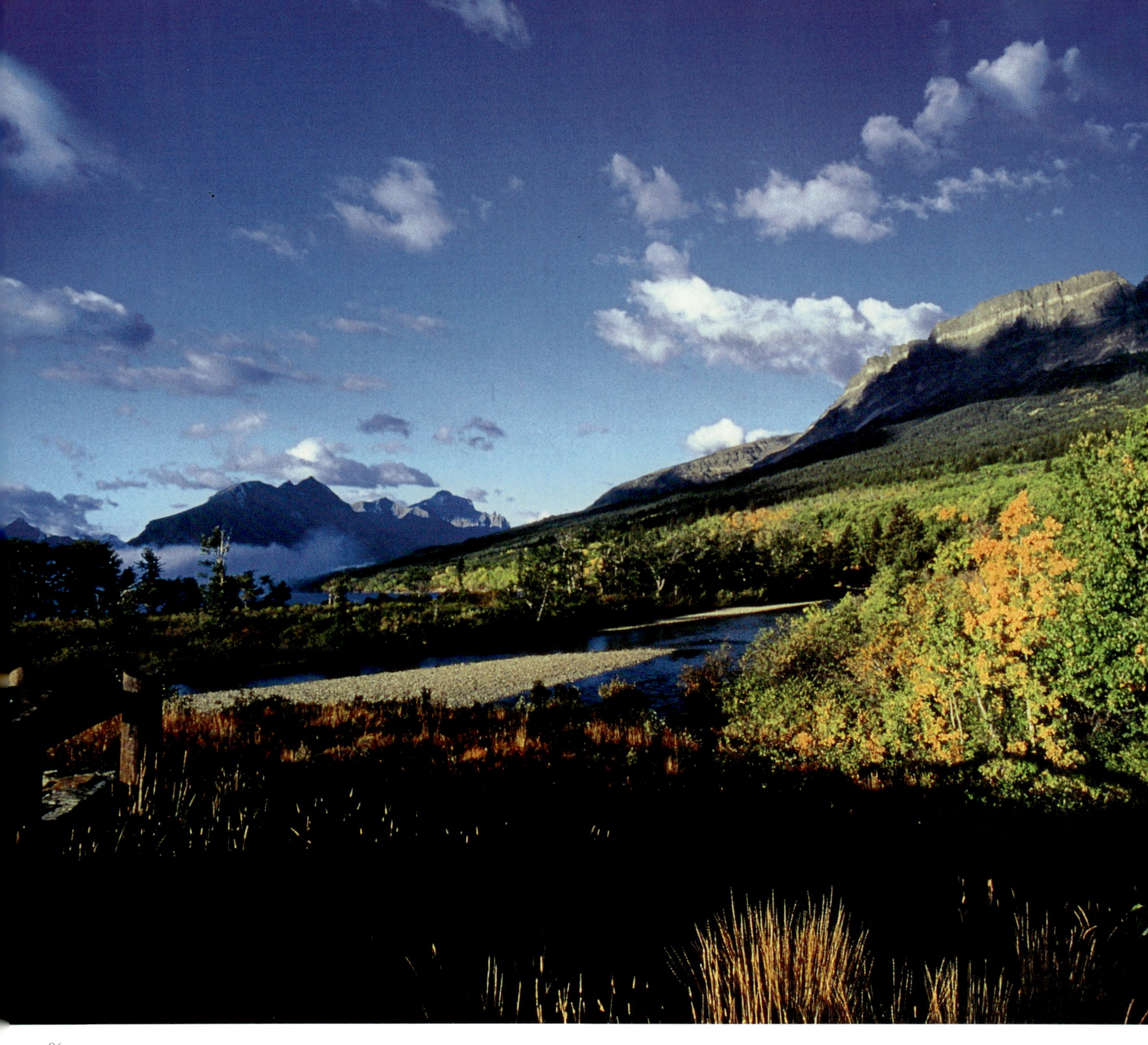

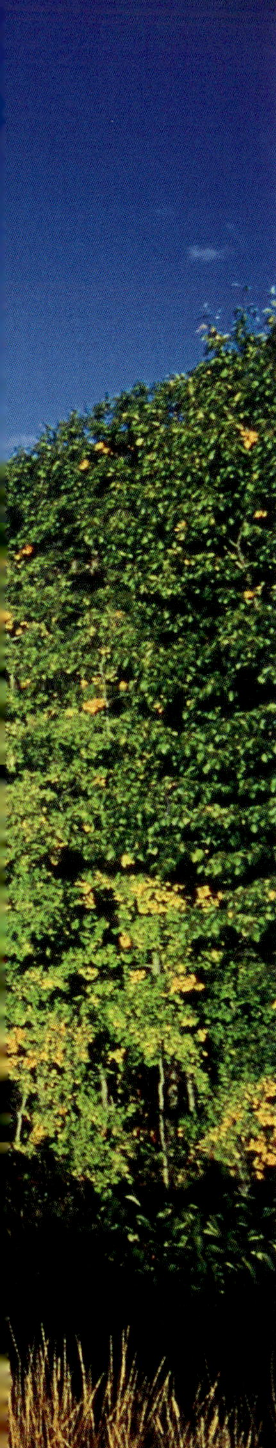

LEFT: ***Mile 16.2.*** This charming, meandering stream is where Saint Mary Lake drains into Saint Mary River—a scene enhanced at nightfall by a glowing sunset.

BELOW: This rock face is actually fossilized algae called stromatolite. There are six species of fossilized algae in Glacier National Park, some nearly one billion years old. This algae first introduced oxygen into our atmosphere.

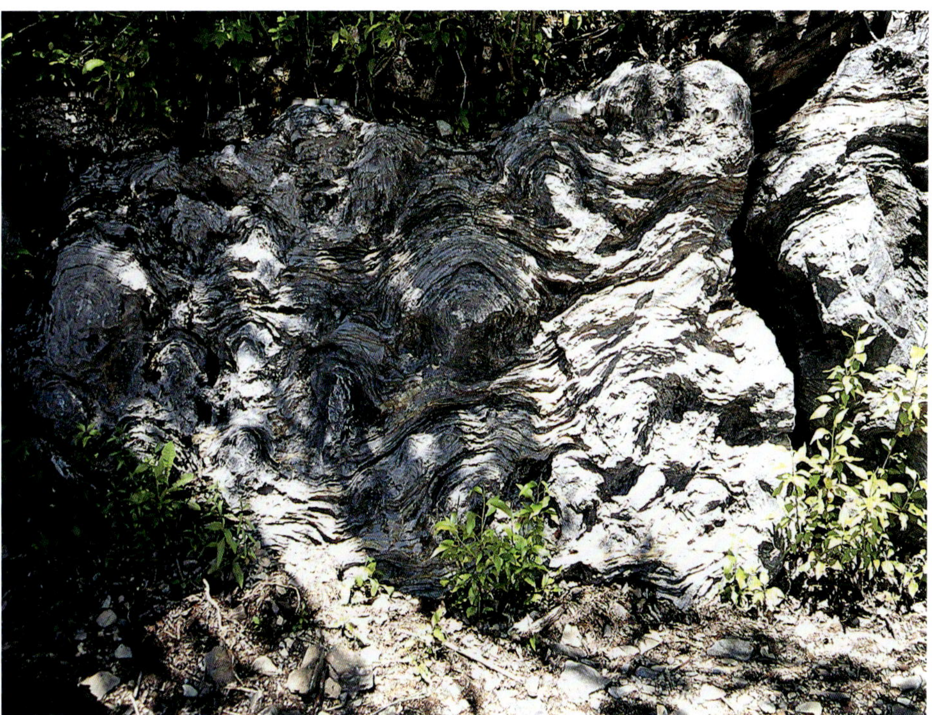

RIGHT: Saint Mary River between Saint Mary and Lower Saint Mary Lakes.

FAR RIGHT: ***Mile 16.2.*** This photo of Saint Mary Lake was taken about 50 feet from the meandering stream on the preceding page.

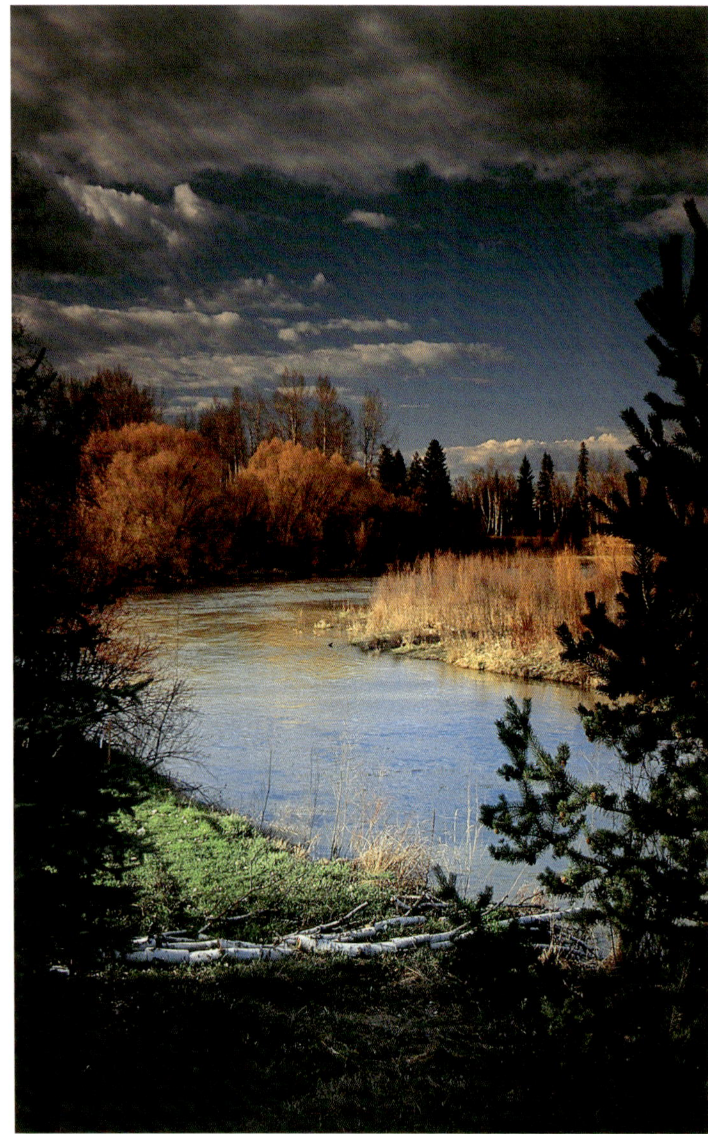

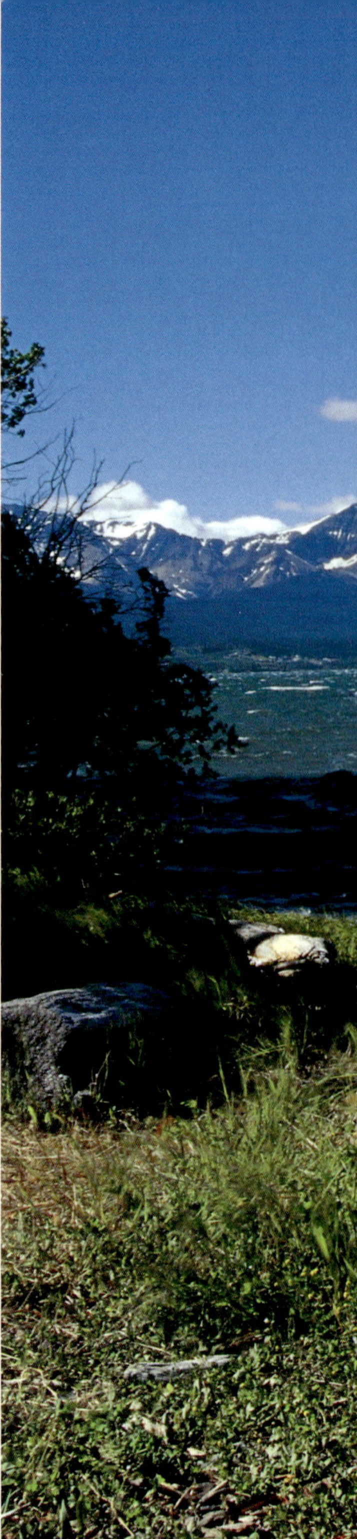

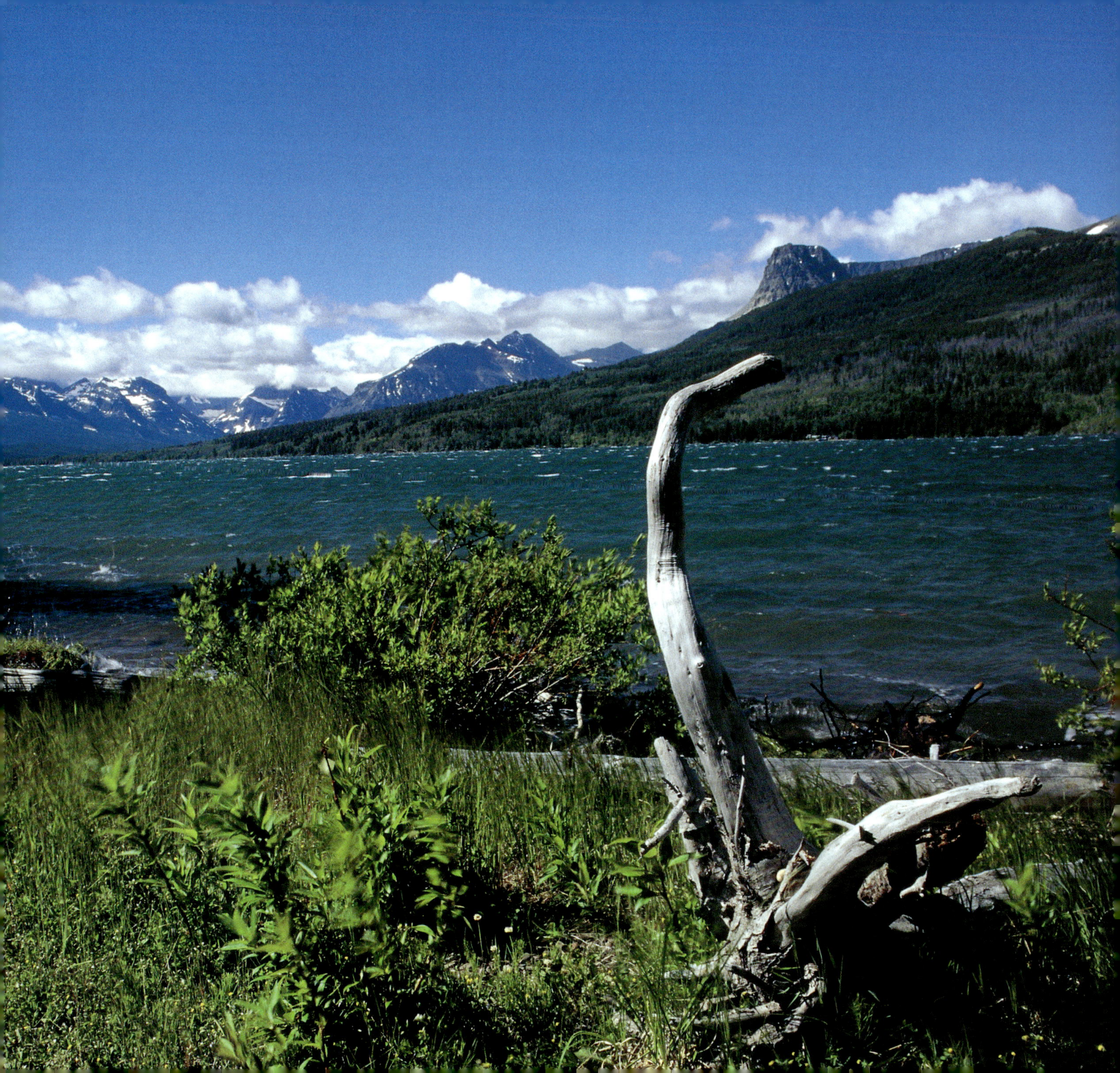

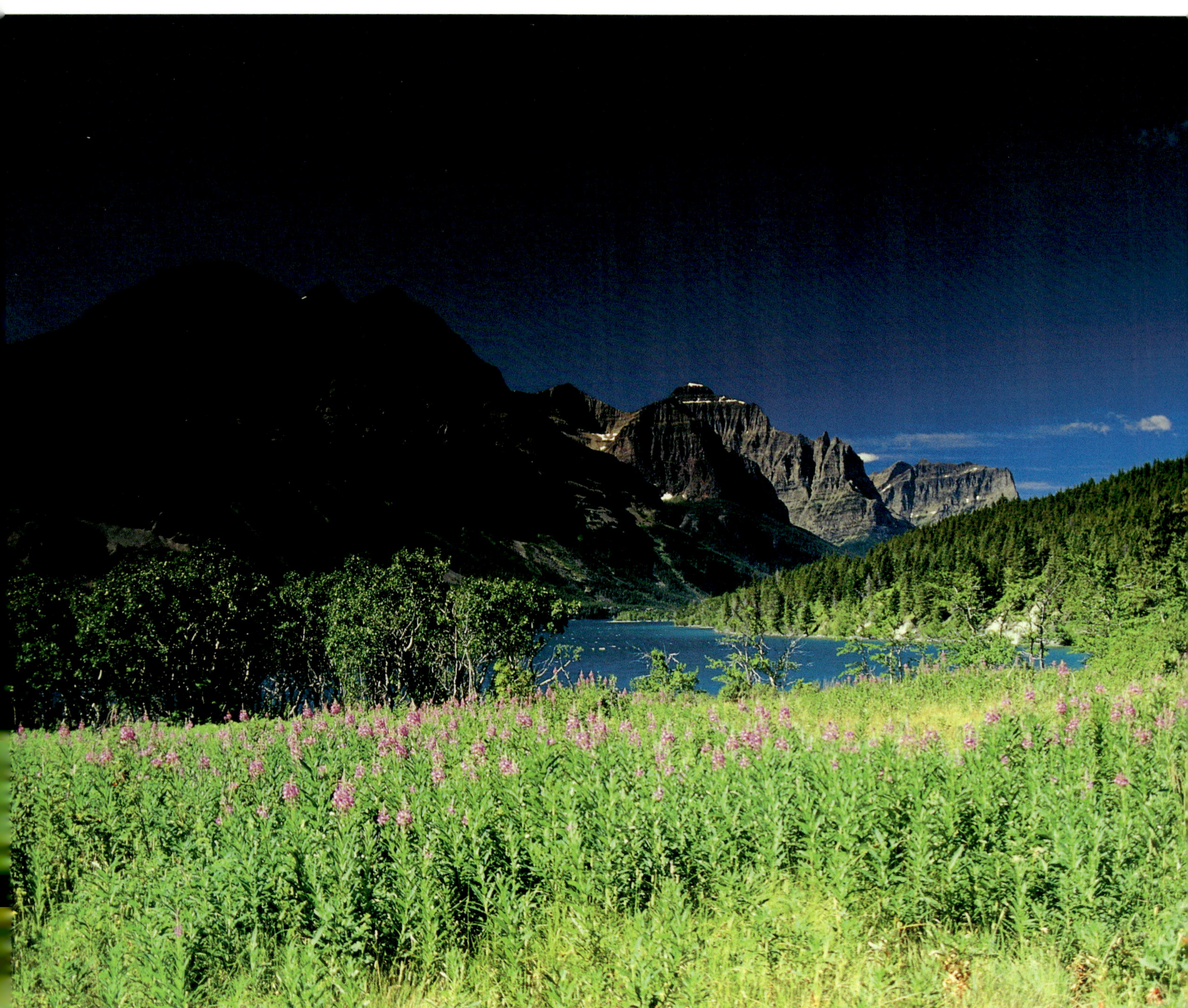

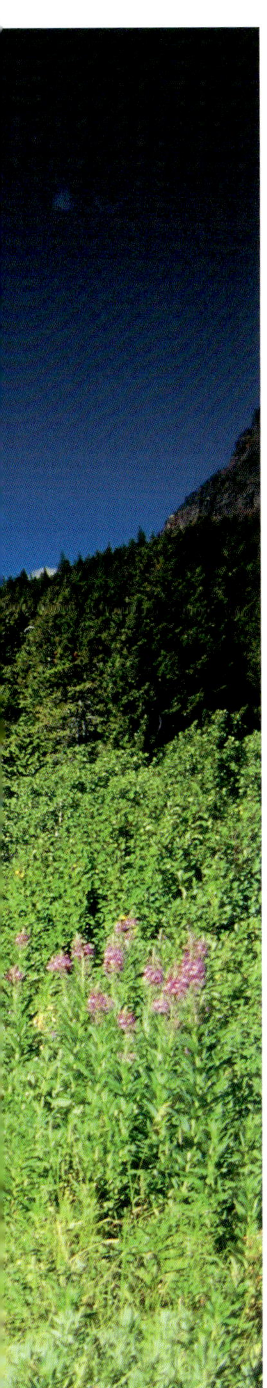

LEFT: Saint Mary Lake with fireweed in the foreground.

BELOW: Saint Mary Lake, with its shoreline dressed in spring green.

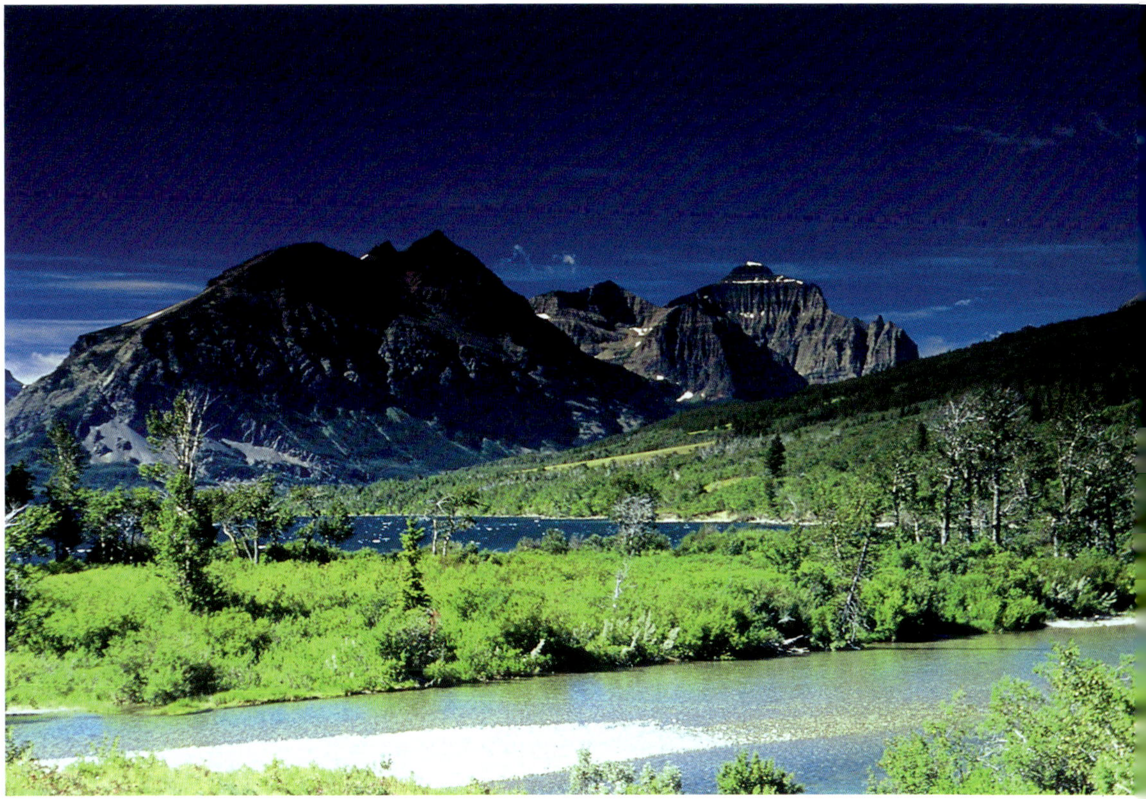

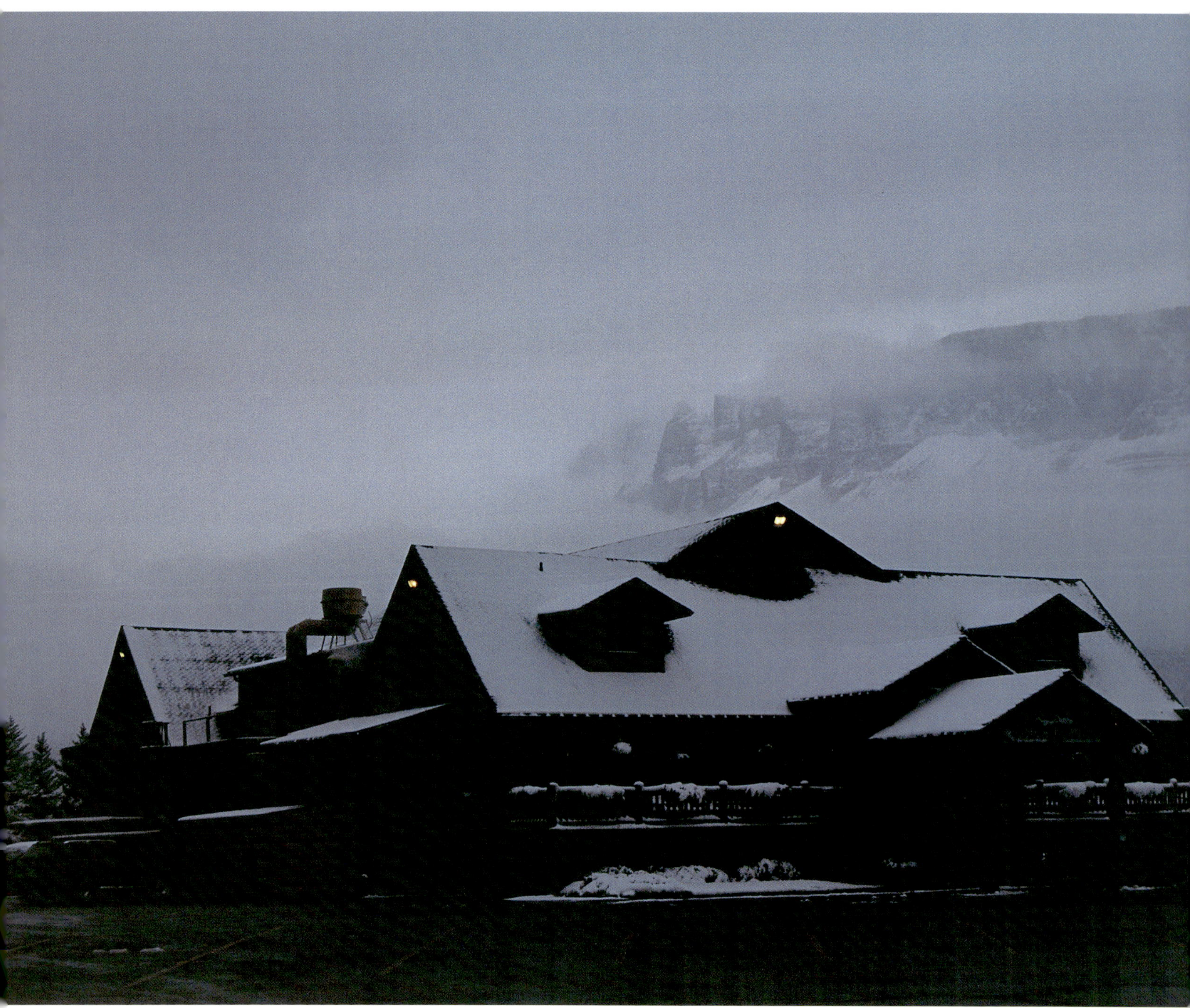

LEFT: ***Mile 18.4.*** You exit the park at Saint Mary, a small town dominated by the Saint Mary Lodge, pictured here. Originally started in 1932, the resort now features a log lodge, restaurant, and gift shop. I call it the east side "center of civilization."

BELOW: A view of snow-capped mountains in Glacier National Park from U.S. Highway 2 East.

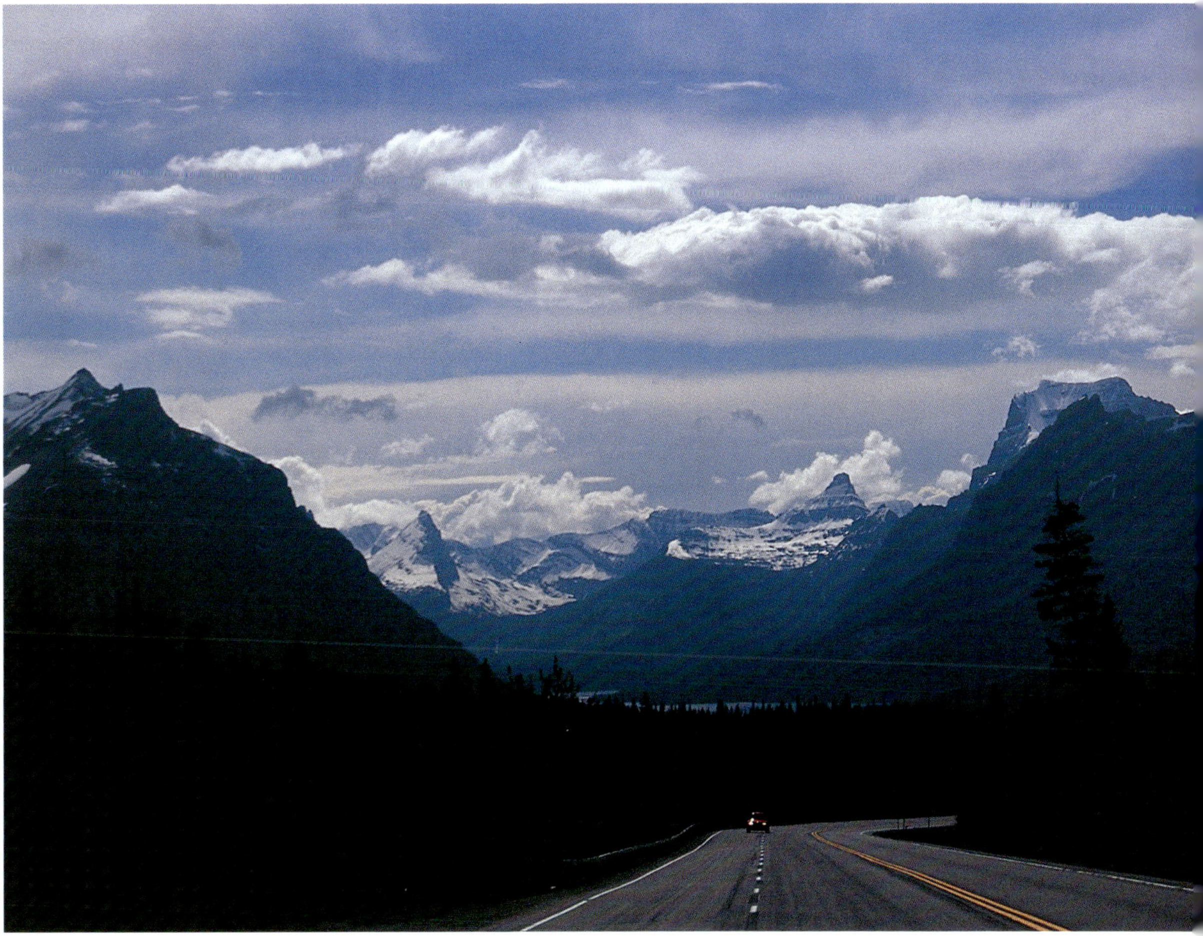

To reach Many Glacier, head north on U.S. 89 along the shore of Lower Saint Mary Lake. Just after Babb, take a left and follow the road to the Many Glacier area. Because this area is so small, we have not included mileage markers.

RIGHT: The spectacular Grinnell Falls and 9,200-foot Grinnell Peak at Many Glacier were named for George Bird Grinnell, who advocated preserving Glacier as a national park.

BELOW: Mountain goats graze along a rocky mountainside.

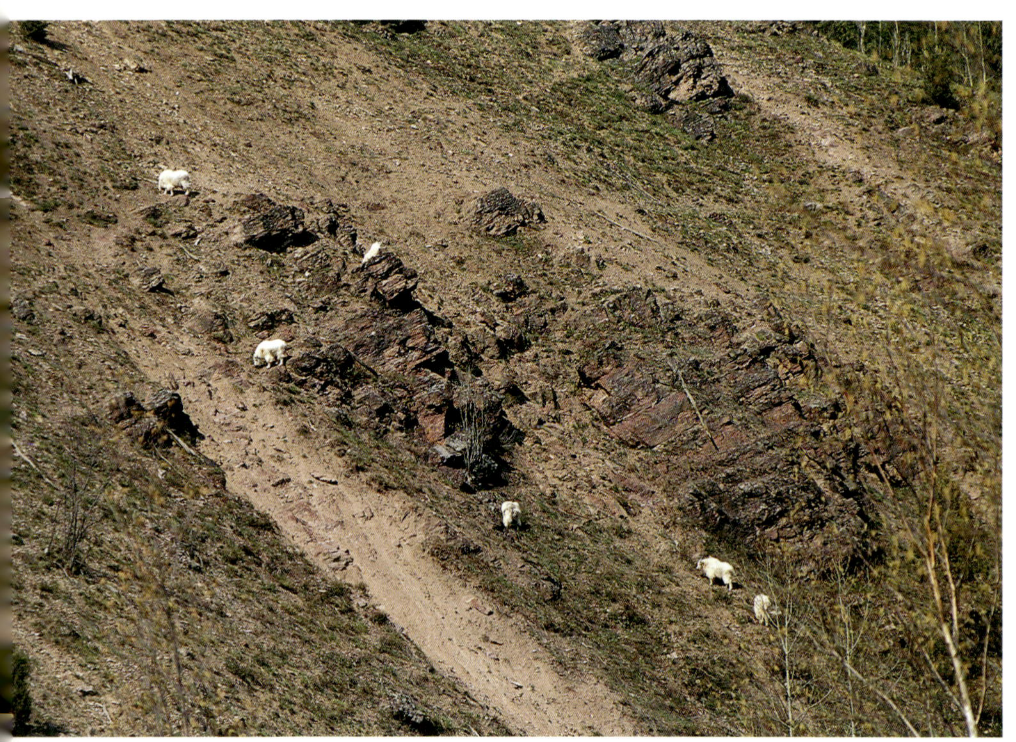

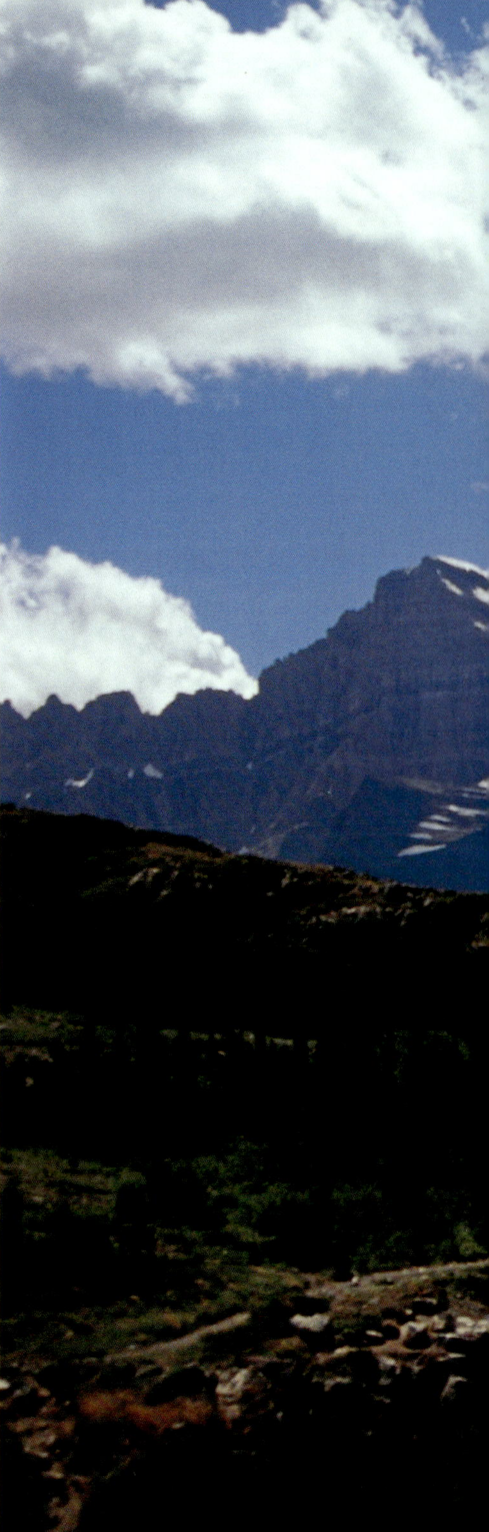

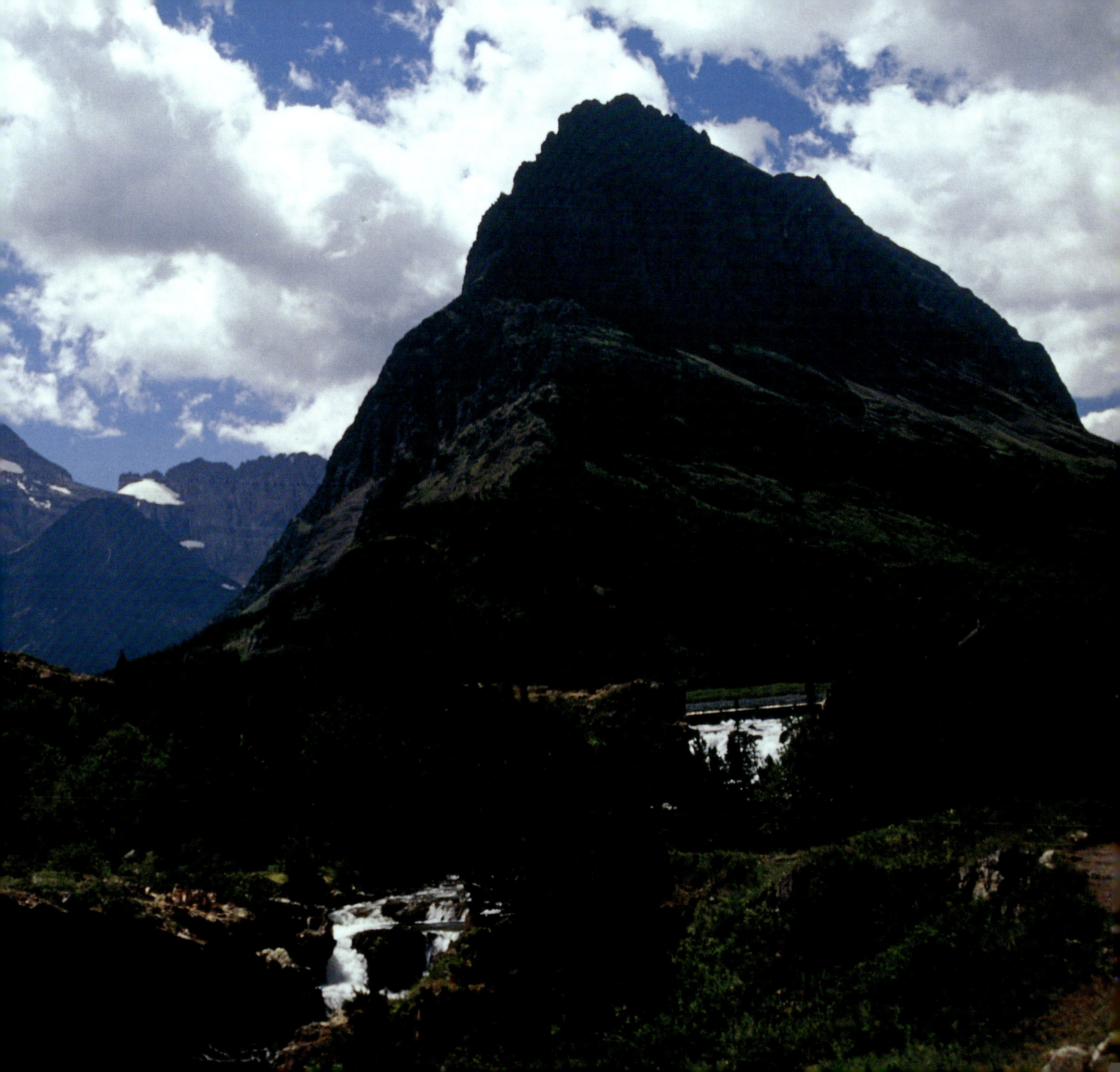

RIGHT: Grinnell Peak rises majestically above Lake Sherburne, which is actually a reservoir.

BELOW: Grinnell Peak with a spring mantle of snow.

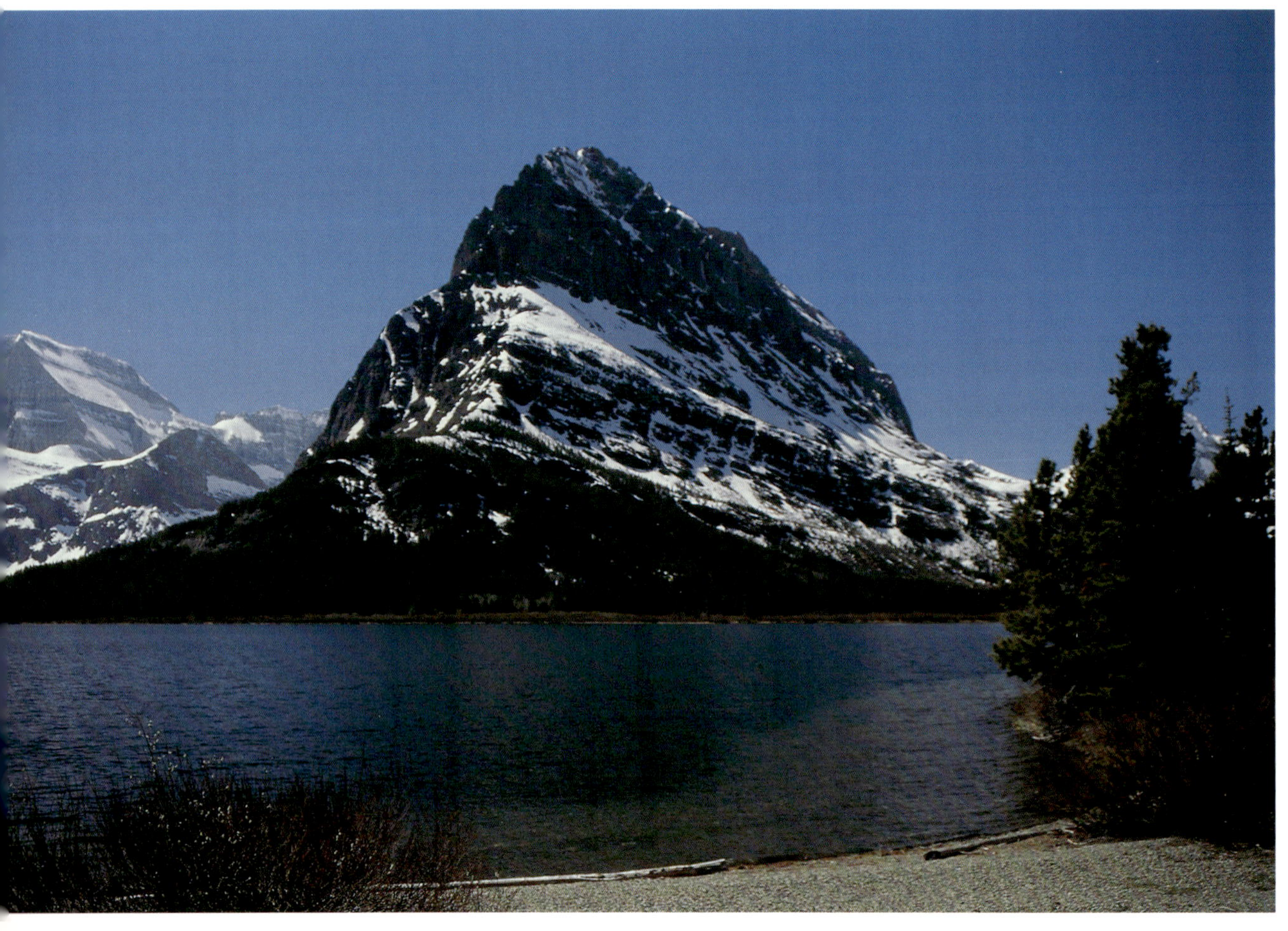

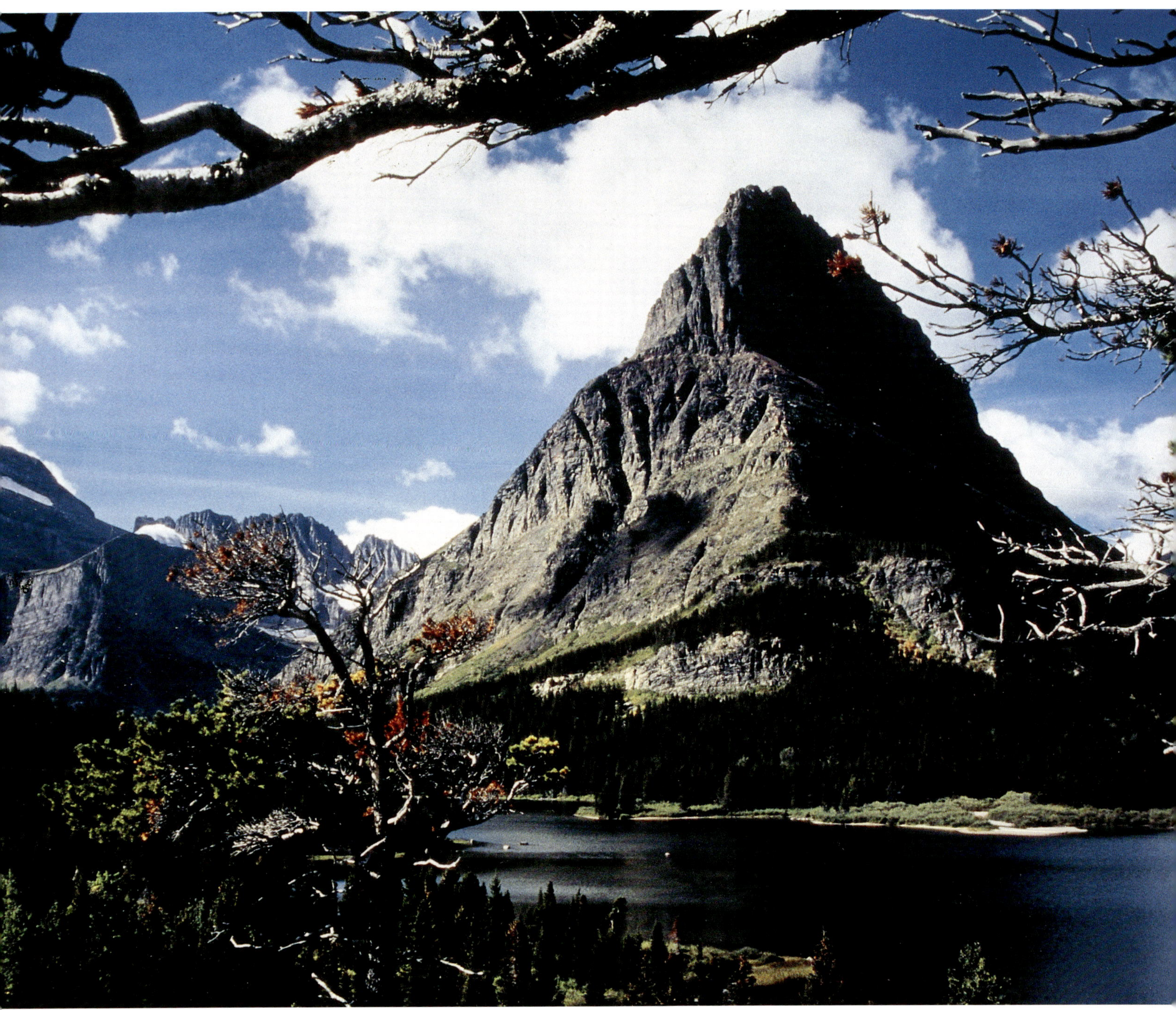

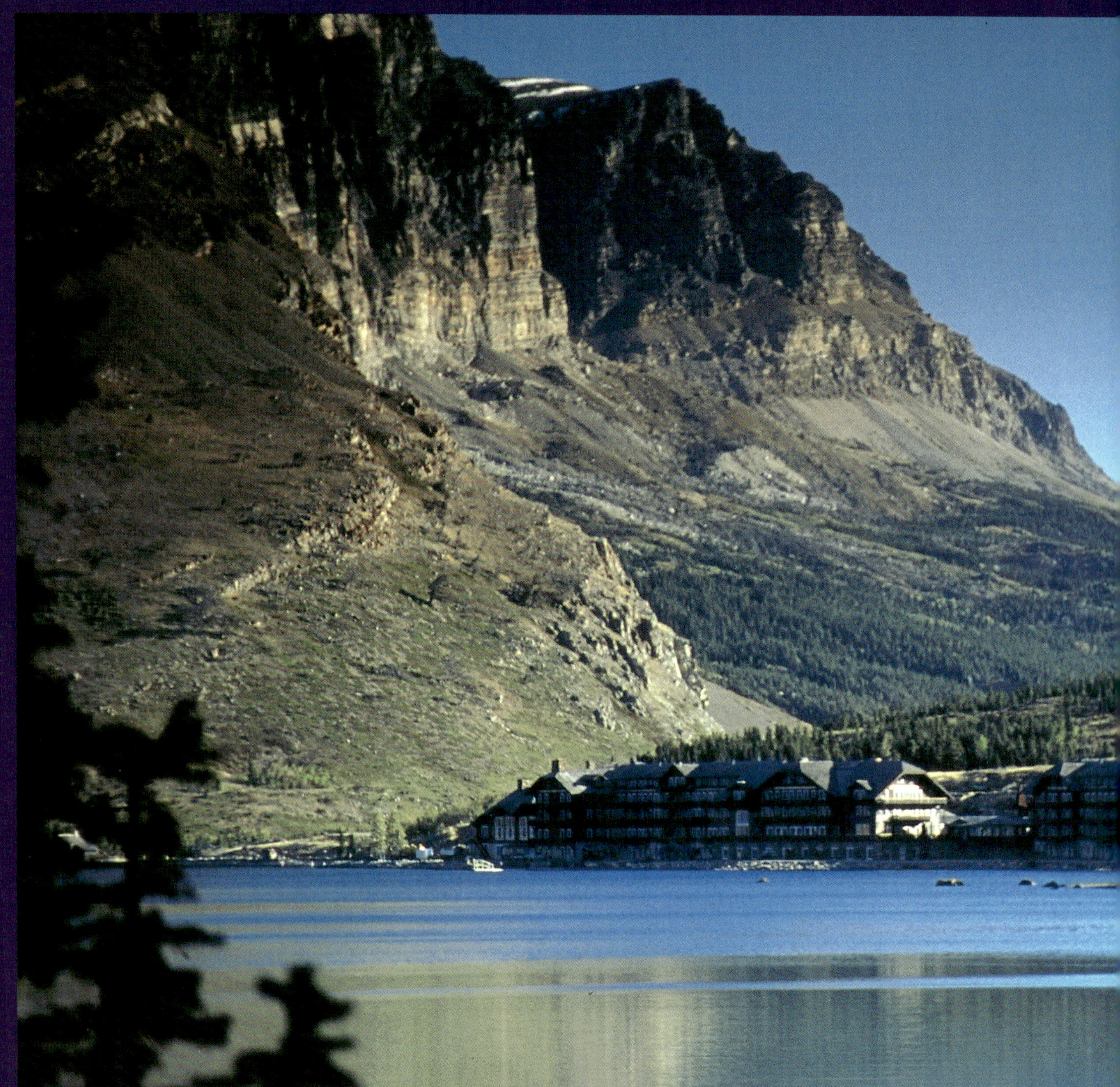

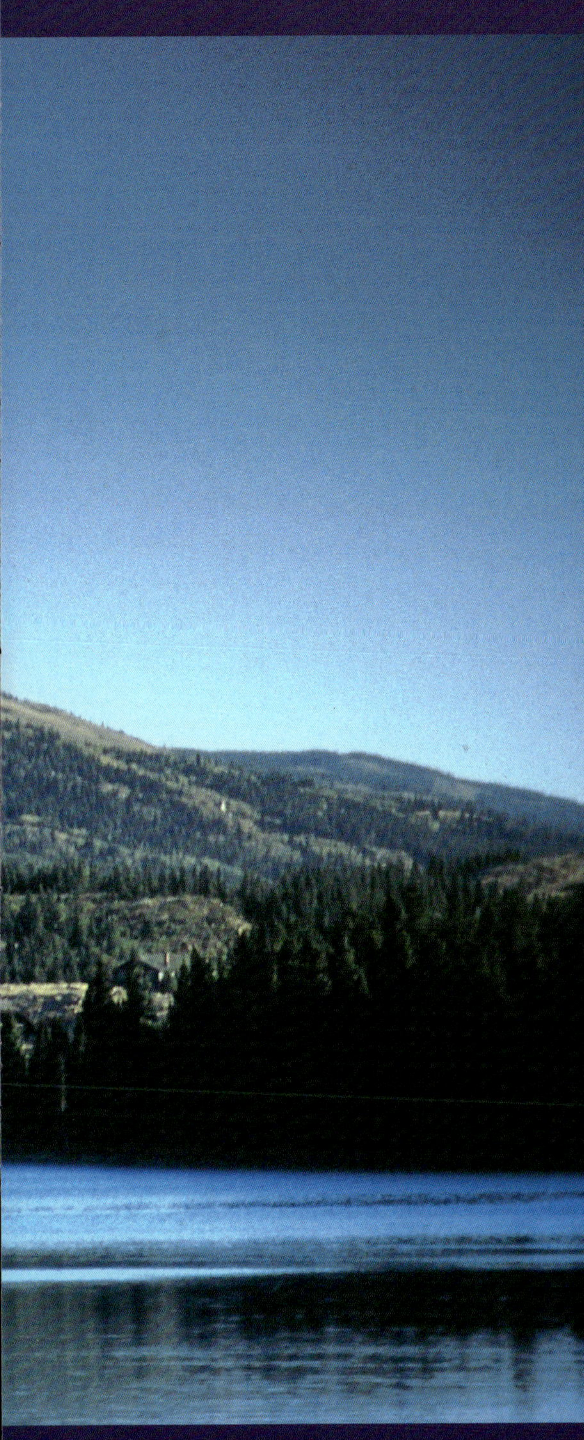

LEFT: Built by the Great Northern Railway in 1914 from native stone and massive logs, the Swiss-style Many Glacier Hotel is situated at the edge of Swiftcurrent Lake and is worth the trip in itself. Here you can take boat rides across Swiftcurrent and Josephine Lakes or you can hike around Swiftcurrent Lake to Josephine Lake.

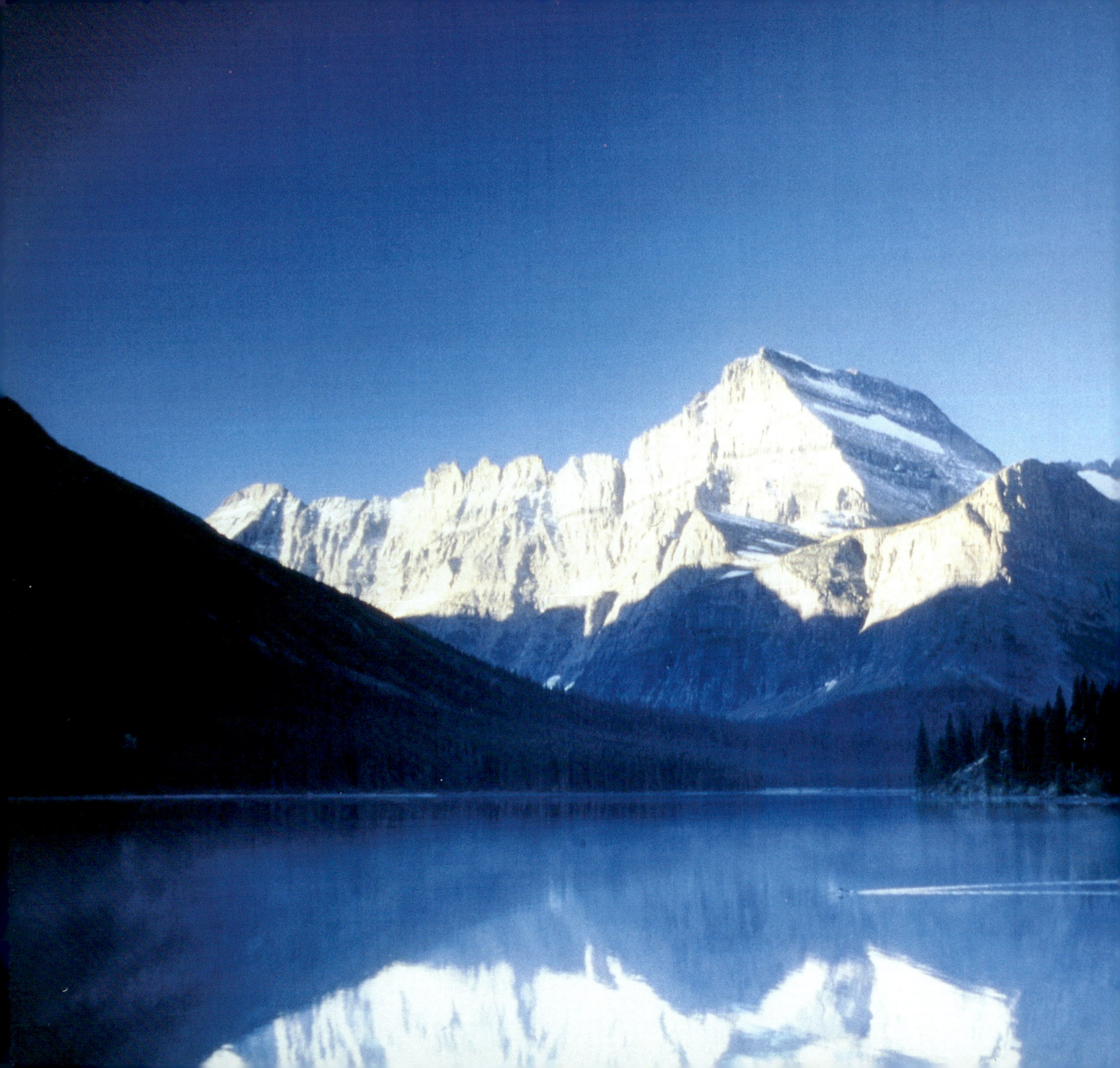

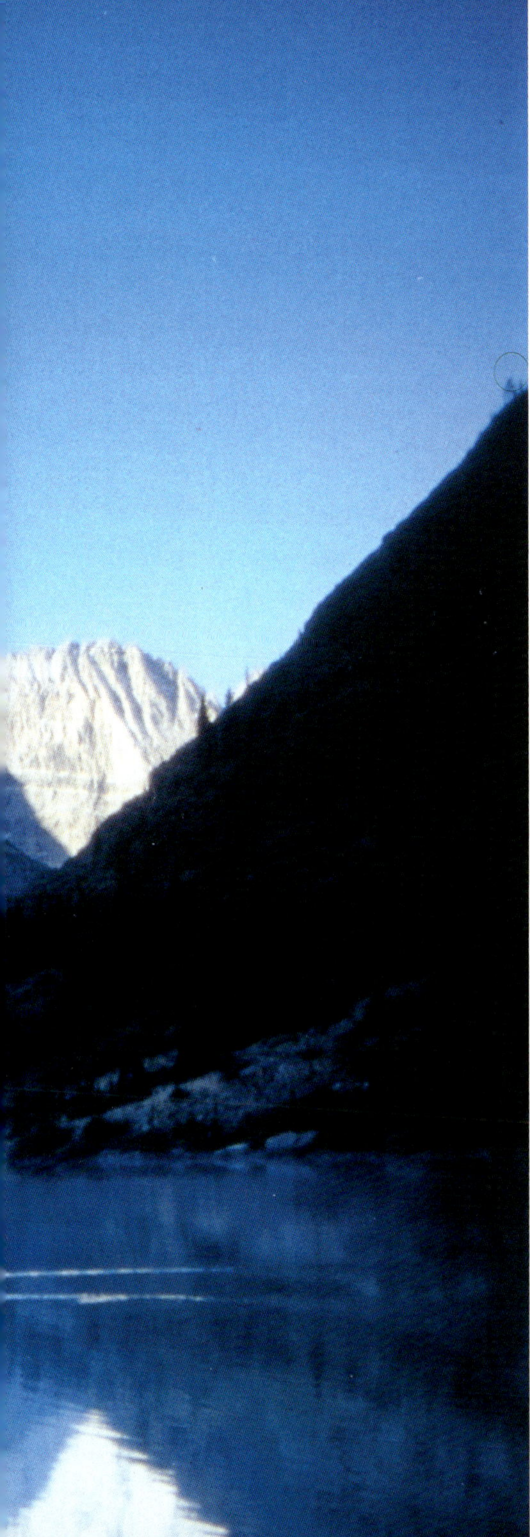

LEFT: A loon swims the waters of Josephine Lake, framed by the snow-covered Mount Gould in the background. Loons can be seen in late spring, summer, and early fall throughout the park.

BELOW: A black bear, silhouetted on a field of snow, digs for food.

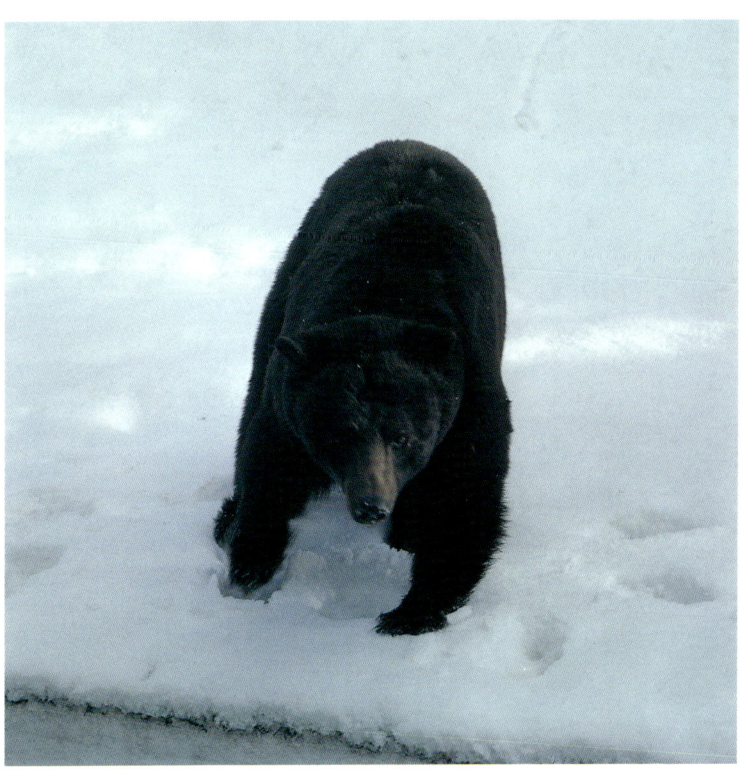

RIGHT: Many Glacier is decked in wildflowers and spring green.

BELOW: Divide Mountain, which is located between Saint Mary Lake and Many Glacier.

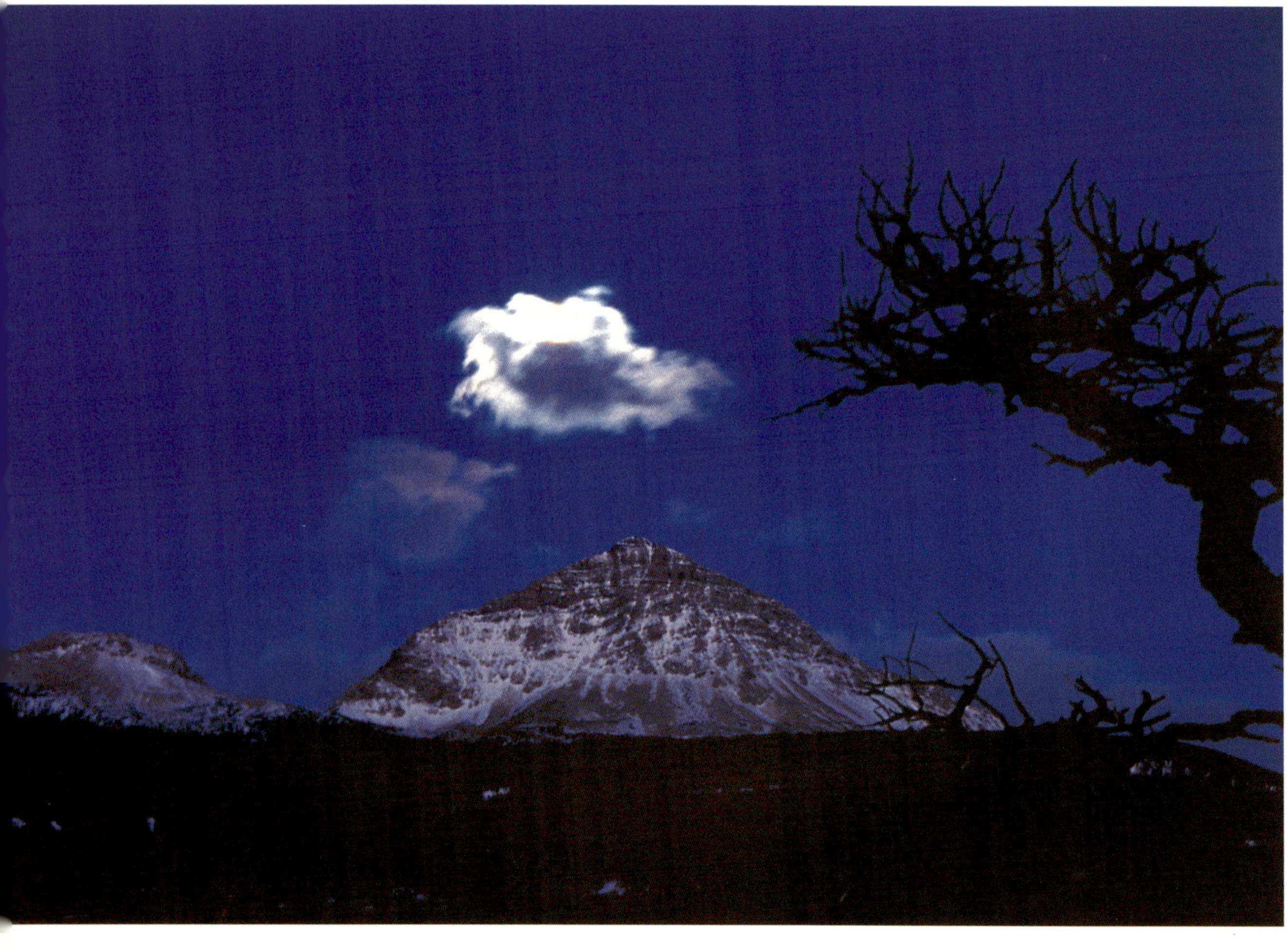

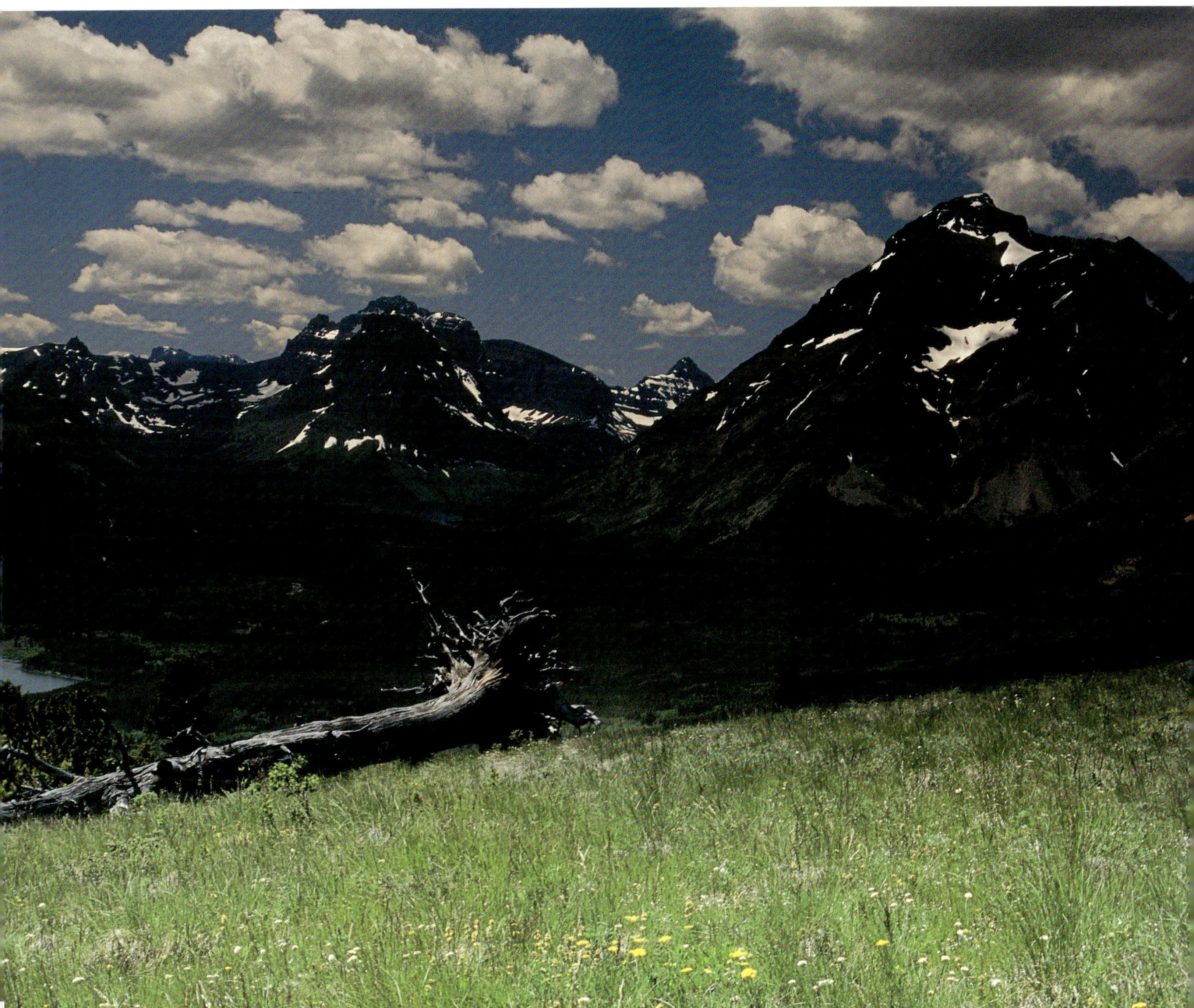

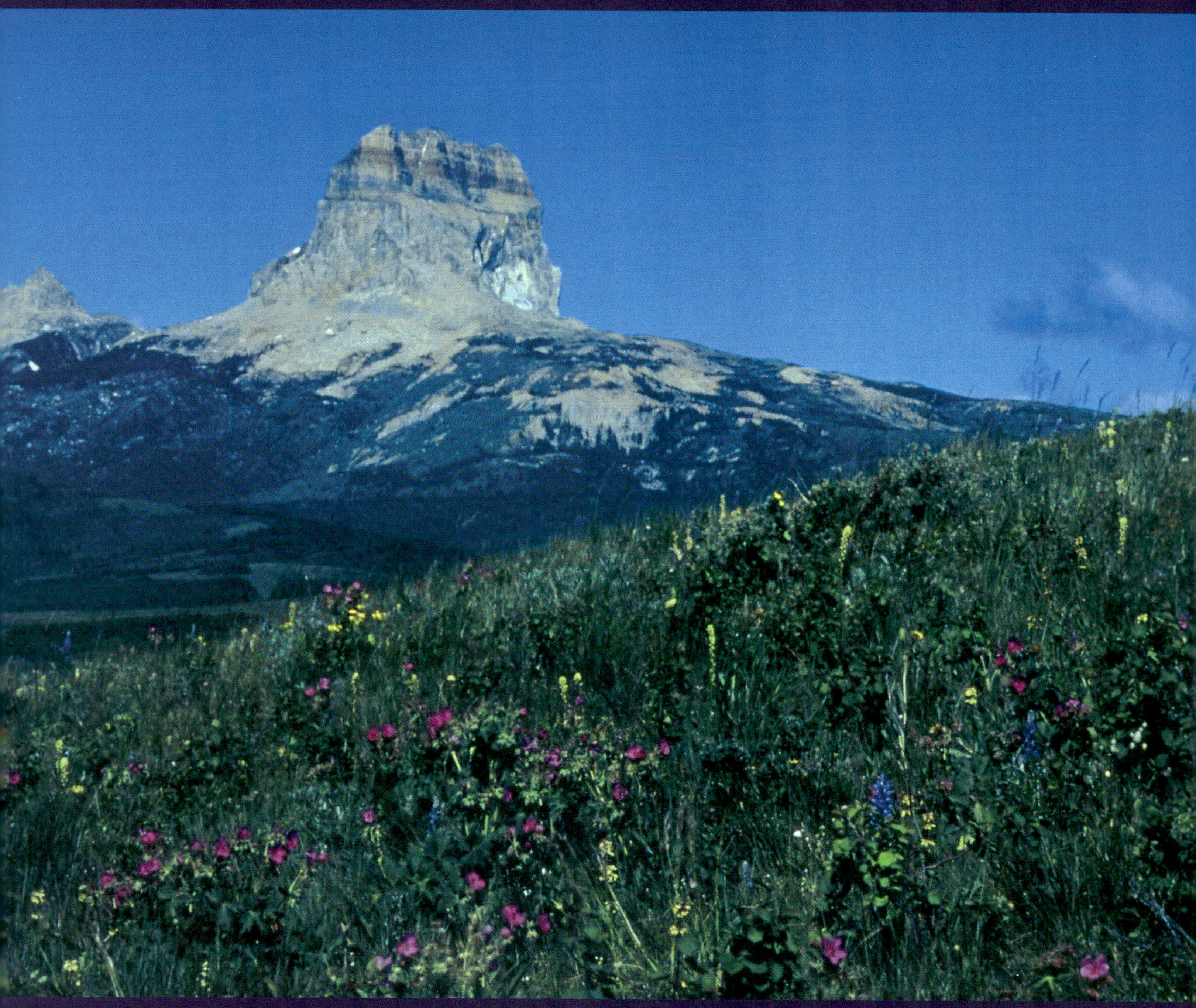

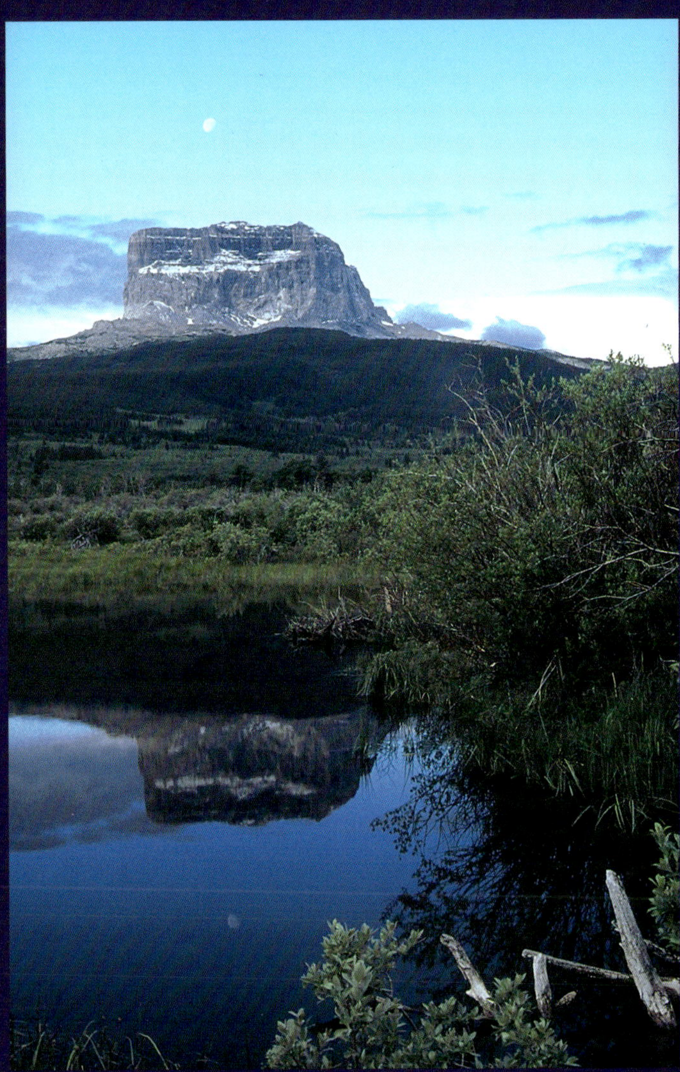

To reach Chief Mountain, return to Babb, Montana, and head north on U.S. 89 for 4 miles until you reach State Highway 17, the Chief Mountain International Highway that links Glacier and Waterton Lakes National Parks.

LEFT: You'll have a variety of opportunities along the way to photograph the 9,080 foot Chief Mountain, one of the park's most unusual and interesting geologic features. Chief Mountain is a rare geologic oddity called a klippe, which is a completely isolated remnant of a glacial plain due to erosion.

FAR LEFT: A scenic photograph of Chief Mountain, the easternmost extension of the Lewis Fault Block, with a blanket of wildflowers in the foreground.

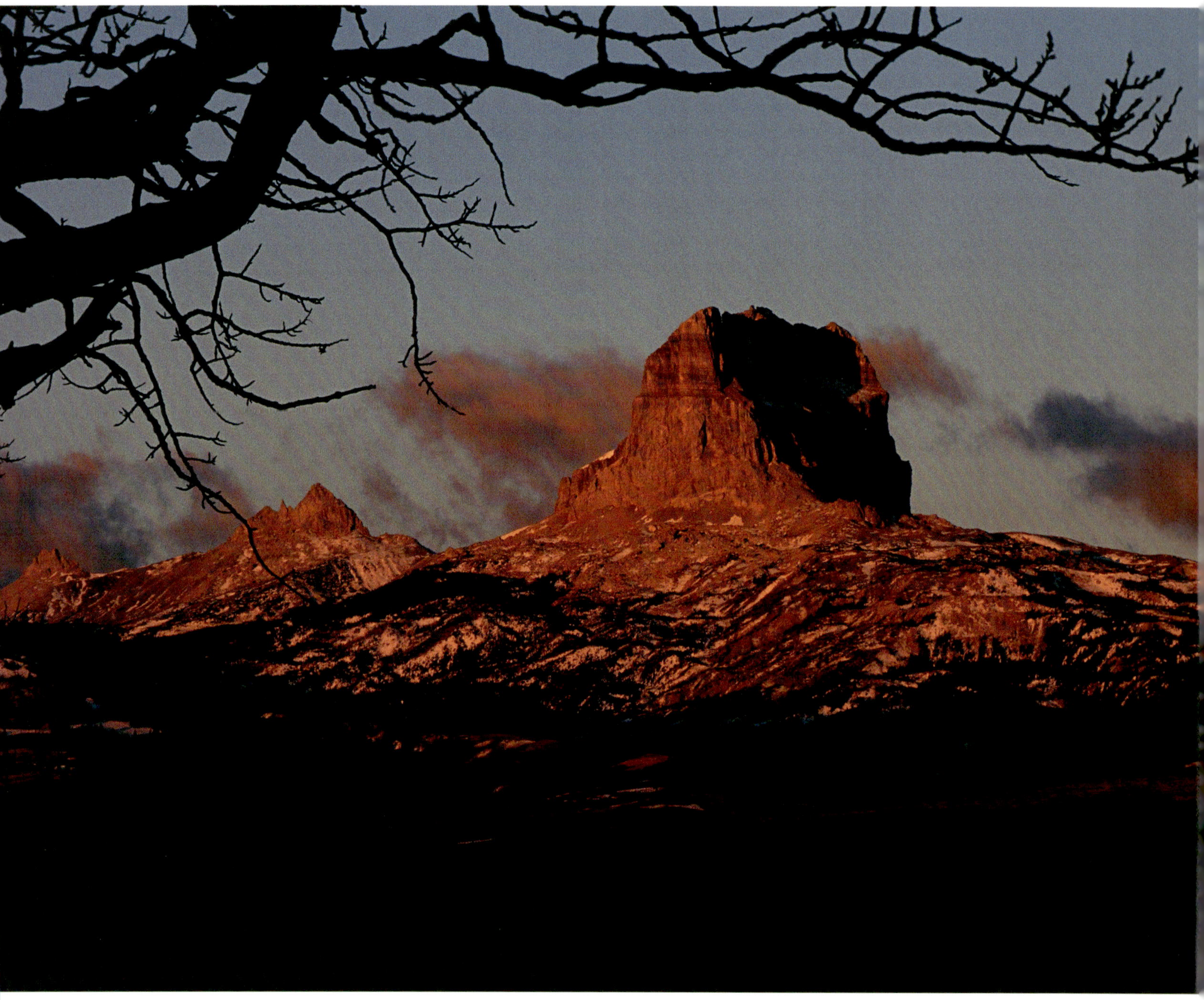

FACING PAGE: Chief Mountain is where the Blackfeet Indians traditionally conducted their vision quests.

BELOW: A sunset paints the skies over Glacier National Park in purples and pinks.

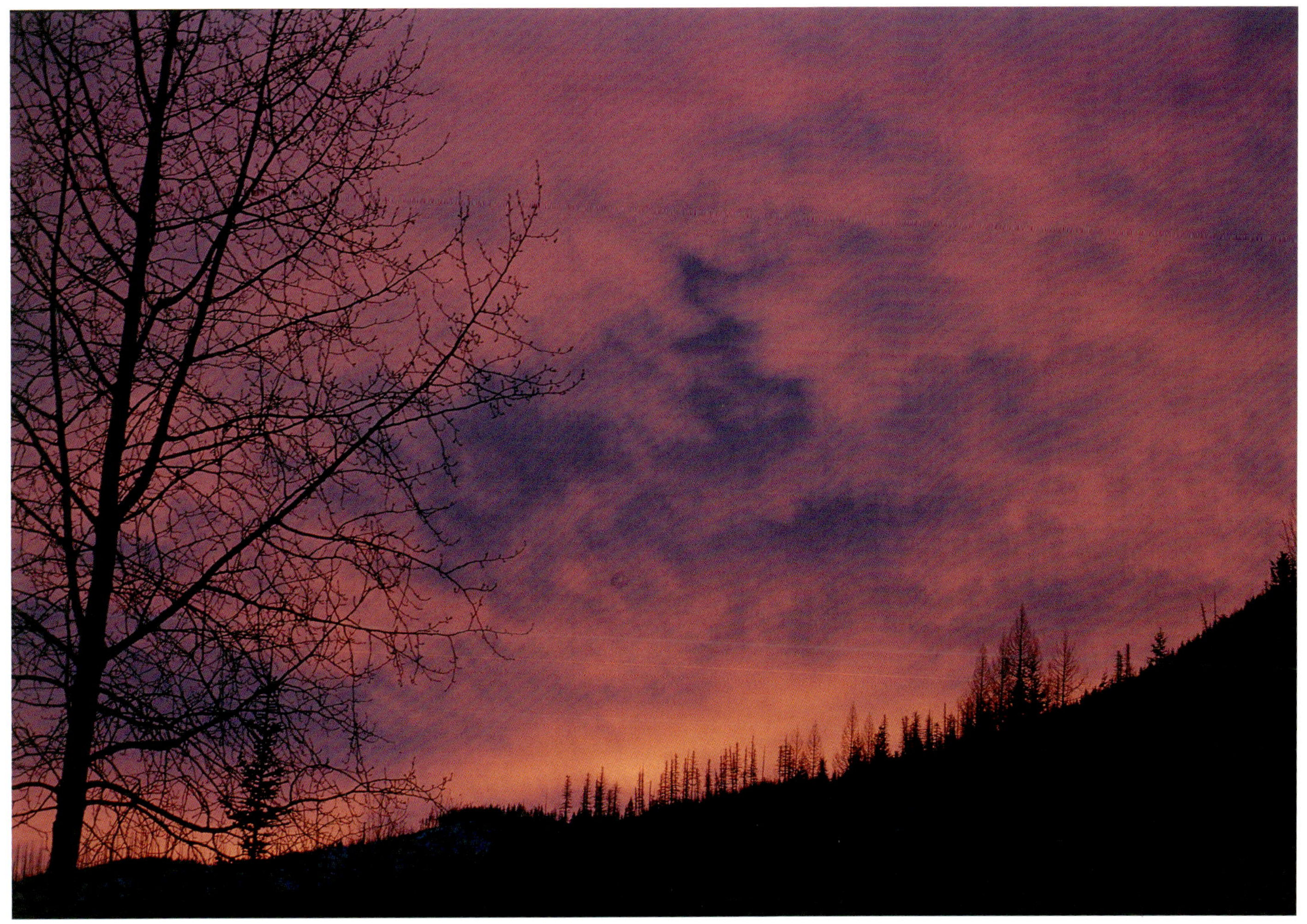

RIGHT: An early morning view of the east face of Chief Mountain with a full moon rising just behind it.

BELOW: The horizontal ridges of the summit of Chief Mountain reveal the mountain's sedimentary origins.

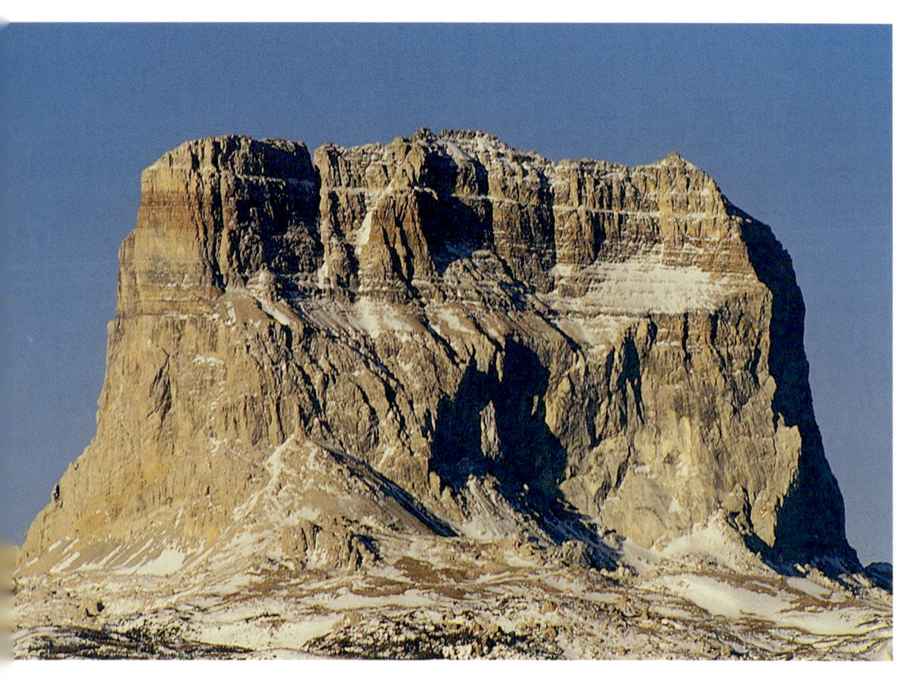

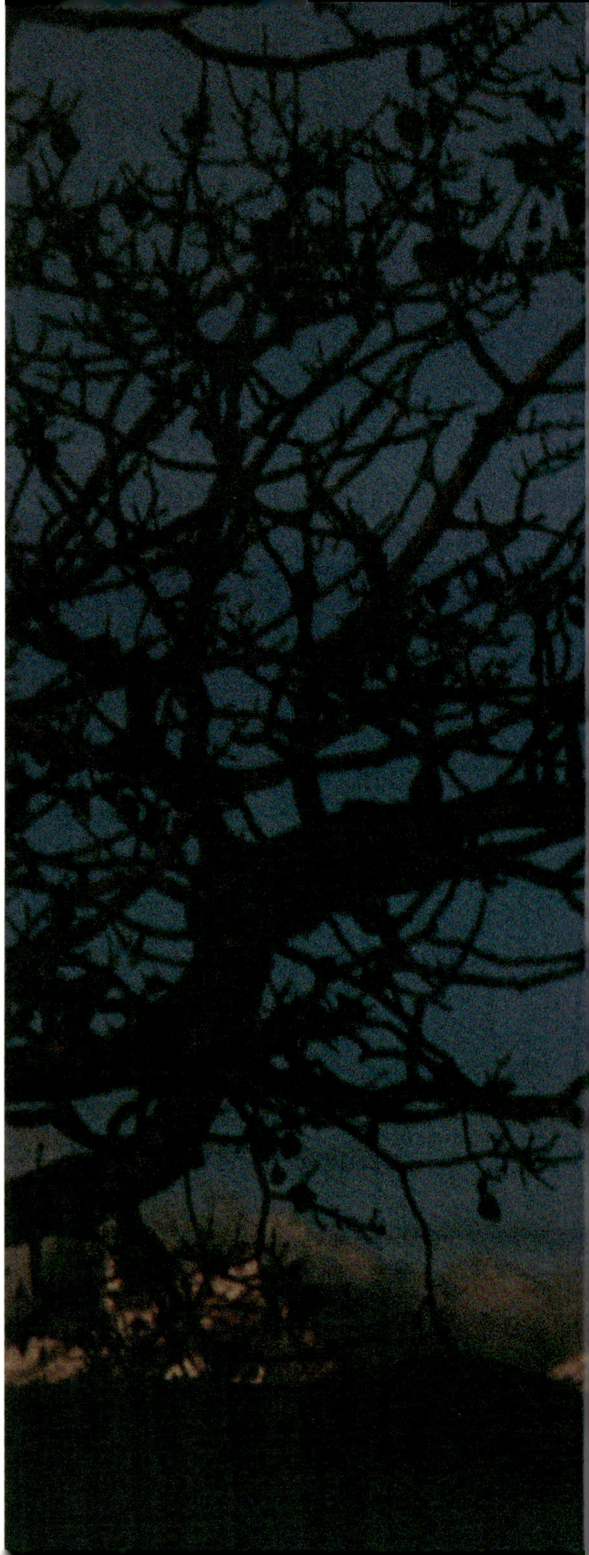

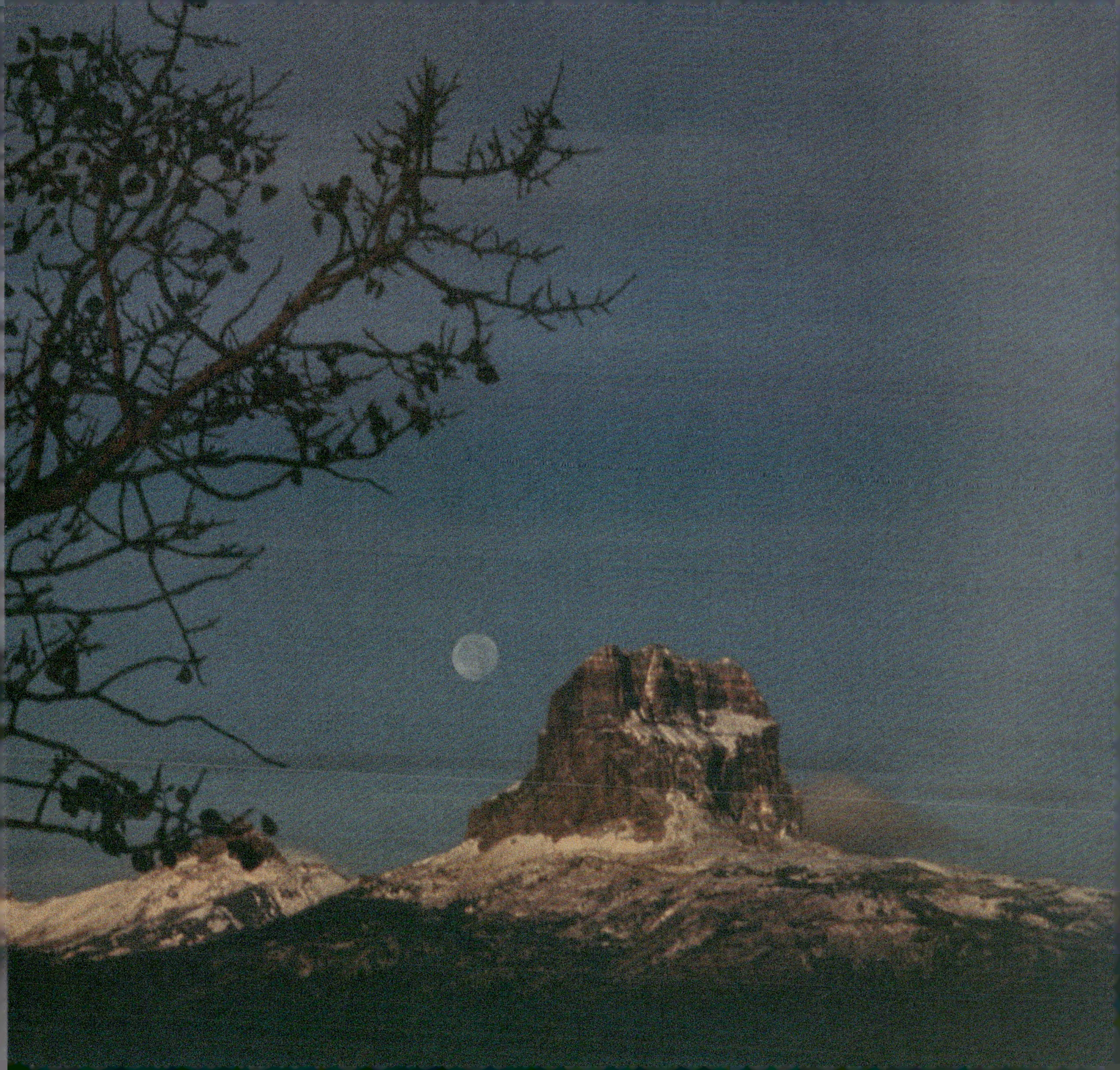

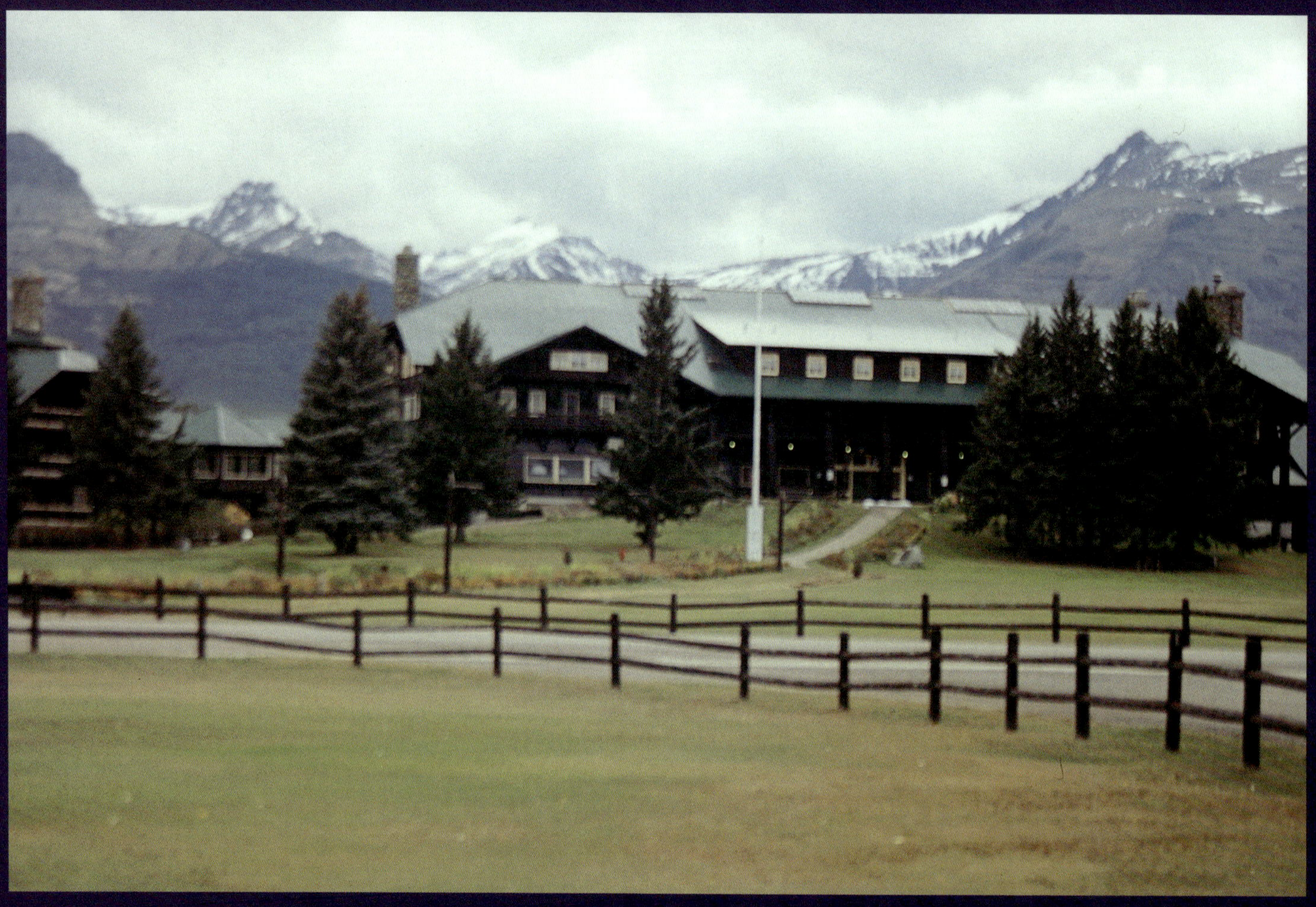

ABOVE: Completed in 1913, the grand Glacier Park Lodge in East Glacier—the first lodge built by the Great Northern Railroad—is also known as the "Big Tree Lodge" because of its dramatic lobby with Douglas-fir columns.

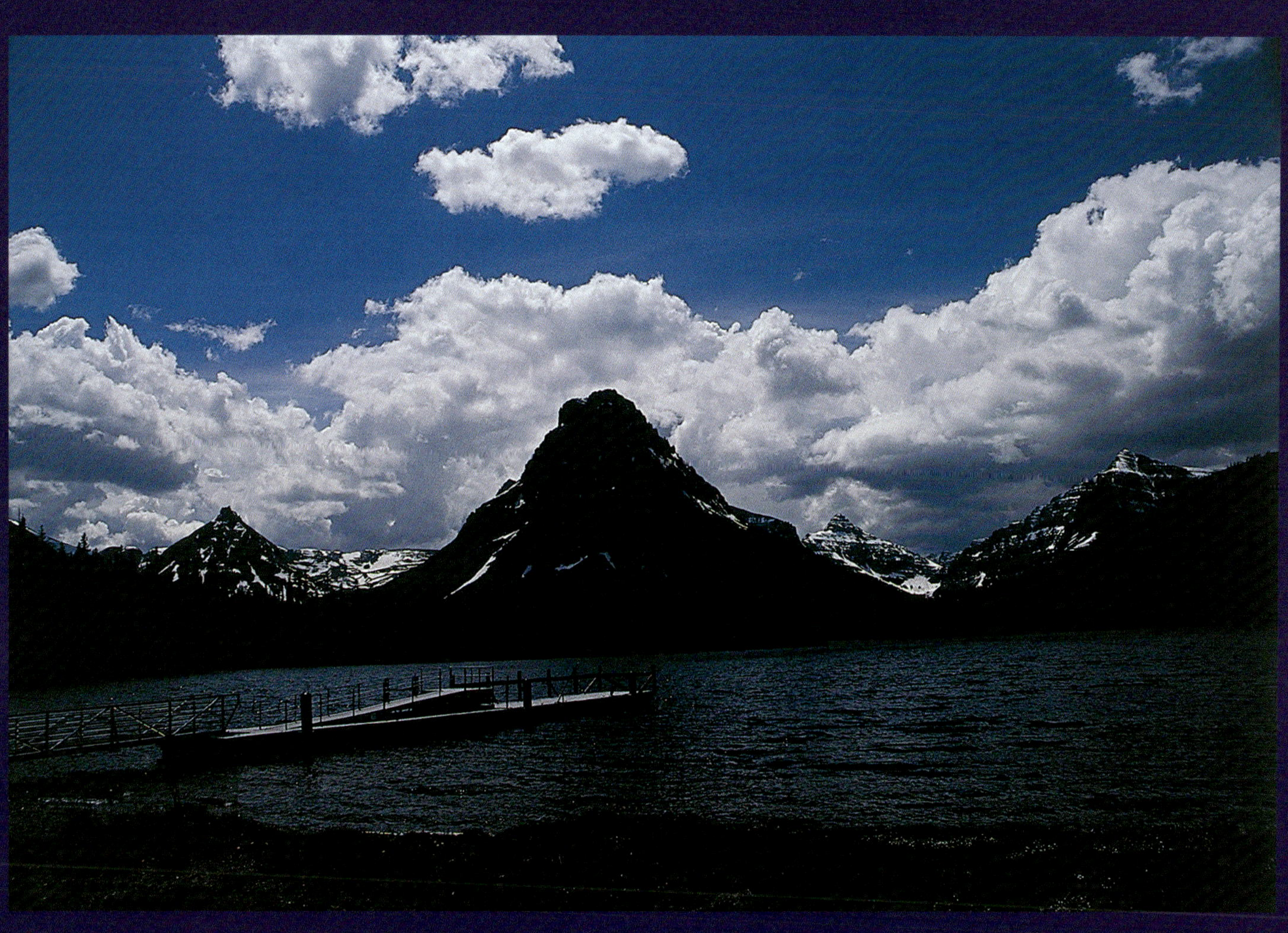

ABOVE: Located north of East Glacier off U.S. Highway 2, Two Medicine Lake was formed by a convergence of drainages and is a lovely spot for camping and hiking.

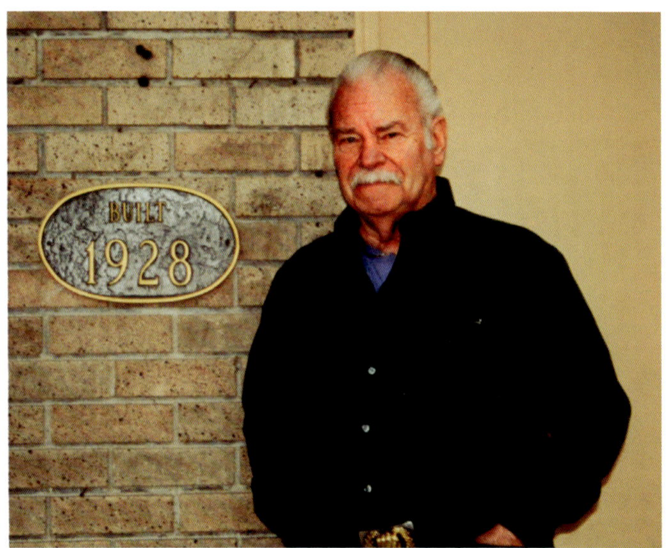

I was born on February 11, 1929, in Kansas City and raised in a rural community near the Lake of the Ozarks in southern Missouri, a reservoir that was created in 1931 when the Osage River was dammed. It's a beautiful place that nurtured in me a lifelong love of the outdoors. When I was six, a family trip to Estes Park in the Colorado Rocky Mountains kindled in me an intense infatuation with mountains. This led to an undergraduate degree in (what else?) geology. But instead of ending up in the mountains, my first job with Conoco Oil landed me a five-year stint that took me from the deserts of west Texas to the bayous of Louisiana. When I was about to be sent to Saudi Arabia, I quit: I was determined to live in the mountains and to be my own boss.

Following in the footsteps of my grandfather, who was a textbook example of an old country doctor, I decided to get a degree in medicine. After I received my medical degree from the University of Kansas in 1960 and completed a one-year internship, I moved to Jackson Hole, Wyoming, in the splendid Teton Mountains. I spent the next seventeen years climbing and hiking these mountains—including the fourth winter ascent of the Grand Teton—which only intensified my awe for the mountains' magnificence. In the small-town atmosphere of the good old days in Jackson Hole, I was a county commissioner, a part-time bouncer at the Cowboy Bar, a camera store proprietor, and a team member of the Teton National Park Rescue Squad, as well as a full-time family physician.

Answering the ever-present call of the mountains, I moved to Montana, where I did emergency room work first in Great Falls, Helena, and then Kalispell. Soon after, my children followed—Dave (D.J.), Ben, and Pilar. This brought me close to one of the most beautiful spots in the nation: Glacier National Park. I was inspired further by an extensive photography workshop organized by Missoula's Rocky Mountain School of Photography with the renowned Galen Rowell, the greatest outdoor photographer of our time. The memories of that inspirational week in Glacier Park with Rowell will last the rest of my life. Without it, this book would have been unlikely.

Photographing mountains is tricky. You must always keep in mind a proper perspective of the elements of the scene. You also have to anticipate the light and its relationship to the mountains. This dictates where you need to be and what time of day you need to be there. To photograph the early morning beauty on the east side of Glacier National Park, I worked night shifts in the emergency room in Browning, Montana, so I could get into the park at the crack of dawn. The results are some of my best photographs so far. I've sold many of these prints, and some of these photographs can also be seen at my gallery, Doc Walker's Photo Gallery, in downtown Kalispell.

Mountains inspire me. As a geologist and a mountain climber, I feel drawn to explore them. Yet, about the time I was retiring from my career in emergency medicine, I was no longer able to make the highest and most difficult ascents. Photography, I have found, provides me with a sense of intimacy with the mountains. It is a way I can explore their intricacies and moods, which change constantly with the vagaries of the light. With my photos, I have recorded these splendors to the best of my ability in order to convey them to others.

It was mountains, too, that—thirty-one years ago—brought me to my wonderful wife and companion, Arlene Zepeda de Walker, with whom I live in Kalispell, Montana. When I lived in Jackson Hole, I ran across a beautiful tourist whom I eventually convinced to marry me. Because of Arlene's foresight, effort, and generosity, I have been able to make photographic forays to mountains around the world, ranging from the European Alps to New Zealand's Fox Glacier, from Alaska's Kenai Peninsula to Tierra del Fuego in Patagonia.

It is to her I dedicate this book.

Dr. Jack Walker